WHY *NOT*
IN MY
BACKYARD?

WHY *NOT* IN MY BACKYARD?

Neighborhood Impacts of Deconcentrating Assisted Housing

GEORGE C. GALSTER
PETER A. TATIAN
ANNA M. SANTIAGO
KATHRYN L. S. PETTIT
ROBIN E. SMITH

CENTER FOR URBAN POLICY RESEARCH
EDWARD J. BLOUSTEIN SCHOOL OF PLANNING AND PUBLIC POLICY
RUTGERS, THE STATE UNIVERSITY OF NEW JERSEY
NEW BRUNSWICK, NEW JERSEY

© 2003 by Rutgers, The State University of New Jersey

Published by the CENTER FOR URBAN POLICY RESEARCH
Edward J. Bloustein School of Planning and Public Policy
Rutgers, The State University of New Jersey
Civic Square • 33 Livingston Avenue
New Brunswick, New Jersey 08901-1982

Printed in the United States of America

Library of Congress Cataloging-in-Publication Data

Why not in my backyard? : neighborhood impacts of deconcentrating
assisted housing / George Galster . . . [et al.].
    p. cm.
Includes bibliographical references and index.
   ISBN 0-88285-176-4 (paper : alk. paper)
  1. Housing policy—United States. 2. NIMBY syndrome—United States.
3. Low-income housing—United States. 4. People with
disabilities—Housing—United States. 5. People with mental
disabilities—Housing—United States. I. Galster, George, 1948–   II.
Title
  HD7293.W52 2003
  363.5'83'0973—dc21

                                     2002073474

*To our families
and all families in America*

*that they may live in communities
of opportunity and justice*

About the Authors

George C. Galster is Clarence Hilberry Professor of Urban Affairs in the College of Urban, Labor, and Metropolitan Affairs at Wayne State University. He has authored more than one hundred scholarly articles and book chapters on topics that include housing policy; neighborhood dynamics; discrimination and segregation in housing, mortgage, and insurance markets; metropolitan opportunity structures for the poor; and urban sprawl. Among his four previous books is *The Metropolis in Black and White: Place, Power, and Polarization* (coedited with Edward W. Hill), published by CUPR Press in 1992. Galster formerly served as director of housing research at the Urban Institute in Washington, D.C.

Peter A. Tatian is a senior research associate in the Metropolitan Housing and Communities Policy Center at the Urban Institute. His research focuses on both domestic and international housing policy, quantitative methods, and developing and using neighborhood indicators as a community-building tool. He previously served as research analyst at the International Food Policy Research Institute.

Anna M. Santiago is professor of social work at Wayne State University. Her research focuses on discrimination and segregation in metropolitan housing markets, racial and ethnic differences in opportunity structures, asset-building in low-income communities, and barriers to help-seeking in communities of color. She is currently coprincipal investigator (with George C. Galster) in a longitudinal research study assessing the effects of participation in homeownership programs on the acquisition of human, financial, and social capital assets by public housing residents and their children.

Kathryn L. S. Pettit is a research associate in the Metropolitan Housing and Communities Policy Center at the Urban Institute. She conducts research on measures of neighborhood change and the role of place in social outcomes. Pettit serves as deputy director of the Institute's National Neighborhood Indicators Partnership. She previously worked at the National Center for Charitable Statistics.

Robin E. Smith is a research associate in the Metropolitan Housing and Communities Policy Center at the Urban Institute. Coauthor of the U.S. Department of Housing and Urban Development's 1997 handbook on community building in public housing, *Ties That Bind People and Their Communities*, Smith's research focuses on community development, fair housing, and public housing transformation. Much of her work involves evaluating federal housing programs, including her current effort assessing HUD's Moving to Work demonstration.

Contents

List of Tables viii

List of Maps ix

List of Figures x

Preface and Acknowledgments xi

1 Introduction: Deconcentrating Poverty or Destabilizing Neighborhoods? 1

2 The Denver Controversies over the Dispersed Public Housing and Supportive Housing Programs 21

3 The Baltimore Controversies over the Section 8 and Moving to Opportunity Programs 50

4 Deciphering the Neighborhood Impacts of Assisted Housing: Methodological Issues 74

5 Patterns of Assisted Housing, Property Values, and Crime Rates 108

6 The Impacts of Dispersed Public Housing in Denver 131

7 The Impacts of Supportive Housing In Denver 143

8 The Impacts of Section 8 in Baltimore County 159

9 Conclusions and Policy Implications: Toward a Neighborhood-Friendly Strategy for Deconcentrating Assisted Housing 175

Appendix: Econometric, Spatial Econometric, and Data Issues 205

References 210

Index 220

Tables

Chapter 2

2.1   Selected Population and Housing Characteristics by Ethnicity,
Denver, 1980–90   22

Chapter 3

3.1   Selected Population and Housing Characteristics by Ethnicity,
Baltimore County, 1980–90   51

Chapter 4

4.1   Maximum Numbers of Assisted Sites and Units (Beds) Observed at
Time of Home Sale, by Proximity   89

4.2   Characteristics of Denver Dispersed Housing Focus Group Sites
and Encompassing Census Tracts   93

4.3   Characteristics of Supportive Housing Sites in Denver Focus Group Areas   97

4.4   Characteristics of Neighborhoods (Census Tracts) Surrounding Denver
Supportive Housing Focus Group Sites   98

4.5   Characteristics of Baltimore County Focus Group Sites and Surrounding
Neighborhoods   102

Chapter 5

5.1   Single-Family Home Sales in Denver and Baltimore County   110

5.2   Denver Crime Rate per 100 Residents   112

5.3   Occupancy Statistics for Section 8 Sites in Baltimore County, 1991–97   117

5.4   Occupancy Statistics for Public Housing Sites in Denver, 1980–97   122

5.5   Public Housing Sites in Denver by Number of Units, 1997   123

5.6   Denver Public Housing Sites, Average Year Built and Number of Housing
Units, by Year of Acquisition   123

5.7   Opening Dates of Supportive Housing Sites in Denver   124

5.8   Supportive Housing in Denver, by Program Type   125

5.9   Supportive Housing Sites in Denver, by Number of Units   126

5.10   Characteristics of Supportive Housing Sites for
Property-Value-Impact Analysis   127

5.11   Characteristics of Supportive Housing Sites for Crime-Impact Analysis   128

Chapter 9

9.1   Summary of Statistical Estimates of Neighborhood Impacts:
The Importance of Context, Concentration, and Scale   178

Maps

Chapter 2

2.1	Percentage Black Population, Denver Census Tracts, 1990	24
2.2	Percentage Hispanic Population, Denver Census Tracts, 1990	25
2.3	Percentage Renter-Occupied Housing, Denver Census Tracts, 1990	28
2.4	Median House Values, Denver Census Tracts, 1990	29
2.5	Percentage Change in Average House Values, Denver Census Tracts, 1990–96	30
2.6	Denver Conventional and Dispersed Housing Sites, by Opening Date	37
2.7	Denver Supportive Housing Sites by Zoning Approval Date	41

Chapter 3

3.1	Percentage Black Population, Baltimore County Census Tracts, 1990	53
3.2	Percentage Renter-Occupied Housing, Baltimore County Census Tracts, 1990	56
3.3	Median House Value, Baltimore County Census Tracts, 1990	57
3.4	Percentage Change in Average House Values, Baltimore County Census Tracts, 1990–96	58

Chapter 4

4.1	Denver Census Tracts, Showing Denver Housing Authority Dispersed Housing Focus Group Sites	92
4.2	Denver Census Tracts, Showing Location of Focus Group Sites	96
4.3	Baltimore County Census Tracts, Showing Section 8 Focus Group Sites	101

Chapter 5

5.1	Violent Crimes, Denver Census Tracts, 1997	113
5.2	Property Crimes, Denver Census Tracts, 1997	114
5.3–7	Locations of Section 8 Households, Baltimore County, 1991–97 (overview and detail maps)	116–121

Figures

Chapter 5

5.1   Home Price Trends in Baltimore County and Denver during the 1990s   111

Chapter 6

6.1   Estimated Price Trends within 2,000 Feet of Any Dispersed Housing Site(s), Denver County   132

Chapter 7

7.1   Estimated Price Trends within 2,000 Feet of Any Supportive Housing Site(s), Denver   145

Chapter 8

8.1   Estimated Price Trends within 500 Feet of Any Section 8 Site, Baltimore County   161

8.2   Estimated Price Trends as Function of Density of Section 8 Sites, Baltimore County   162

Chapter 9

9.1   Countervailing Externality Functions with Assisted Housing Rehabilitation Policy, High-Value, Less-Vulnerable Neighborhoods (One Site)   180

9.2   Countervailing Externality Functions with Assisted Housing Rehabilitation Policy, High-Value, Less-Vulnerable Neighborhoods (Number of Sites Greater than Threshold)   181

9.3   Countervailing Externality Functions with Assisted Housing Rehabilitation Policy, Low-Value, More-Vulnerable Neighborhoods (One Site)   182

9.4   Countervailing Externality Functions with Assisted Housing Rehabilitation Policy, Low-Value, More-Vulnerable Neighborhoods (Number of Sites Greater than Threshold)   183

Preface and Acknowledgments

Assisted housing policy increasingly has been concerned with providing residential opportunities for low-income and special needs households outside areas of concentrated poverty. In recent years, this concern has dominated policymaking at the U.S. Department of Housing and Urban Development and has been manifested in several ways. Households receiving Section 8 rental certificates or vouchers in selected metropolitan areas have been provided with housing information and mobility assistance through the Regional Opportunity Counseling initiative. Several longstanding public housing desegregation suits have been settled by the construction of scattered-site public housing and/or the issuance of Section 8 assistance to minority households in conjunction with mobility counseling. HOPE VI plans to revitalize distressed public housing have often called for the deconcentration of former residents into neighborhoods in which they have not previously resided. And special-needs households, such as those suffering from mental illness or physical disabilities, have been increasingly provided with less-institutionalized, small-scale apartment buildings placed unobtrusively in good-quality residential neighborhoods.

Several studies, notably those associated with the Gautreaux and Yonkers public housing desegregation suit settlements in Chicago and New York, have shown the beneficial consequences for assisted households when they can live in these low-poverty, decent-quality residential settings. The replication and extension of these findings is the goal of HUD's Moving To Opportunity demonstration, now under way in five metropolitan areas. Preliminary results have thus far supported the conventional wisdom: Deconcentrating assisted housing is beneficial to residents.

Relatively few studies, however, have investigated what this new generation of deconcentrated assisted housing efforts has meant for the neighborhoods into which assisted households are placed. The few studies that have investigated local property-value impacts suffer from severe methodological shortcomings that put their conclusions in doubt. Further, no previous study has probed the potential impacts on neighborhood crime levels.

This glaring knowledge gap in a crucial arena of public policy motivated the research that is reported here. This book provides a comprehensive evaluation of the neighborhood property-value and crime impacts of three deconcentrated assisted housing programs: (1) the Section 8 program in Baltimore County, MD; (2) the scattered-site public housing program in Denver, CO; and (3) the supportive housing program for special needs households in Denver. In all three cases, much public debate erupted about their neighborhood impacts, which resulted in significant policy modifications. In this book, we use the term "assisted housing" to refer generically to all three types of housing programs we examined. Otherwise, we refer to each individual program by its name.

We employed a multi-method research strategy that previously has not been applied to this topic. We combined archival research, key informant interviews, econometric analyses, and focus group discussions. Our goal was to explain more fully the nature of the opposition to deconcentrating assisted housing, the sorts of programmatic restrictions that were imposed on the programs by local politics, and whether there was any empirical support for the fears that motivated this opposition. Drawing upon this deeper understanding, our goal was to derive relevant recommendations for policymakers across the country who are currently implementing programs to deconcentrate assisted housing. In particular, we have drawn out the implications of our findings for site selection and concentration, landlord monitoring, tenant selection and monitoring, collaboration with neighborhoods, public education, and a host of other practical and strategic features of deconcentrated assisted housing policy.

This book is based largely on research supported by the U.S. Department of Housing and Urban Development through contracts with the Urban Institute's Metropolitan Housing and Communities Policy Center. We thank HUD for its generous support. The analyses and opinions expressed in this book are ours and do not necessarily reflect those of HUD, the Urban Institute, Wayne State University, or their respective trustees.

A study of this scope and complexity obviously could not have been accomplished without the support and participation of a large number of people. Hetty Barthel, Mary Cunningham, John Marcotte, Sheila O'Leary, Kevin Thornton, and Charlene Wilson, researchers at the Urban Institute, and Sandra Newman of Johns Hopkins University contributed to this work. Subro Guhathakurta, Susan Popkin, Janet Smith, and Tom Thibodeaux provided helpful comments on early drafts of sections of the book. Ron Malega and Jackie Cutsinger provided invaluable editorial and manuscript production assistance.

The research on supportive housing benefited from a distinguished advisory panel, which provided input on policy context and study design. The members of this panel were Roger Clay, Howard Goldman, Marty Cohen, Susan Weaver, and Mark Elliot.

We also would like to recognize the numerous contributions made by many organizations and individuals in Baltimore County and Denver. First, we are grateful for the support given to us by officials at local housing authorities and public agencies. In particular, we thank Lois Cramer, administrator of the Baltimore County Housing Office (BCHO); Ruth Crystal, director of the Moving To Opportunity program (Baltimore); David Fields, director of the Baltimore County Office of Community Conservation; Gary Markowski, director of rental and assisted housing for the Housing Authority of Baltimore City; and Salvadore Carpio, executive director of the Housing Authority of the City and County of Denver (DHA). Bob Bromley and Jill Miller of the BCHO and Stella Madrid and Karen Spruce of the DHA gave us invaluable assistance in securing the data files on their agencies' programs that we needed for our analysis. Chuck Funayama, zoning program manager at the Department of Zoning, and Sadie Norman of the Department of Public Safety, both of the City and County of Denver, graciously provided us with data on supportive housing and crime reports. Roe Davis and Harold Reid of the BCHO provided helpful background information on the sites where we conducted focus groups in Baltimore County. Bobby Anderson at the DHA provided data on maintenance expenditures for the dispersed housing program.

To organize and conduct the focus groups in Denver, the Urban Institute subcontracted with the Latin American Research and Service Agency (LARASA). LARASA not only gave crucial assistance in completing the focus groups but also provided us with useful insights into the neighborhoods of Denver. The work at LARASA was initially directed by Susan Gallo, assisted by Jeff Garnas, and subsequently directed by Lisa Waugh. Glenda Swanson Lyle was the coordinator and facilitator for several of the Denver focus groups.

Once the research is completed it is, of course, another giant leap to transform it into a polished book. We were extremely fortunate in this regard to work with a team of first-rate editors and typesetters under the flawless direction of Arlene Pashman, senior editor at the Center for Urban Policy Research Press in the Edward J. Bloustein School of Planning and Public Policy at Rutgers University. We greatly appreciate the remarkable care lavished upon this manuscript, and the result will be clear to all readers. None of this would have been possible, of course, had not Robert W. Lake, editor in chief of CUPR Press, shown faith in our manuscript, so many thanks are due him as well.

Finally, we offer our thanks to the many key informants and focus group participants in Denver and Baltimore County who candidly shared their views and opinions on their neighborhoods and local communities. We hope that this book serves to guide assisted housing policy in ways that improve all of their neighborhoods.

George C. Galster
Peter A. Tatian
Anna M. Santiago
Kathryn L. S. Pettit
Robin E. Smith

1

Introduction: Deconcentrating Poverty or Destabilizing Neighborhoods?

Promoting the geographic mobility of low-income persons is a policy priority for HUD.
—Henry Cisneros, former secretary of the U.S. Department of
Housing and Urban Development (quoted in Hogan 1996)

I need some more space, . . . more green, . . . more oxygen, that's what I need for my
children. We're looking at [a new, nonpoverty neighborhood] and hoping and
praying they'll accept us as human beings.
—Isaac Neal, low-income resident of assisted housing in an
inner city neighborhood (quoted in Otto 2000)

Once you start messing around with people's property values
[by bringing in assisted housing], you're asking for trouble.
—Ellen Sauerbrey, Republican candidate for Governor
of Maryland (quoted in Waldron 1994)

I will not allow the public housing authority to ruin nice neighborhoods.
—Frank Rizzo, former mayor of Philadelphia
(quoted in Hogan 1996)

Neighborhoods across the United States are roiling with a conflict created by public policy. Policymakers who wish to deconcentrate assisted housing for low-income and special-needs households into areas where these households are underrepresented are at odds with citizens who wish to keep such housing out of their neighborhoods. One side sees the evils of concentrated poverty and the expanded opportunities and quality of life for residents when their assisted housing is located in low-poverty neighborhoods. The other side sees an invasion of undesirable neighbors who will undermine their quality of life, security, and property values.

Both sides have been myopic. In their zeal to deconcentrate assisted housing, policymakers at both federal and local levels have often ignored legitimate concerns of affected neighbors, sometimes dismissing their complaints out of hand as uninformed or purely prejudicial. In their knee-jerk, "not in my backyard" opposition, prospective neighborhoods have often ignored the fact that deconcentrated assisted housing can have neutral or even beneficial effects on the neighborhood, when it is done well.

In this book, we try to expand the field of view from both sides. We start from a middle-ground premise: There are persuasive reasons to offer assisted housing options in nonpoverty neighborhoods, but there are equally persuasive reasons for formulating deconcentrated housing policy in ways that recipient neighborhoods are not harmed. It is unsound public policy either to provide all assisted housing in poor neighborhoods or to allow assisted housing to be delivered in such a way that it destabilizes lower-poverty neighborhoods, thereby eventually re-creating poverty concentrations anew. Our goal in this book is thus to help inform the development of public policy that achieves the social benefits of assisted housing deconcentration with the least possible social costs to recipient neighborhoods. Ideally, this new public policy would produce a situation in which a neighborhood, facing the prospect of assisted housing, would respond "Why *not* in my backyard?"

There is no doubt that numerous communities across the nation *believe* that the social costs associated with the in-migration of any sort of low-income, assisted households spell disaster for their neighborhood (Evans 1996; HUD 2001). Well-publicized incidents of public protest crystallized around this issue have erupted during the past decade in such diverse metropolitan areas as Buffalo, Dallas, Chicago, Minneapolis, Oakland, Philadelphia, and Pittsburgh.[1]

Perhaps nowhere, however, has this belief been better illustrated than in Baltimore County and Denver. The City and County of Denver are coterminous, so we simply will refer to the jurisdiction as Denver. Baltimore County is a local jurisdiction entirely separate from the City of Baltimore, so we will always refer to it as Baltimore County. Though the jurisdictions differ in many respects, innovative efforts during the late 1980s and early 1990s to spatially deconcentrate assisted households of various types met with vocal, well-organized community opposition in both locales. In Denver, scattered-site public housing and the supportive housing for special needs populations programs were targeted. In Baltimore County, the Section 8/Moving to Opportunity rental assistance program proved a lightning rod for protest. The political opposition was sufficiently powerful that these programs were threatened with abolition; in the end, they were significantly cut back in scale or otherwise limited in the manner in which they operated.

In this book, we seize upon the analytical opportunity provided by these three programs in Denver and Baltimore County to explore the fundamental issues at the heart of the controversy over deconcentrating assisted housing. *Does assisted housing of various types cause negative neighborhood impacts? Do impacts vary across different sorts of neighborhoods? How does the spatial concentration of assisted housing or the scale of the facility affect impacts? What are the mechanisms through which these impacts transpire? How can deconcentration policies be revised to minimize any negative impacts?*

This book provides answers to these questions by bringing to bear a variety of qualitative and quantitative research methods. On the basis of our analysis, we advance this central thesis:

> *Most neighborhood fears regarding assisted housing are unfounded, but in certain circumstances (low value neighborhoods, high concentrations, large scales) they are justified. These circumstances must be avoided by significant reforms in the way assisted housing deconcentration policy is currently implemented.*

We acknowledge that our evidence is based on three assisted housing programs operated in two locales. Clearly, additional research on more programs in more sites is required before we can be assured of the generality of our findings.

The National Policy Context for Deconcentrating Assisted Housing

Policymakers at all levels of government have come to the conclusion that many past efforts to assist the needy with their housing have been misguided. During the past several decades, there has been a swelling consensus that concentrating low-income families, mentally ill individuals, or those with other special needs in large-scale developments designed exclusively for such people is usually a bad idea. It is especially bad policy when these large developments—be they called public housing projects, mental hospitals, or special care institutions—are located in neighborhoods where poverty, crime, decay, and other social problems are rampant. We consider the scientific basis of this conclusion below.

In response to this consensus, multifaceted efforts at various levels of government have been initiated to increase opportunities for assisted households to live in far less dense residential clusters of similar households that are located in far superior neighborhoods than have been typical in the past. The programmatic particulars of these deconcentration efforts differ according to whether low-income or special needs (e.g., mentally ill, disabled, frail elderly) individuals are concerned.

Before turning to the programmatic particulars and the supportive evidence upon which they are based, we note that the case for deconcentrating low-income populations is not airtight. We are only in the initial stages of attempting rigorous social benefit–cost analyses, which weigh the benefits of deconcentrated assisted housing programs to their costs of administration and impacts on recipient neighborhoods (Galster 2002; Johnson, Ladd, and Ludwig 2002). Indeed, this book provides vital raw material for such a benefit–cost analysis.

But to debate the merits of the deconcentration case is to miss our point: Policy decisions clearly *have* been made to deconcentrate assisted housing, whether justifiable on the basis of research or not (HUD 2001). Our purpose here is not to defend these initiatives, but to evaluate objectively how and why they have affected neighborhoods and, if necessary, how they should be modified to minimize harmful impacts.

The Perils of Poverty Concentrations

Regardless of the population being assisted or the programmatic particulars, deconcentration efforts have been motivated by an abiding abhorrence of concentrated poverty.[2] The guiding belief is that the physical, social, and economic conditions in a neighborhood contribute in important ways to the life chances of individuals, especially children and youth, beyond the contributions of one's family background and personal attributes (Kotlowitz 1991). By shaping what options for income, education, marriage, and the like are feasible and the expected payoffs from each, the neighborhood functions as a key component of one's "opportunity structure" (Galster and Killen 1995).

In neighborhoods characterized by concentrated poverty, chronic joblessness, and welfare use, the limitations on opportunity are especially horrific (Wilson 1987, 1996). If few of one's neighbors work, there is little chance of learning through informal networks about job vacancies that may arise in employees' firms. If one's children play in a friend's home that is filled with lead paint dust, their mental capacity can be impaired. If students who are not ready to learn dominate the local public school, the quality of education received by other students will be harmed. If neighborhood norms tolerate or even encourage teen childbearing out-of-wedlock, boys and girls will be more likely to become sexually active. If there is little social cohesion and collective efficacy, control of public spaces may default to criminal elements, whereupon some members of households may fear to leave their homes for work or recreation.

Commonsensical arguments such as these have garnered some support from statistical work undertaken during the 1990s (Ellen and Turner 1997; Gephart 1997; Leventhal and Brooks-Gunn 2000). Several studies have shown that, controlling for many (though certainly not all) parental and individual characteristics of importance, outcomes for people living in places of concentrated disadvantage are much less positive. A variety of social maladies—violence, crime, substance abuse, dropping out of school, not participating in the labor market, out-of-wedlock childbearing—will be intensified in circumstances of concentrated poverty.

There also is new evidence that the likelihood that people will engage in such socially undesirable behaviors grows disproportionately as the percentage of disadvantaged neighbors exceeds a threshold point (Quercia and Galster 2000). The bulk of the evidence, albeit limited, implies a threshold around 20 percent poor in the neighborhood (Galster 2002, 2003). This would be particularly important were it to garner an empirical consensus, for it suggests that deconcentrating poverty will not merely "move social problems around" while keeping their aggregate level unchanged. Rather, if low-income households were moved from neighborhoods exceeding the threshold to others well below it, the overall incidence of social problems throughout the metro area as a whole would be dramatically reduced (Galster and Zobel 1998; Galster 2002, 2003).

In fairness, it must be noted that the literature on concentrated poverty neighborhood effects is not without its weaknesses. Not all scholarly studies find that the characteristics of one's neighborhood have any identifiable impact on behavior, others find identifiable but only small impacts, others find impacts on only certain low-income population groups, and all studies of neighborhood effects have important methodological weaknesses (Brooks-Gunn, Duncan, and Aber 1997; Ginther, Haveman, and Wolfe 2000; Popkin et al. 2000).

The Push to Deconcentrate Housing for Low-Income Households

Policymakers' concerns about the location of low-income households who receive governmental housing assistance have traditionally been articulated in themes related to the aforementioned social problems of concentrated disadvantage. Since the 1990s, however, the issue has been framed more positively by those espousing deconcentration strategies (Polikoff 1994; Rosenbaum 1995; Cisneros 1995; Turner 1998). Housing subsidy programs, advocates argued, should be restructured to give low-income households more spatial options than they have had previously, for both equity and efficiency reasons. This enrichment of residential alternatives would improve not only the opportunities and well-being of recipients in the short run, it is claimed, but also their prospects for economic self-sufficiency in the long run, by enhancing their access to employment, job information networks and better-quality education. It would also expose them to community social norms more supportive of education and employment, which should have especially large payoffs for succeeding generations.

Programmatic manifestations over concerns regarding the locations of assisted households have assumed different guises, depending on whether the assistance took the form of demand-side (tenant-based) or supply-side (building-based) strategies (Nenno 1997). Tenant-based subsidies issued through the auspices of the Section 8 program emerged as the prime delivery vehicle for assisted housing in the early 1980s (Hartung and Henig 1997; Nenno 1997). Today the program assists approximately 1.5 million households, more than any other federal low-income housing assistance program. As of fiscal 2001, the program had witnessed three consecutive years of increasing appropriations involving tens of thousands of additional assisted households annually. Under the program, qualified households pay 30 percent of their adjusted gross income toward rent, whereas the federal government provides an additional subsidy equal in value to the difference between this tenant contribution and the "fair market rent" for an appropriately sized apartment of medium quality.[3]

Given that the tenant's location choices were not prescribed in the Section 8 program, policymakers concerned about deconcentration focused on how tenants could best be provided mobility information and counseling and how housing authorities could be encouraged to adopt procedures that would open up the widest feasible range of residential options. By 1990, a set of new legislative and rule changes was in place that permitted recipients of Section 8 certificates and vouchers to use their subsidies elsewhere than in the issuing local housing authority's jurisdiction (Goering, Stebbins, and Siewert 1995;

Peterson and Williams 1995). Local housing authorities were also required to provide information and counseling designed to encourage Section 8 recipients to move to low-poverty neighborhoods.

Two additional initiatives in the 1990s signaled the increasing federal commitment to deconcentrate Section 8 recipients (HUD 2001). In 1992, Congress authorized the Moving to Opportunity (MTO) demonstration program (Ludwig and Stolzberg 1995; Goering et al. 1999). In five metropolitan areas, this experimental program provided randomly selected, inner-city public housing residents with Section 8 subsidies, moving assistance, and mobility counseling supplied by a nonprofit agency. This experimental group was required to use their Section 8 subsidy in census tracts having no more than 10 percent poverty rates as of 1990. Similar public housing residents who applied were randomly assigned either to another treatment group receiving a Section 8 subsidy but no mobility assistance or requirement that they move to a low-poverty neighborhood, or to a control group remaining in public housing from which they applied. The results are to be evaluated over 10 years to assess the efficacy of different mobility-enhancing strategies and the long-run impacts on recipients of having greater mobility (HUD 1996; Goering et al. 1999).

In 1997, the U.S. Department of Housing and Urban Development (HUD) began another tenant-based mobility demonstration program in 16 metropolitan areas. Titled the Regional Opportunity Counseling demonstration program, it involved infusing the regular Section 8 program with exemplary mobility assistance strategies, recruitment of more landlords into the program, and inter–housing authority collaboration within a metropolitan area. It sought a comprehensive approach to help Section 8 households select the most appropriate dwellings and neighborhoods from a wide array of jurisdictions across their metropolitan area (Turner and Williams 1998).

As for supply-side strategies, efforts to head off further concentration of assisted housing developments were instituted as early as the 1970s. HUD promulgated "neighborhood impaction" standards that forbade the construction of subsidized housing in neighborhoods that exceeded certain percentages of low-income and minority residents (Gray and Tursky 1986). Fears that the scales of some public housing developments were so gigantic that they would create concentrated poverty regardless of the neighborhoods in which they were placed led to initiatives for constructing small-scale, widely scattered public housing complexes (Hogan 1996). Such "scattered-site housing" initiatives continue to this day, with local public housing authorities across the nation utilizing small apartment buildings, duplexes, and even single-family units for their tenants. Some buildings are newly constructed, whereas others are developed through acquisition and subsequent rehabilitation (Turner and Williams 1998).

Two additional reforms of the public housing program in the 1990s generated increasing pressure to deconcentrate assisted tenants: federal desegregation suits and HOPE VI. During the 1980s, a host of suits were filed by minority residents against local public housing authorities and HUD, alleging various types of discriminatory and segregationist behaviors. Of course, the long history of such actions by public housing authorities has been well documented (Hirsch 1983; Goering 1986; Goldstein and Yancy 1986; Bauman 1987; Coulibaly, Green, and James 1998).

What was unusual about the 1990s was that an exceptional number of such long-standing suits (more than a dozen) were settled in short order during the early years of Bill Clinton's administration. Most of these settlements involved the construction of scattered-site public housing and/or the issuance of Section 8 assistance to minority households in conjunction with mobility counseling (Popkin et al. 2000). Often there was a court-mandated requirement that such Section 8 subsidies be used in low-poverty, low-minority neighborhoods.

The second important public housing reform was the Urban Revitalization Demonstration, conventionally called HOPE VI. Begun in 1992, HOPE VI focused on the most distressed, large-scale public housing developments, with goals to integrate them better into the surrounding neighborhood, create a more mixed-income environment on-site that promoted family self-sufficiency, and leverage a variety of funds to achieve area-wide revitalization. By 2000, the program's roster included 129 developments in 80 cities (Kingsley, Johnson, and Pettit 2001). Program guidelines were flexible, and local public housing authorities developed idiosyncratic redevelopment schemes based on perceived needs and opportunities (Epp 1996). Of most importance here, however, is that many HOPE VI plans called for deconcentration of former public housing residents into neighborhoods in which they had not previously resided, either through scattered-site new construction or Section 8 subsidies (Kingsley, Johnson, and Pettit 2001).[4]

Thus, with both demand- and supply-side strategies, federal housing policy in the 1990s witnessed increasing emphasis on deconcentrating low-income households receiving housing assistance (HUD 2001). This emphasis belies a tacit assumption that deconcentration is greatly beneficial for participating low-income households.

Perhaps the best-known supportive evidence was produced by Rosenbaum and his many collaborators during their multiple investigations of the Gautreaux program in Chicago. As a remedy to the 1969 lawsuit filed by Dorothy Gautreaux and other tenants of the Chicago Housing Authority, the court ordered HUD to help thousands of black public housing residents move to neighborhoods with low concentrations of blacks that were located within the metropolitan area (Goering 1986). Although scattered-site public housing was part of the original settlement promulgated in 1976, neighborhood opposition slowed its production.

So Section 8, coupled with intensive mobility counseling and moving assistance, became the largest component of the settlement (Davis 1993). Ultimately, 7,100 families participated, with most moving to suburban areas with low concentrations of poverty and minorities. Interviews revealed that, compared to those remaining in the city, participants (1) felt significantly safer and their children were less vulnerable to gang recruitment; (2) were (eventually) socially integrated to some degree and not isolated; and (3) had children who were more likely to be attending four-year colleges, taking college-track courses in high school, and working at a job with good pay and benefits (Rosenbaum 1995; Rubinowitz and Rosenbaum 2000).

Recent evidence emerging from the ongoing MTO demonstration echo many of the Gautreaux findings of positive impacts, though the research methods and findings vary across the experimental sites in a way that generalizations are rendered precarious. Moreover, the studies thus far have only been able to ascertain short-term impacts within a few years of program startup; perhaps more impressive long-term effects will be observed henceforth.

Nevertheless, the results to date suggest that compared with the control group, the experimental MTO group moving to low-poverty neighborhoods experienced (1) social interactions with neighbors that were not significantly different from their neighborhood of origin; (2) better physical health and fewer reports of depressive or anxious behavior; (3) reductions in self-reported criminal victimization; (4) lower rates of welfare receipt; (5) increased standardized achievement scores of their young children; (6) lower rates of criminal offending and arrests for violent crimes for their young boys; and (7) fewer instances of behaving punitively toward their children or engaging in restrictive parenting practices (Leventhal and Brooks-Gunn 2000; Katz, Kling, and Liebman 2001; Ludwig, Duncan, and Pinkston 2000; Ludwig, Ladd, and Duncan 2001).

Studies of the impacts upon households participating in scattered-site public housing programs have generally reinforced the conclusions derived from research on tenant-based subsidy programs, though they have typically not been as comprehensive or methodologically rigorous (Varady and Preiser 1998). Tenants living in scattered-site public housing generally (1) experienced few problems with their move and felt welcome in their homes, (2) strongly preferred their new homes and neighborhoods to their former ones; (3) were generally satisfied with accessibility and public services, with the exception of public transportation; (4) had minimal social interactions with their middle-class neighbors, but were not socially isolated; and (5) expected their children to benefit in the long-term from the superior educational opportunities and neighborhood safety (Hogan 1996; Briggs 1997).

The Push to Deconcentrate Assisted Housing for People with Special Needs

In contrast to the long-standing experience supplying assisted housing to low-income populations in general, such aid to those with special needs—such as persons with physical or developmental disabilities and the severely mentally ill—has been relatively recent. Prior to the 1970s, "housing policy" for these groups consisted almost exclusively of confinement in large-scale institutions, typically operated by the states or, in the case of frail elderly, private, for-profit providers. These institutions, of course, often produced maximum concentration of the group in question.

With the wave of de-institutionalization came the realization that not only did many with special needs require affordable housing, they also required supervision and a package of supportive services tailored to their needs, perhaps but not necessarily delivered in conjunction with the housing (Dear and Wolch 1987; Mechanic and Rochefort 1990; S. J. Newman 1992). "Supportive housing facilities" were the result.

Prior to the 1980s, supportive housing facilities were subsidized primarily by states or private philanthropies. The one long-standing exception was housing for the frail elderly, which was financed under the HUD Section 202 program initially authorized in 1954. The dramatic growth in the homeless population during the 1980s, however, led to the passage of the Stewart B. McKinney Act in 1987 (amended in 1988 and 1990) and, for the first time, the availability of significant federal resources for housing and services programs for homeless persons.

During the Clinton administration, supportive housing was emphasized heavily (Fuchs and McAllister 1996). Innovations in the field were encouraged by the HUD Supportive Housing Program Competition beginning in 1994. HUD's goal was to establish a programmatic continuum along which the needs of various sorts of homeless and disabled individuals could be met effectively (HUD 1995). Supportive housing became the mainstay of this effort in communities across the country (Guhathakurta and Mushkatel 2000).

At the present time, the main public-sector sources of governmental funding for supportive housing include state supplements to the Supplemental Security Income (SSI) program, two optional programs under Medicaid (Targeted Case Management and Rehabilitative Services), the Social Services Block Grant, the HUD 811 Program,[5] and a broad range of McKinney Act programs (e.g., Projects for Assistance in Transition from Homelessness, Shelter Plus Care). Despite the upsurge in public resources, the development of supportive housing typically requires a complex financing scheme whereby multiple sources are packaged (S. J. Newman 1992). SSI, for example, can be used for some clients' rental expenses, but not capital costs. Medicaid can pay for case management, but not housing costs. Grants from state governments have provided the bulk of the developers' hard and soft costs.

In general, supportive housing initiatives subscribe to one of two different approaches on how to best meet special needs: the "level of care" or "residential continuum" approach, and the "independent housing" or "housing as housing" approach (S. J. Newman 1992). The concept guiding the former is to accommodate the heterogeneity of client needs by establishing a continuum of residential settings that varies in the level and intensity of staff supervision and in program structure.[6] By contrast, the second approach views housing fundamentally as a decent, affordable place to live, not a place to be treated. Thus, efforts to "normalize" the dwellings and neighborhood surroundings are stressed, with no requirement of on-site service provision and direct supervision.[7]

The supportive housing facilities developed under both the "housing as housing" strategy and the less supervised/intensive segments of the "continuum of care" strategy share common features related to deconcentration. They typically are composed of buildings of a comparatively small scale and/or with relatively few special-needs individuals sharing the same building. These characteristics often arose due to a confluence of limited funding sources and emerging beliefs on the part of sponsors of improved therapeutic benefits for residents. Increasingly, the development of supportive housing facilities has involved the construction or acquisition and rehabilitation of buildings in nonpoverty residential areas that previously had no such facilities.

Research has focused on comparing resident outcomes in supportive housing with those obtained in more traditional, institutionalized settings or in the unsupported private housing market, not on the effects of location or neighborhood conditions per se. Given the diversity of those with special needs, it is understandable that no consensus has emerged about the optimal mix of housing, neighborhood, and service characteristics for clients fitting a particular profile, other than that "a range of options" is desirable (S. J. Newman 1992). The available evidence indicates, however, that supportive housing can provide a humane, therapeutically effective environment for groups with even the most challenging special needs. Its application to those with severe mental illness, even those who were homeless, has proven remarkably effective in many circumstances (Shern et al. 1997; Ridgway and Rapp 1998), and has led to significant reductions in residents' subsequent use of shelters and in-patient psychiatric services, and rates of incarceration (Metraux, Culhane, and Hadley 2000).

Answers to the question of the optimal neighborhood environment for supportive housing are less clear and are indeed conflicting. On the one hand, Earls and Nelson (1988) suggest that residency in a good-quality environment may be one way that those with special needs, much like other individuals, can satisfy their "pain-avoidance needs" and thereby experience therapeutic benefits. On the other hand, neighborhoods of modest socioeconomic status, racial and ethnic diversity, mixed land uses, and social disorganization may be less likely to reject or isolate special-needs populations (Hall, Nelson, and Fowler 1987; S. J. Newman et al. 1994; Segal, Silverman, and Baumohl 1989; Taylor, Hall, and Hughes 1984; Trute and Segal 1976). This greater sense of belonging may translate into tenant benefits. Certainly, no one suggests that there are benefits to special-needs tenants from concentrating them in unhealthy, unsafe neighborhoods. But no consensus has been reached about the degree of deconcentration and the relative quality position of the destination neighborhood.

The Nature of NIMBY

From the perspective of many prospective neighbors, whether deconcentrated assisted housing is good for the needy households participating is beyond the point. "It probably is *not* good for me, my property values, and my neighborhood," goes the conventional wisdom.

Neighborhood opposition to moving in low-income tenants or subsidized housing facilities is hardly new. Indeed, it has been present from the earliest days of the public housing program (Hirsch 1983; Bauman 1987; Sugrue 1996; Hogan 1996). In the past decade, however, opposition has grown so much more strident and widespread (and perhaps more effective) that researchers and practitioners commonly use an acronym for it: NIMBY (not in my backyard) (Freudenberg and Pastor 1992; Dear, Takahashi, and Wilton 1996; Takahashi and Dear 1997). In extreme cases, NIMBY has turned into attitudes of: NIABY (not in anybody's backyard), BANANA (build absolutely nothing anywhere near anyone) and NOPE (not on planet Earth).

Roots of Opposition

The resistance to low-income and supportive housing facilities results from two types of processes—economic and noneconomic—though in practice the two are often not easily separable (Lake 1993; Kaufman and Smith 1999).[8] The economic reasons for opposing assisted housing relate to the alleged impact of these facilities on property values within the neighborhood. It is widely accepted that property values reflect the overall quality of life in the neighborhood as well as the mix of local amenities (Grieson and White 1989). Therefore, by purportedly reducing aspects of the quality of life in the neighborhood, opponents claim that assisted housing will contribute to lower property values.

For instance, any development, whether it is for assisted housing or not, can create unwanted noise and congestion. Assisted housing may represent the introduction of different racial and ethnic groups or lower socioeconomic class populations into a neighborhood. These groups may have difficulty integrating into the social structure of their environment. Another conventional idea is that residents of the new facility are more prone to criminal activity, especially if they are males, members of certain racial or ethnic groups, convicted felons, or recovering substance abusers. A final reason is associated with the anticipated inferior management of the assisted housing, which results in poor upkeep of the building and grounds and inadequate supervision and monitoring of tenant behaviors. All of these effects, it is argued, will lower the quality of life and be negatively evaluated by the housing market, resulting in psychic and pecuniary losses for property owners in the area.

Empirical studies in a wide variety of contexts have emphasized that, indeed, such fears of eroding quality of neighborhood life constitute the foundation of opposition (Rocha and Dear 1989; Hogan 1996). For example, the National Law Center on Homelessness and Poverty (1997) polled 89 supportive housing programs from around the nation and found that 41 percent had experienced NIMBY opposition from either prospective neighbors or their local governments prior to beginning their operations. The most prevalent reason cited (64 percent) was anticipated loss of property values; potential increase in crime was next in frequency (61 percent). Other major sources of opposition stemmed from expectations of increased traffic and parking problems (39 percent of the cases), an unsightly facility (21 percent), and greater noise (18 percent). Concerns over supervision of residents were voiced in a few additional cases. Analogous community concerns about Section 8 were revealed in eight recent case studies (HUD 2001). By far the most frequent areas of worry related to disruptive tenant behavior and poor upkeep of the Section 8–occupied apartments. Declines in property value and increases in crime also emerged as issues.

Although much community opposition has an economic motivation, there are also noneconomic issues related to prejudices and ethics that can create staunch opposition to assisted housing. Prospective neighbors may harbor biases against low-income people in general, especially if they are in certain racial or ethnic groups. They also may dislike the in-movers because they deem them on moral grounds to be unworthy recipients of aid, and thus would be better housed in marginal or nonresidential parts of a city. Or residents may not oppose assisted housing or households in general, but may believe on the grounds of fairness that the proposed neighborhood already has its "fair share." When it comes to supportive housing for special-needs populations, community residents are even more likely to express highly emotional reasons for opposition. These include a fear of people with disabilities—particularly a fear of living near or coming into contact with people with mental illnesses, HIV/AIDS, or substance abuse problems (Dear 1992; Takahashi and Dear 1997).

The above-mentioned National Law Center on Homelessness and Poverty survey (1997) is also informative in this regard. In five sites, the respondents cited NIMBY motivated by opposition to "those people," substance abusers, persons with HIV/AIDS, pregnant teens, or homeless people. In two more sites, neighbors voiced a concern that there already was an overconcentration of social service agencies and facilities in the area. Similar concerns have been expressed regarding "overconcentrations of Section 8" (HUD 2001).

Ironically, concerns over the reconcentration of supposedly "deconcentrated" assisted housing and the resulting detrimental impacts on neighborhoods have been voiced not only by community opponents but also by some researchers and policymakers (HUD 2001). Evidence from a variety of sources—the Freestanding Voucher Demonstration and administrative data from local Section 8 programs, MTO, the vouchering out of assisted housing projects, and HOPE VI site demolitions—have consistently revealed that Section 8 subsidy recipients tend to move into relatively few neighborhoods unless they are strongly assisted in doing otherwise (Goering et al. 1995; Hartung and Henig 1997; Fischer 1999; Turner and Williams 1998; Pendall 2000; Turner, Popkin, and Cunningham 2000; Kingsley, Johnson, and Pettit 2001). There is also limited evidence to suggest that the clustering of Section 8 recipients reinforces the spatial pattern of supportive housing programs (Guhathakurta and Mushkatel 2000). Thus, neighborhood concerns about the entrance of assisted housing may implicitly tap a (not unrealistic) fear that "once the door is opened, they all will come in."

The potential "overconcentration" of assisted households participating in reputedly deconcentrated housing programs is a recurrent theme in this book. We will explore both theoretically and empirically the forces that tend to cluster assisted households and facilities. Our empirical analyses will investigate the degree to which assisted housing starts to create negative neighborhood impacts when it exceeds a threshold concentration. Were such thresholds to be identified, it would suggest not only that the fears of some neighborhoods may be justified but also that the practice of delivering deconcentrated assisted housing needs improving, topics we address at length in chapter 9.

Variations in Opposition

However motivated, resistance to the siting of assisted housing is not monolithic. Opposition depends on the characteristics of the host community and the assisted housing program or assisted households in question (Dear 1992). Resistance typically has been strongest in middle- and upper-income communities and nondiverse suburban areas, especially those containing households with children (Graham and Logan 1990). Areas with mixed land uses appear just as prone to opposition as exclusively residential ones (National Law Center on Homelessness and Poverty 1997). By contrast, tolerance of more diverse residential environments seems to be higher among those who are better educated, renters, and younger (Dear 1992; Hogan 1996).

Regardless of the host community, the type of assisted housing in question is strongly predictive of the degree of opposition. Low-income families may be virtually invisible to host neighborhoods when they use Section 8 to occupy a well-managed, long-established apartment building in the area, but they may be opposed when they are to be housed in a newly constructed public housing development. The types of facilities sited under HUD-funded supportive housing programs often serve even more unacceptable populations, as perceived by incumbent neighborhood residents. For instance, facilities such as group homes and homeless shelters are consistently rated in polls as being unwelcome additions to any neighborhood (Takahashi and Dear 1997). Moreover, the National Law Center on Homelessness and Poverty (1997) survey of 92 supportive housing providers found that the likelihood of community opposition to supportive housing varied with the character of the client population served. The two most likely to engender opposition were adult recovering substance abusers (50 percent of the cases met opposition), and adults with severe mental illness (37 percent).

Forms of Opposition

When opposition has surfaced, it has taken several forms. Prospective neighbors have raised objections at local zoning or planning board meetings, mounted public demonstrations, organized petition drives, and filed lawsuits. The National Law Center on Homelessness and Poverty (1997) survey of supportive housing providers discerned that opposition in the majority of cases took the form of protests at a public meeting or hearing (82 percent of the cases) and/or neighbors conveying disapproval to public officials through various means (58 percent). Neighbors voiced opposition to the media in 30 percent of the cases and organized petition drives in 21 percent; in only 6 percent were suits filed.

Typically in response to their constituents' wishes, local politicians have also mounted various forms of opposition, including media events, legal restrictions, and injunctions. The most common tactics involve land use regulations that impose onerous procedural or permitting requirements, tightly limit areas in which certain building types or occupancy classifications may be applied, or otherwise constrain how scattered certain supportive housing facilities must be or how many residents each building may contain. In some cases, developers of proposed supportive housing facilities have been required to prove that the proposal will not harm the recipient neighborhood (National Law Center on Homelessness and Poverty 1997).

The final form of protest used by a few opponents of assisted housing is, unfortunately, extreme. These constitute cases of violent threats, harassment, and arson (Henig 1994; National Law Center on Homelessness and Poverty 1997). Though rare, such a radical form of protest is emblematic of the sort of passions that the NIMBY syndrome may engender.

Many of the above-mentioned forms of opposition are clearly illegal, and others have been attacked on legal grounds. The most commonly applied federal legal bases for challenging certain forms of opposition to supportive housing have been the Fair Housing Amendments Act of 1988 and the Americans with Disabilities Act of 1990, which prohibit discrimination against people with disabilities. For example, the Supreme Court ruled in 1995 in the case of *City of Desmonds v. Oxford House, Inc.*, that a restrictive definition of "family" could not be used by communities to exclude group homes from residential areas. The Justice Department under the Clinton administration initiated suits in several towns across the country to enjoin residents from protesting the establishment of group homes through distributing leaflets, contacting local representatives, and filing lawsuits. The department contended that First Amendment rights should not apply when such actions are pursued for illegal ends, such as excluding disabled citizens from their neighborhoods (Colwell, Dehring, and Lash 2000).

Many state laws have also been applied to overturning local restrictions. Some state fair housing laws go further than federal statutes in extending protections, most notably to those receiving government assistance as the primary source of income. In these cases, landlords' refusal to rent to Section 8 subsidy holders may be judged illegal. Other states have legislatively constrained localities' ability to limit supportive housing through restrictive zoning and permitting practices. California and New Jersey, for example, preempt local land use controls over the siting of particular sorts of facilities (National Law Center on Homelessness and Poverty 1997), and Illinois requires that localities submit plans to assure adequate availability of sites for supportive housing facilities (Colwell, Dehring, and Lash 2000). A large number of states and counties have passed inclusionary zoning ordinances requiring developers of new subdivisions to set aside a share of new units for lower-income households, thereby trumping potential local opposition (Mallach 1984; Calavita and Grimes 1998).

Innovative Deconcentration Efforts Meet NIMBY: An Overview of Three Case Studies

Push has come to shove. Housing policymakers at various levels of government have increasingly adopted strategies for deconcentrating low-income and special-needs populations. Correspondingly, neighborhood opposition to this deconcentration of assisted housing has become equally widespread, typically founded on the expectation that such housing will spawn social problems and erode property values in the vicinity. Legal skirmishes have intensified as federal and state governments have attacked forms of local opposition through the courts. Something has to give.

Three recent examples provide quintessential illustrations of community opposition—based on fear of detrimental neighborhood impacts—to creative policy initiatives to deconcentrate subsidized households. In all these cases, the opposition resulted in considerable modifications to the original programmatic initiatives. The three examples involve a supply-side, low-income housing strategy in Denver; a supply-side supportive housing strategy in Denver; and a demand-side, low-income housing strategy in Baltimore County. These three cases are the subject of this book, and we introduce them below as a prelude to the detailed histories provided in chapters 2 and 3.

The Denver Housing Authority's "Dispersed" Public Housing Program

In 1969, the Housing Authority of the City and County of Denver (DHA) began operating a public housing "dispersal" program involving 100 single-family and duplex units acquired at foreclosure sales, which were then renovated and occupied by DHA tenants. The program grew slowly, yet was able for almost two decades to "stay below the radar" of public opposition or political visibility. All that abruptly changed in 1988, when HUD ordered the DHA to notify publicly the Denver City Council about the site-by-site details and obtain its approval for any dispersed housing plans. By contrast, DHA housing acquisitions needed to be described only in general terms to the council and required only the mayor's consent.

In 1988, therefore, the DHA was forced to reveal the details of its proposed second-phase dispersal plan, which involved purchases of more than 400 additional homes in middle-class neighborhoods. An inflammatory political skirmish erupted, centering on the concerns of the local citizenry regarding the perceived deleterious effects of moving public housing residents into middle-class neighborhoods. In response to these concerns, a council-appointed task force drafted a set of guidelines regulating further DHA acquisitions. These guidelines stipulated that the DHA could not acquire more than one unit per block face and no more than 1 percent of the units in any census tract. Moreover, the DHA was to target the "nonimpacted" areas of Denver for these purchases.

This concession did little to defuse the controversy. Opponents persisted in their argument that the dispersed public housing plan would increase crime and erode property values in recipient neighborhoods, and that the plan was inequitable inasmuch as poor families could occupy better-quality homes than working-class families currently living in these areas. Proponents argued that the plan was crucial for improving the quality of life for DHA tenants, enhancing the geographic diversity of their residential options, and creating an environment where their chances of economic self-sufficiency were enhanced. After much acrimonious debate, the Denver City Council approved the dispersed public housing plan with restrictive siting guidelines and formulated an intergovernmental agreement that has been in operation since late 1989.

The Supportive Housing Initiatives in Denver

During the 1980s and 1990s, the pace of developing supportive housing sites by a wide variety of public and private entities in Denver also intensified. The most significant local event shaping this growth was the *Goebel* case, in which chronically mentally ill plaintiffs sued governmental service providers for supplying inadequate care. The trial court found for the plaintiffs in 1985 and ordered the defendants to submit a plan for delivery of appropriate community mental health services. The Community Development Agency devised a plan to use Denver funds to leverage state and other monies aimed at developing 250 units of supportive housing.

As is detailed in chapter 2, there were several highly visible and contentious debates over this expanding number of supportive housing facilities that were proposed throughout Denver's residential areas. In response to these controversies, the Denver City Council passed the Large Residential Care Use Ordinance in 1993. This law sought to ameliorate concerns related to the facilities of both supportive housing advocates and host neighborhoods (City and County of Denver 1998a, 1998c). Among other things, the ordinance specified minimum separation requirements among facilities, much as had been done for dispersed public housing; limited facility scale; and established a mechanism of consultation between the developer and the host neighborhood, mediated by city officials. Moreover, the ordinance gave Denver's zoning administrator the power to approve, approve with conditions, or deny a permit for supportive housing.

HUD-Sponsored Section 8 and MTO Programs in Baltimore County

The Section 8 program has operated for a quarter of a century, providing needy recipients with a subsidy allowing them, in principle, to rent decent-quality apartments anywhere in a metropolitan area. A major controversy over attempts to deconcentrate low-income, former public housing tenants through the use of Section 8 subsidies erupted during the summer of 1994 in Baltimore County. Much of the opposition crystallized around a newly initiated Section 8 demonstration and research program, HUD's Moving to Opportunity demonstration. During its first phase, MTO was designed to assist 143 subsidized tenants in moving from Baltimore City public housing developments to Baltimore County. Subsequent planned waves would quadruple this number.

Despite the small scale of the Baltimore City MTO program, especially compared with Baltimore County's own Section 8 program involving more than 3,000 households, it became a lightning rod for opponents of deconcentrating assisted housing because it arrived at the unfortunate confluence of several local events, which we detail in chapter 3. A Fourth of July parade in blue-collar Dundalk, Maryland, a community adjacent to Baltimore, turned into a de facto rally where spectators could vocally air their fears surrounding deconcentrated assisted housing. A spate of anger-filled public meetings and protests followed. The local political pressure ultimately proved irresistible, even at the national level. Maryland Democratic senator Barbara Mikulski, a native of Dundalk, was persuaded to use her influence as chair of the Senate Appropriations Subcommittee for HUD to cut short funding for MTO. As a result, the eagerly anticipated longitudinal study on the tenant impacts of deconcentration was scaled back not only in Baltimore but in the other four demonstration sites as well.

Does Deconcentrating Assisted Housing Harm Neighborhoods? An Investigative Strategy

This book provides some answers to the fundamental neighborhood impact questions that have swirled around deconcentrated assisted housing programs. Through a mixture of qualitative and quantitative analyses, we have established a framework that provides an in-depth analysis of the extent and nature of these impacts in specific contexts. In particular, we address the following:

- Does the Denver Housing Authority's dispersed housing program, the supportive housing programs in Denver, or the Section 8 / MTO program in Baltimore County significantly reduce the sales prices of single-family homes in the vicinity?
- Do these Denver programs significantly increase the rate of reported violent, property, and other crimes in the vicinity?[9]
- Does context matter? Are there particular sorts of recipient neighborhoods for which the answers to the above questions change?
- Do concentration and scale matter? Are there threshold concentrations of assisted housing sites past which negative impacts ensue? Do impacts vary by the scale of the assisted housing facility?
- How do neighborhood impacts happen? What are the mechanisms through which these impacts transpire? What lessons can be learned that can usefully guide future deconcentration efforts in ways that minimize harmful neighborhood impacts?

To answer these questions, we have undertaken a three-pronged investigative strategy in both Denver and Baltimore County case study sites: a community and policy reconnaissance involving key informant interviews and archival analysis, multivariate statistical analyses, and focus group analyses.

Community and Policy Reconnaissance

Through the analysis of archival and published sources and interviews with key informants, we have developed a context for understanding any observed neighborhood impacts. Specifically, this book provides (1) a profile of the economic, demographic, and political landscape of the local communities and housing markets in Denver and Baltimore County; (2) a detailed description of the policy history, administration, and operation of the deconcentrated assisted housing programs; (3) a historical narrative describing the opposition to the programs; and (4) an analysis of the NIMBY syndrome based on key community members' hypotheses about the relationship between the housing programs and neighborhood changes.

Quantitative Property-Value and Crime-Impact Analyses

We performed comprehensive multiple regression analyses to ascertain whether sales prices of single-family homes are adversely affected by proximity to dispersed public housing units or supportive housing facilities in Denver, or Section 8 households in Baltimore County. We performed similar analyses to ascertain whether crime rates are affected by proximity to dispersed public housing or supportive housing sites in Denver. Our econometric specifications involved a "pre/post" model that measures both levels and trends of the given impact variable before and after the opening of an assisted housing facility. This model represents an important analytical advance, for it allowed us to sort out directions of causation between the assisted housing and the neighborhood.

Focus Group Analysis

We conducted focus groups with homeowners in a wide variety of neighborhoods where assisted housing existed to gather more qualitative information on the possible interactions among house prices, neighborhood quality, crime, and the location of assisted housing. The focus groups also allowed us to collect additional, policy-relevant information on homeowners' perceptions of the changes taking place in their communities, their opinions about the impact of assisted housing, and their views on what makes neighborhoods more or less vulnerable to negative impacts.

A Guide to This Book

The next two chapters provide the results of our community and policy reconnaissance: a geopolitical background to the NIMBY controversies over deconcentrating assisted housing in our Denver and Baltimore County study sites. Chapters 2 and 3 paint a demographic and economic portrait of Denver and Baltimore County, respectively. They give extensive descriptions of the three deconcentrated assisted housing programs constituting the focus of this book, maps of the locations of the assisted units, and political histories of the controversies that swirled around them. They make it clear that the fears about neighborhood impacts of these housing programs were remarkably similar, despite distinct differences in the communities, the programs, and their clientele.

Chapter 4 describes the quantitative and qualitative research methods used in our second two research prongs. It probes the methodological challenges in deciphering the neighborhood impacts of assisted housing programs. Previous statistical approaches fall short of supplying unambiguous answers; chapter 4 explains how our method overcomes these shortcomings. The chapter provides at the outset a nontechnical overview of our econometric approach for those who wish an intuitive understanding of our method without considering more advanced statistical issues. Clearly denoted sections of chapter 4 and an appendix contain more technical material. Finally, the chapter describes our focus group sites, protocols, and associated qualitative methods.

Chapter 5 offers descriptive statistical data on housing prices, crime rates, and the location of deconcentrated assisted housing programs in Denver and Baltimore County. Data are presented in both tabular and map forms to provide a comprehensive yet comprehensible portrait of the data we have analyzed.

The statistical findings related to neighborhood property value and crime impacts are presented in chapters 6, 7, and 8. These chapters provide a detailed quantification of the neighborhood impacts of, respectively, dispersed public housing in Denver, supportive housing in Denver, and Section 8 in Baltimore County. Statistical results are conveyed in graphical form to make them accessible to a wide readership. The Denver analyses involve impacts measured in terms of both housing prices and crime rates; data limitations allow us to analyze only housing prices in Baltimore County. Impacts across the entire sample and for particular subsets of neighborhoods are considered. The qualitative focus group results are woven throughout these chapters to provide richer interpretations and deeper understandings of the statistical patterns.

Chapter 9 provides concluding observations and draws implications from our work for policy and practice. By synthesizing the quantitative and qualitative evidence of the previous chapters, it draws a powerful portrait of neighborhood impacts that vary by context, concentration, and scale. On the basis of these findings, the chapter then provides a comprehensive set of practical suggestions for those who devise and operate deconcentrated assisted housing programs. These holistic recommendations constitute what we term a "neighborhood-friendly" program for deconcentrating assisted housing in ways that minimize negative impacts while maximizing positive ones. Our policy is designed to confound the conventional negative public stereotypes about deconcentrated assisted housing programs by significantly enhancing their performance in numerous dimensions implied by our analyses. We hope that these recommendations make deconcentrated assisted housing efforts better both for assisted households and for their new neighbors.

Notes

1. For illustrations and details, see Schill 1992; Husock 1994; Bovard 1994a, 1994b; Montgomery 1994; Goetz, Lam, and Heitlinger 1996; Hogan 1996; Nichols and McCoy 1997; Varady and Walker 2000; and Popkin et al. 2000.

2. Concentrated poverty has not been the only grounds for concern. Others believe that spatially concentrating subsidized households facilitates their stigmatization and the withdrawal of private and public capital from their neighborhood (Rainwater 1970; Massey and Kanaiaupuni 1993; Schill and Wachter 1995; Leavitt and Loukaitou-Sider 1995). Still others see a social cost in clustering assisted households in the form of perpetuated racial and ethnic segregation and isolation (Goering and Coulibably 1989; Massey, Gross, and Eggers 1991; Bauman, Hummon, and Muller 1991; Massey and Denton 1993).

3. The program details of Section 8 differ slightly, depending on whether it is the certificate or voucher variant. For more, see Goering, Stebbins, and Siewert 1995.

4. Note that another form of supply-side program faced challenges during the 1990s that added yet further pressure to move assisted households. Earlier generations of federal programs assisted developers of new and substantially rehabilitated housing set aside for a contractual period units for occupancy by low-income households. Several of such complexes had fallen into such serious disrepair that HUD "vouchered them out"; tenants were given Section 8 vouchers for use with different apartments (Varady and Walker 2000). However, this does not represent a powerful example of federal efforts to deconcentrate assisted households. There were no restrictions on where displaced tenants could move, nor was mobility emphasized; tenants were only given the option of relocation counseling (Varady and Walker 2000).

5. Nonelderly disabled individuals who previously were eligible for the Section 202 program are now separated into this program.

6. E.g., in the early 1990s, New York relied on a four-level system for the mentally ill: supervised, intensive supportive, supportive, and crisis; Massachusetts used a three-level approach; and Missouri had a two-level system. For more examples and details, see S. J. Newman (1992).

7. E.g., the Santa Clara County Clustered Apartment Project, started in the late 1980s and targeted toward persons with serious mental illness, has a housing component consisting of individual rental units that are located within walking distance of one another, and on-demand service support and treatment elements. The attempts of several cities, including Los Angeles, New York, and San Diego, to reclaim, preserve, and upgrade single-room-occupancy hotels is also a "housing as housing" approach (S. J. Newman 1992).

8. Kaufman and Smith (1997) provide finer-grained distinctions: functional consequences, economic consequences, environmental consequences, and social consequences.

9. Unfortunately, crime data coded by individual address of report are not available for Baltimore County, so we were unable to conduct a crime-impact analysis there.

2

The Denver Controversies over the Dispersed Public Housing and Supportive Housing Programs

Neighborhood opposition to local efforts to deconcentrate low-income and supportive housing in Denver was well orchestrated and contentious. Denver homeowners—incited by fears of declining property values and diminished quality of neighborhood life, and abetted by local politicians—successfully launched campaigns in the 1980s against two distinctive housing initiatives: the Denver Housing Authority's (DHA's) Dispersed (scattered-site public) Housing Program and the supportive housing units mandated as a result of the settlement of the *Goebel* court case. These actions led to the near demise of the Dispersed Housing Program and delayed action on the implementation of the supportive housing remedy for nearly a decade. Though both initiatives survived community opposition, it was not without significant restrictions on their operations.

In this chapter, we examine various demographic, housing, and political characteristics and trends operative in Denver during the 1980s and into the 1990s that undergird these controversies. We then trace the history of the Dispersed Housing Program and describe the conditions that fueled the 1989 controversy. Next, we provide a history of the supportive housing initiatives in Denver and their associated controversies. The chapter concludes with a brief discussion of the lessons learned from these policy histories.

A Profile of Denver

To place our study of dispersed and supportive housing in its proper context, this section provides a general overview of the demographic and housing trends in Denver for 1980 and 1990. Table 2.1 summarizes census data on population, education and employment, income and poverty, and housing characteristics for Denver by race and ethnic groupings. Because the spatial distribution of these features is vitally important to this project, we have also created a series of maps that highlight the geographic distributions of key indicators in census tracts throughout the county (see maps 2.1 through 2.5).

Table 2.1

Selected Population and Housing Characteristics by Ethnicity, Denver, 1980–90

Characteristic	1980 All	White	Black	Hispanic	1990 All	White	Black	Hispanic
Population								
Total population	492,365	326,554	58,408	92,348	467,610	287,162	57,793	107,382
Median age (in years)	30.2	32.2	25.9	23.0	33.8	37.3	30.3	26.0
Percentage of households headed by females	18.7	14.9	35.8	25.7	22.2	15.3	41.3	30.2
Percentage foreign born	6.2	5.0	1.7	9.9	7.4	3.8	2.3	15.2
Education and employment								
Percentage with less than high school degree	25.3	22.0	29.9	57.2	20.8	12.6	25.0	49.6
Percentage college graduates	24.8	27.9	12.0	6.1	29.0	37.1	14.5	6.9
Labor force participation rate	66.4	66.4	68.5	64.1	67.6	67.6	66.9	68.4
Unemployment rate	5.0	4.2	8.1	8.9	6.8	4.6	11.5	11.5
Income and poverty status								
Median family income	19,527	21,062	15,211	13,945	32,038	38,501	24,619	20,863
Percentage of households receiving public assistance	7.4	5.4	15.7	17.6	7.6	4.5	15.2	15.3
Percentage of families living in poverty	10.3	6.6	21.2	22.9	13.1	6.2	23.0	27.9
Percentage of persons living in poverty	13.7	10.2	23.3	23.9	17.1	9.8	27.0	30.6
Percentage of female-headed families living in poverty	30.2	21.5	41.2	49.3	34.1	21.1	41.0	51.5
Housing								
Total year-round housing units	227,806				239,636			
Occupied housing units	211,566	170,406	21,587	27,887	210,952	148,238	23,785	34,358
Housing vacancy rate	7.1				12.0			
Percentage owner occupied	50.2	52.7	43.6	41.5	49.2	52.9	42.5	39.9
Percentage renter occupied	49.8	47.3	56.4	58.5	50.8	47.1	57.5	60.1
Percentage of housing units built prior to 1940	29.4	29.8	23.4	33.4	25.7	25.7	19.1	28.8
Percentage of housing units in 20+ unit structures	N/A	N/A	N/A	N/A	26.1	24	17.8	13.3
Median housing value	62,000	63,700	55,700	51,300	78,300	84,100	68,000	62,700
Median contract rent	213	222	195	175	338	362	302	294

Note: N/A means not available.

Sources: Various published tables were used from the following sources: U.S. Bureau of the Census (1983). *1980 Census of Population and Housing. Population and Housing Characteristics for Census Tracts: Denver–Boulder, CO.* Washington, DC: U.S. Government Printing Office; U.S. Bureau of the Census (1993). *1990 Census of Population and Housing. Population and Housing Characteristics for Census Tracts and Block Numbering Areas: Denver–Boulder, CO.* Washington, DC: U.S. Government Printing Office.

Population Characteristics

Denver serves as the economic, political, and social center of not only the metropolitan area but also Colorado. In Denver, the city and county boundaries are geographically congruent and have a single, county-level government.

During the 1980s, while the metropolitan population grew by one-tenth of a percent, the population of Denver declined by 5 percent.[1] The population of Denver was 467,610 in 1990. Significant decreases in the white (i.e., non-Hispanic white) population (−12 percent) and modest declines in the non-Hispanic black population (−1 percent) in Denver were only partially offset by substantial increases in the Hispanic population (+16 percent) during the 1980s. These population shifts were reflected in the changing ethnic composition of Denver. By 1990, 61 percent of Denver residents were white, 23 percent were Hispanic, and 12 percent were black. The 1980s also witnessed the growth of foreign-born Hispanics. By 1990, one out of every six Hispanics was foreign born.

The City and County of Denver, as well as the larger metropolitan area, remain highly segregated along ethnic lines. Although only 23 percent of all metropolitan-area whites lived in the City of Denver in 1990, 51 percent of Hispanics and 63 percent of blacks were Denver residents. Though this concentration within the central city decreased during the 1980s for all groups, the declines were most pronounced for blacks. Nonetheless, minority segregation from whites is marked, and a number of majority white census tracts experienced considerable racial change with the in-migration of black and Hispanic residents. In 1980, 72 percent of all blacks and 57 percent of all Hispanics would have had to move from their place of residence in Denver to live in integrated neighborhoods with whites (Santiago 1996). During the 1980s, black segregation from whites decreased substantially—59 percent of black residents in Denver would have had to move from their place of residence in 1990 to live in integrated neighborhoods. In contrast, Hispanic segregation from whites declined slightly. In 1990, 57 percent of all Hispanics would have had to move to live in integrated neighborhoods with whites. Black residents in Denver tend to be concentrated in Northeast Denver, whereas Hispanic residents tend to be concentrated in Northwest Denver as well as in some neighborhoods in central Denver.

Map 2.1 shows the percentage of black residents in 1990 in Denver City and County census tracts. Most tracts in the area (102 out of 142) have fewer than 10 percent black residents. The black population is largely concentrated in the northeast part of the city, with 13 tracts having a majority of black population.

Map 2.2 provides similar geographic distributions for the Hispanic population. Map 2.2 shows a quite clear division of Denver into Hispanic and non-Hispanic areas. The western portion contains mostly tracts with more than 40 percent Hispanic populations. A second concentration of Hispanics can be found in the northeastern corner of the city. These areas also experienced the most rapid growth in the proportion of Hispanics during the 1980s.

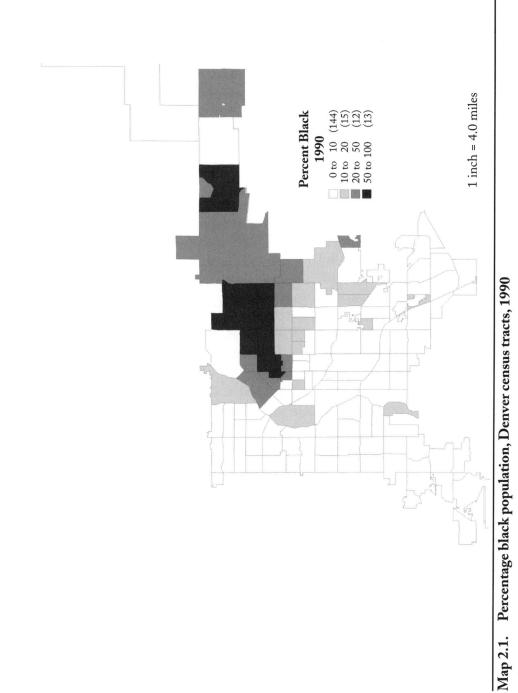

**Percent Black
1990**

	0 to 10	(144)
	10 to 20	(15)
	20 to 50	(12)
	50 to 100	(13)

1 inch = 4.0 miles

Map 2.1.   Percentage black population, Denver census tracts, 1990

Source: U.S. Bureau of the Census, *1990 Census of Population and Housing,* Summary file 3

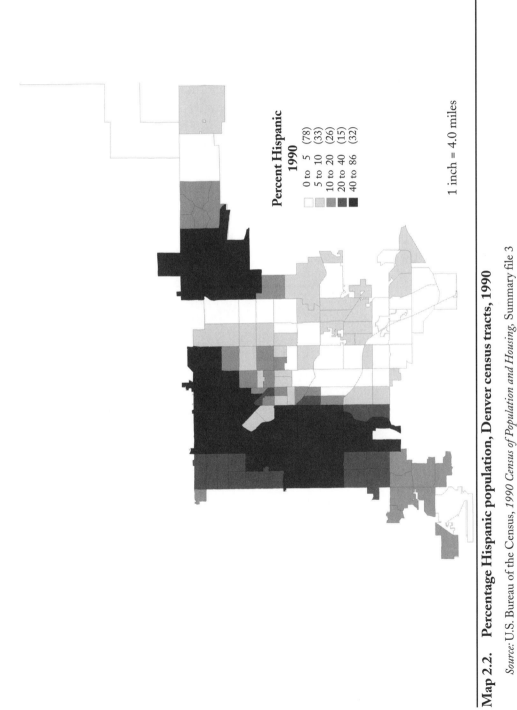

Map 2.2. **Percentage Hispanic population, Denver census tracts, 1990**

Source: U.S. Bureau of the Census, *1990 Census of Population and Housing*, Summary file 3

Percent Hispanic
1990

0 to 5 (78)
5 to 10 (33)
10 to 20 (26)
20 to 40 (15)
40 to 86 (32)

1 inch = 4.0 miles

Education and Employment Characteristics

There are marked ethnic differences in the levels of educational attainment in Denver. Although the fraction of individuals with college degrees increased and the fraction of individuals with less than high school degrees decreased in the 1980s, the results presented in table 2.1 underscore the very low levels of educational attainment of Hispanics in Denver. In 1990, nearly one-half of all adult Hispanics above the age of 25 years had not completed high school. Only 7 percent held college degrees. In contrast, fewer than 13 percent of white and 25 percent of black adults had not finished high school. Moreover, 37 percent of whites and nearly 15 percent of blacks held college degrees.[2]

Although the lower levels of educational attainment of minority, and particularly Hispanic, residents might account for their significantly higher unemployment rates (12 percent) relative to whites, they do not translate into markedly different rates of labor force participation. Across all groups, approximately two-thirds of persons above the age of 16 were in the labor force. In 1980, blacks had the highest rate of labor force participation (69 percent); by 1990, Hispanics had the highest rate (68 percent). During the 1980s, unemployment rates increased for all groups, although the increase was almost negligible for whites. Further, the unemployment rates of blacks and Hispanics were nearly 2.5 times higher than those of whites.

Income and Poverty Status

In 1990, the median family income in Denver was $32,038. However, there was considerable variation by race and ethnicity. On the upper end, white median family income was $36,501. On the lower end, Hispanic median family income was $20,863. Relative to white residents of Denver, blacks and Hispanics experienced substantial erosion in their income during the 1980s. In 1980, black and Hispanic median family incomes were 72 and 66 percent, respectively, of white median family income. By 1989, black median family income had fallen to 64 percent of white median family income; for Hispanics, the gap had widened to 54 percent of white median family income. Thus, it is not surprising that 1989 family poverty rates for blacks and Hispanics were 3.7 and 4.5 times higher, respectively, than the rate for whites. By 1989, 23 percent of black and 28 percent of Hispanic families were living in poverty. Although the ethnic differentials are not as pronounced for individual poverty rates, blacks and Hispanics were approximately three times more likely to experience poverty than were whites.

Housing Characteristics

As is typical of newer, western cities, only 26 percent of the housing units in Denver were built before 1940. Hispanics were more likely to live in these older units (29 percent) than whites (26 percent) and blacks (19 percent). However, the scale of the housing was unusually large for the region, with 26 percent of the housing stock constructed in complexes with 20 or more units. Though 24 percent of all whites lived in these larger housing complexes in 1990, only 18 percent of blacks and 13 percent of Hispanics did. Although new housing construction added modestly to the housing stock in the 1980s—an increase of 5 percent of total units—the fall in housing starts mirrored the collapse of the Denver economy during the latter half of the 1980s. Vacancy rates climbed markedly, from 7 percent in 1980 to 12 percent by 1990.

The weakness of the local economy in the late 1980s was reflected in the decrease in homeownership, particularly among minority residents. By 1990, less than one-half of all households owned their homes. Homeownership rates varied from a high of 53 percent among whites to a low of 40 percent among Hispanics. Nevertheless, according to map 2.3, there were only a few areas with a high concentration (more than 80 percent) of rental housing, primarily in the northwestern quadrant of the city.

Despite the slump in the latter half of the decade, median housing values increased slightly overall from 1980 to 1990, though at a markedly slower pace for blacks and Hispanics. Further, there were sizable differences in the 1990 median value of homes across ethnic groups. For whites, the median value was $84,100, whereas for blacks and Hispanics it was $68,000 and $62,700, respectively. The median contract rent in Denver was $338, ranging from a low of $294 for Hispanics to a high of $362 for whites. The areas with the highest house values in 1990 were in the southeastern quadrant of the city (map 2.4). Starting in 1992, there was an explosion in housing prices, with prices in 61 census tracts increasing 75 percent or more from 1990 to 1996 (map 2.5).[3]

Summary: The Demographic Context of the Controversy

By the close of the 1980s, Denver had witnessed increased polarization along ethnic, economic, and neighborhood lines, which made it a locale ripe for controversy. High rates of minority unemployment and significantly lower incomes resulted in increased income inequality. In turn, the lower economic status of Hispanics, coupled with their rapid growth within the metropolitan area, triggered neighborhood succession in some white neighborhoods, thereby abetting anxieties while maintaining high levels of residential segregation between the two groups. As we will see below, during this time of economic downturn and stagnant or eroding property values, tensions were high on issues of local control and preserving neighborhood quality of life. Thus it is not surprising that local residents, particularly those residing in vulnerable neighborhoods, viewed the dispersed and supportive housing programs as potential threats to community life as they envisioned it.

Pct. Renter Occupied Housing 1990

0 to 20	(63)
20 to 40	(39)
40 to 60	(33)
60 to 80	(27)
80 to 100	(22)

1 inch = 4.0 miles

Map 2.3. Percentage renter–occupied housing, Denver census tracts, 1990

Source: U.S. Bureau of the Census, *1990 Census of Population and Housing,* Summary file 3

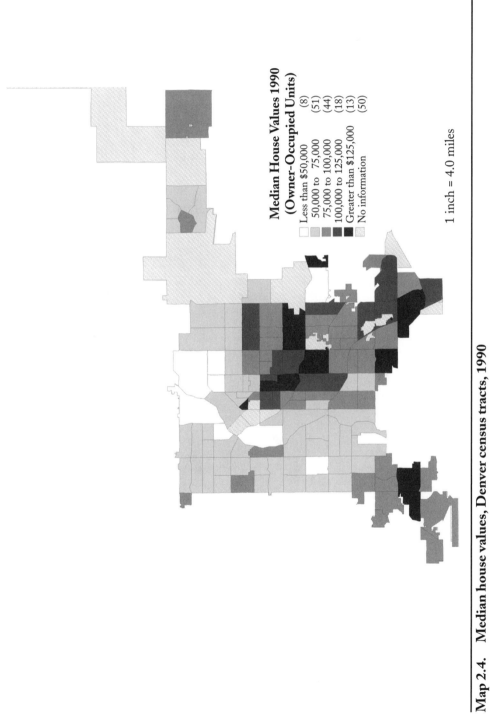

**Median House Values 1990
(Owner-Occupied Units)**

Less than $50,000	(8)
50,000 to 75,000	(51)
75,000 to 100,000	(44)
100,000 to 125,000	(18)
Greater than $125,000	(13)
No information	(50)

1 inch = 4.0 miles

Map 2.4.   Median house values, Denver census tracts, 1990

Source: U.S. Bureau of the Census, *1990 Census of Population and Housing,* Summary file 3

**Pct. Change in Average
House Values, 1990–1996**

	0 to 50	(54)
	50 to 75	(51)
	75 to 100	(41)
	100 to 280	(20)
	No information	(18)

1 inch = 4.0 miles

Map 2.5.   Percentage change in average house values, Denver census tracts, 1990–96

Source: Authors' analysis of Experian home sales data

Dispersed Housing Initiatives in Denver

A Brief History of Deconcentration Strategies

Denver was strongly influenced by the national debates regarding the optimal design of scattered-site public housing that crystallized at the close of the 1950s. Indeed, over the course of the next 37 years, the DHA would implement three different initiatives under the rubric of "dispersed housing" that would generate approximately 1,300 units of scattered-site public housing by the end of 1997.[4] These program initiatives included (1) the acquisition and conversion of homes on which the U.S. Department of Housing and Urban Development (HUD) had foreclosed;[5] (2) the construction of dispersed, clustered housing on vacant lots in existing neighborhoods; and (3) the DHA replacement housing program, which purchased small-scale residential properties through the local real estate market. Each of these initiatives is described below.

VA–FHA Acquisition Program

Although the precise origins of, and reasons for, the development of the Dispersed Housing Program in Denver are not well documented, discussions about the feasibility of the program emerged as a regular agenda item at the monthly DHA Board of Commissioners meetings during the fall of 1960.[6] Indeed, by the end of 1960, the DHA had identified 20 areas in the city suitable for the development of newly constructed, dispersed public housing, presented a proposal to the City Council on the plan, and obtained City Council permission to release bids for the construction of these new dispersed units.[7] Despite City Council concerns regarding the program (i.e., density, proximity to existing public housing), the DHA received council approval to develop an initial 250 units of new dispersed housing in March 1961.[8] This initial support for the Dispersed Housing Program solidified after the results of a DHA and Denver Health and Hospitals Corporation–sponsored needs assessment for large families underscored the serious problems confronted by large families seeking low-rent housing in Denver.[9]

Despite the reported interest in the program, it would not be until the end of the decade that the first dispersed units would be built. What caused the delay? In part, new construction of large-family units was delayed by a protracted debate about the development of 250 units of elderly housing—a debate that was finally resolved in the latter part of the 1960s. However, the primary factor cited for the delay was the enormous land costs in the city that inhibited the construction of these units.[10] Others speculated that homeowner fears regarding the impact on property values of building units to house disadvantaged minority persons was a major reason for delaying new construction.[11]

The DHA—dogged by low vacancy rates and long waiting lists—sought to reduce the costs of developing dispersed units and to speed their delivery. The DHA investigated the use of foreclosed Department of Veterans Affairs (VA) or Federal Housing Authority

(FHA) homes to achieve these ends.[12] In 1968, the DHA received the unanimous endorsement of the City Council to acquire 100 units of VA or FHA foreclosed properties—mainly single-family homes.[13] One of the pioneering features of this plan was that, for the first time, many of the proposed units would be located in Southwest Denver.[14] By December 1970, the first 100 FHA homes had been purchased.[15]

Infill Construction Program

As mentioned above, the DHA early on expressed considerable interest in developing dispersed public housing via new construction. It was not until 1969, however, that the authority was authorized to build the first 200 dispersed units. Responding to HUD-supported urban renewal programs, the DHA ultimately constructed approximately 800 units of "clustered dispersed" housing during the period between 1970 and 1974. Using turnkey style construction, these dispersed developments consisted of clusters of 20 to 50 multi-family units built on vacant lots scattered throughout already built-up parts of the city.[16]

Replacement Housing Program

In the 1980s, the DHA, like many housing authorities across the country, began to feel the pressures associated with the obsolescence of its conventional housing stock. To upgrade its housing stock and reduce densities in some of its oldest housing projects, the DHA proposed a five-year modernization plan in 1989 that would include the demolition of approximately 400 units of existing public housing. These would be replaced through the acquisition of existing single-family units, duplexes, condominiums, townhouses, and scattered site, multifamily unit clusters across Denver (City and County of Denver 1989). These replacements were designed primarily to accommodate persons dislocated from the demolished North Lincoln Park (and later, the Stapleton Homes) projects.

Three elements made this particular DHA initiative unique: (1) the sheer scale of the acquisition plan; (2) the proposed purchase of preexisting units from a particularly soft local real estate market; and (3) the passage of a HUD regulation in 1988 that not only mandated the one-to-one replacement of public housing units but also required the consent of the local governing body for the purchase of these replacement units. All of these elements rendered a heretofore relatively invisible program highly visible and subject to intense public scrutiny.[17] This led to a prolonged, contentious public debate regarding the entire Dispersed Housing Program and, some might argue, to its near demise.

The Geopolitical Context of the 1989 Dispersed Housing Program Controversy

For most of its 28-year history, the Dispersed Housing Program had received considerable support from the leadership and staff of the DHA, the DHA Board of Commissioners, and the City Council. Yet in 1989, the program was at the heart of an intense, highly publicized political controversy. For nearly one year, the program served as the lightning rod that polarized Denverites: the DHA versus the City Council; the poor versus the affluent; minorities versus whites. After 20 years of functioning with limited visibility and fanfare, why was the Dispersed Housing Program suddenly the center of attention? What was the political fallout of this controversy? What has since happened to the program?

During our interviews with community leaders, several suggested that at the heart of the controversy was the sheer magnitude of the demolitions involved as part of the five-year replacement housing plan proposed by the DHA in 1989. As one community leader observed, "The primary concern was, where would DHA residents be moved?" The large-scale reductions in densities of conventional projects made it clear that many people would need to be relocated and raised the specter in the minds of many white homeowners of "what would be done with all of *them*?"

In Denver during the late 1980s, the potential relocation sites for displaced DHA residents were considerably more varied than those that had previously been available. Denver was in the middle of a substantial economic downturn in the local economy, provoking, among other things, the destabilization and deterioration of the local housing market. Housing prices had declined significantly and, for the first time, housing units in more affluent neighborhoods located in Southwest and Southeast Denver potentially were available for purchase by the DHA.

A seemingly innocuous letter written by Ron Paul, the DHA's director of redevelopment, in 1989 to area real estate agents may have been the spark that inflamed the public. On January 11, Paul informed area real estate agents that the DHA would be replacing 132 units of obsolete, row-type housing under a recently approved development plan.[18] Paul sought their assistance in identifying "solid, attractive, low-maintenance homes that met the following criteria: one or two story homes, livable functional floor plans, adequate storage space, good carpeting, and space for a laundry room." Excluded from consideration were properties located outside the Denver city limits, in industrial areas or deteriorated neighborhoods, on busy streets, or in areas with unpaved alleys or roads. HUD-owned properties were excluded from consideration because the DHA only purchased said homes via foreclosure sales. Properties without city water or sewer or with structural problems, flat roofs, lead pipes, high levels of lead-based paint, or electric heat were excluded as well.

Paul told the real estate agents that the DHA would be looking for homes in the $55,000–70,000 price range, contingent upon the condition of the structure and the amount of cleanup and rehabilitation required. The statement that reputedly triggered the negative public response was the indication that the DHA would be targeting home purchases in more affluent, predominantly white areas located south of Mississippi Avenue. Although Paul went on to emphasize that the DHA would be restricted from purchasing more than two houses in any single block and that a high concentration of units in any one neighborhood would not be allowed, this statement would be used by real estate agents, neighborhood homeowners' associations, and several elected officials to incite resident fears about the deleterious effects of moving poor people into these middle-class neighborhoods.

Indeed, the NIMBY attitudes of certain City Council members and their constituents were viewed by a number of respondents as the catalyst for the contentious debate that would follow.[19]

According to one public housing administrator, the resultant skirmish reflected three distinctive political positions regarding assisted housing. The first position was that of individuals and groups who were opposed to the development of *any* assisted housing in their neighborhoods. Several prominent leaders of Southwest Denver homeowners' associations, as well as their representatives on the City Council, led the opposition to the acquisition of any dispersed housing units in their neighborhoods.

The second position was that of individuals who wanted a *truly dispersed* program. Several City Council members, as well as local community leaders, were concerned about the historical concentration of dispersed units within poor and working-class, older neighborhoods and wanted to see the deconcentration of these units into all Denver neighborhoods to maximize opportunities of the poor. Finally, the third position (closely related to the second) reflected concerns that some city districts already had *more than their "fair share"* of low-income housing. Council members and the constituents in these heavily impacted neighborhoods felt that it was now time for other areas in Denver to share the burden of providing affordable housing to low-income families.

Residents of Southwest Denver were mobilized into action during the spring and summer of 1989 to oppose the DHA's acquisition plans on the basis of fears about declining property values and neighborhood degradation. As a community leader noted, "Opponents skillfully played to the fears of the public and created a hot button issue." Residents were led to believe that the DHA was engaged in a new social-engineering experiment that would be conducted in their neighborhoods for the first time, even though small numbers of dispersed housing units had been operating quite successfully in these neighborhoods for some time. Leaders from several homeowners' associations suggested that the DHA had acted illegally and covertly in the acquisition of dispersed units. Indeed, one community leader suggested that the program had been deliberately hidden from public scrutiny.

Also implicit within the rhetoric were sentiments of class and ethnic inferiority. Political opponents played on white stereotypes about the poor—particularly the minority poor—to incite community residents.[20] Residents of Southwest Denver were particularly concerned about the provision of good-quality housing to "people on welfare." How could people who were not working live in homes that were better than theirs?

Tensions reached a fever pitch at a neighborhood meeting in April 1989. At that time, representatives of the city government—including the mayor, Frederico Peña, DHA officials, and other supporters—attempted to allay residents' fears. Unfortunately, these constituencies were verbally ambushed at that meeting—and were totally unprepared for the intense backlash against the DHA and the Dispersed Housing Program. There were frequent calls for the elimination of the program as well as for the ouster of DHA officials during the fractious debates that spring. Indeed, after the April meeting, Mayor Peña halted the replacement housing plan, held the DHA accountable to the City Council, and appointed a Citizens Task Force to study (and, it was hoped, diffuse) the issue.

The Citizens Task Force was charged with the mandate to quickly develop a new replacement housing plan. The task force—made up of 30 representatives (2 per council district) and four mayoral appointees—met during May 1989 to draft its recommendations. Interestingly, most task force members supported the concept of dispersed housing, and the debate centered only on the implementation of the program. Acting on consensus, the task force sought to develop a policy that would both avoid impacted areas and find noncontroversial locations for DHA units. The task force developed 29 policy recommendations, which were submitted to the mayor at the end of May 1989 and presented to the City Council during public meetings in June 1989. A series of stringent regulations were proposed. Some viewed these as major concessions to opponents of the Dispersed Housing Program, offered to prevent the demise of the program. Included among the recommendations were guaranteed spatial dispersion of units by virtue of strict density and spatial distance requirements, as well as the addition of four members to the DHA Board of Commissioners to provide additional oversight to the DHA.[21]

Although observers noted that there was strong consensus among task force members, these recommendations fueled additional controversy when presented to the City Council. Public hearings on the Dispersed Housing Program spanned a four-day meeting of the council from June 12 to 16, 1989, at which more than 500 opponents or supporters registered to address the council. In addition, opponents of dispersed housing were able to convince a task force member to present a *minority report*, which essentially summarized ongoing opposition to the program.[22] Not until the fall of 1989 would the City Council finally approve a version of the dispersed housing plan with substantial restrictions through an intergovernmental agreement with the DHA.

The DHA's insensitivity to community residents' concerns and its failure to consider the intense opposition that the replacement program might generate are now recognized by both public housing administrators and community leaders as a major error by the agency. As several administrators acknowledged during the course of our interviews, DHA officials were taken completely by surprise by the vehement negative reactions to the program. Moreover, because they had not engaged in dialogues with community residents prior to program implementation, there had been a breakdown in communication between the DHA and local residents. The DHA had no significant prior experience with community relations and had generally maintained a stance of limited involvement in dealing with larger community issues. As a result, the public meetings held about the Dispersed Housing Program were explosive.[23] One public housing administrator even suggested that it was the DHA's arrogance and bumbling of public relations that led to the controversy in the first place.

Fallout from the 1989 controversy was swift. The perceived inept handling of the matter led to the resignation of the executive director and other significant changes in the DHA's administrative staff. Moreover, the DHA was faced with the task of rebuilding its

public image. Perceptions of DHA misconduct ran deep; as a result, the authority was sub-
jected to intense scrutiny, particularly during the first 18 months after the controversy had
subsided. The DHA would now be held under strict accountability to the City Council.
At one point in 1990, attempts were made to bring the DHA under the direct control of
either the mayor or the City Council, but those efforts were unsuccessful.[24]

Perhaps the most far-reaching effects of the controversy revolve around the restrictions placed on the DHA via the intergovernmental agreement reached with the City
Council. The continued HUD mandate for dispersing conventional public housing while
at the same time complying with the nonimpaction and unit separation distance requirements of the City Council agreement has made it increasingly difficult for the DHA to
find affordable housing to acquire.

Adaptations in the DHA Dispersed Housing Program in the 1990s

Despite the serious threat to the continued survival of the Dispersed Housing Program
posed by the 1989 controversy, the program thrived in the 1990s.[25] According to several
public housing administrators, the DHA was able to regain the trust of the City Council
and the public at large through its strict compliance to the intergovernmental agreement.
One administrator contended that the program was not considered a substantive public
issue at that time. Indeed, during the 1990s the DHA acquired approximately 500 units
of dispersed housing. The agency initiated another five-year replacement plan in 1996 to
upgrade the conventional public housing stock. In sharp contrast to 1989, the intergovernmental agreement was renewed in 1996 with little or no public concern voiced.

How could there be such a sea change in less than a decade? We believe that the
answer lies in programmatic adaptations the DHA was required to make in 1989 and others
it voluntarily made. The three key areas of adaptation involve siting, neighborhood outreach, and tenant selection.

Site Selection

Prior to 1989, the selection of acquisition homes or lots for infill construction under the
Dispersed Housing Program was predicated primarily on budgetary constraints. As a result, a sizable fraction of dispersed units was concentrated in poor and working-class neighborhoods of Northeast, Central, and Northwest Denver, where land and housing values
were lowest (cf. maps 2.4, 2.5, and 2.6). However, as a result of the public scrutiny of the
Replacement Housing Program in 1989 and the nascent movement of DHA tenants into
middle-class neighborhoods, additional regulations were introduced that constrained the
site selection process. These included (1) the purchase of units in nonimpacted census tracts;
that is, low poverty concentrations (fewer than 20 percent of housing units were occupied
by poor and/or public housing residents); (2) a minimum distance requirement of at least
950 feet between DHA properties in any given census tract; (3) a maximum DHA own-

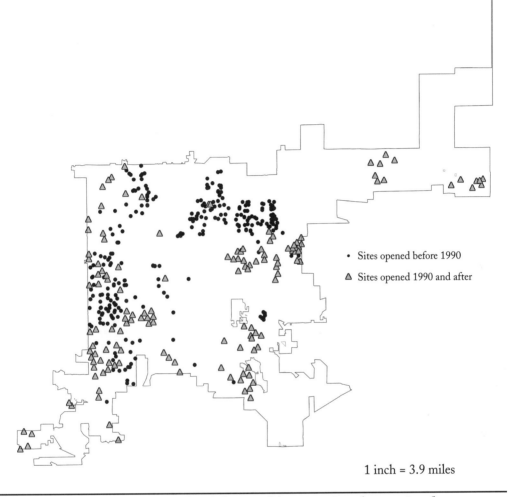

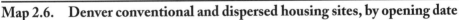

Map 2.6.   Denver conventional and dispersed housing sites, by opening date

Source: Unpublished data from the Denver Housing Authority

ership threshold of 1 percent of all units or eight DHA properties (whichever is less) in any given census tract; and (4) a DHA preference for the purchase of vacant or foreclosed homes.[26]

These siting restrictions clearly led to a more scattered pattern of dispersed housing in Denver. Map 2.6 compares the locations of DHA sites before and after the restrictions went into effect. The post-1989 pattern avoids further concentrations in the core and near-north areas, instead pushing into more peripheral neighborhoods.

Neighborhood Outreach

Since 1990, the DHA has engaged in considerable community outreach in advance of the purchase of new acquisitions. Meetings with neighbors, homeowners' associations, politicians, and others have helped to defuse opposition to the program. Dispersed Housing Program managers, as well as other central administration staff, have become actively involved in addressing neighborhood concerns before they become major problems. Moreover, prompt attention to citizen concerns about problems with existing units and aggressive maintenance policies have led to a general public satisfaction with the program, according to many of our informants.

Tenant Selection

Prior to 1987, Dispersed Housing Program units were only filled with families transferring from DHA conventional public housing. Eligible tenants during that period included those with excellent rent and housekeeping histories as well as those perceived as being more independent and highly motivated.[27] Beginning in 1987, however, all applicants for conventional and dispersed housing programs began to be screened in the same manner and placed on the same public housing waiting list, thereby giving them access to both conventional and dispersed housing as their first DHA unit. Accompanying this shift was the adoption of a more stringent set of tenant selection criteria. These tenant selection criteria are as follows:[28]

- Adherence to HUD income guidelines for program participation as well as the 30 percent income caps for rental payments: The tenant must demonstrate the ability to meet the financial obligations associated with living in the dispersed unit, including costs of lawn maintenance and snow removal.
- No history of criminal activity: There is particular concern for previous drug use or dealing, gang activity, or other criminal acts.
- Proof of acceptable rent payment history: The tenant must have a history of paying rent in full and on time. If the applicant is not a DHA resident, he or she must provide landlord references on rent payment history. If the tenant is a current DHA resident, there must not be an outstanding DHA debt.
- Acceptable housekeeping record: The tenant must furnish a housekeeping report from either a private landlord or from the DHA. Implicit in this criterion is the notion that the applicant can and will work with others in terms of accepting preventive maintenance responsibilities for both the inside and outside of the unit.
- Proof of identity regarding citizenship, relationship to children, and legal custody of children.
- Adherence to federal preferences for standing on the waiting list: Applicants who are involuntarily displaced from their homes are given the highest priority. Applicants residing in substandard housing receive the second preference. The third preference is for applicants who are rent burdened.

In addition, DHA expectations include a high degree of motivation toward self-sufficiency and community involvement. Evidence of these characteristics would include positive attitude and self-esteem, open communication and cooperation with housing management personnel, and participation in local resident councils or other community organizations.[29]

Once applicants are deemed eligible to participate in DHA conventional housing, they are placed on a waiting list according to the HUD preference guidelines described above.[30] Though at one point the waiting list exceeded 2,000, the waiting list as of 1998 numbered only approximately 250. As tenants move to the top of the waiting list, they are referred to the appropriate property manager. If the applicant has been referred to the Dispersed Housing Program, an interview with the manager is completed (whenever possible, this is a home-based interview).[31] At that interview, the applicant is provided with information regarding rental responsibilities and rental rates. The terms and conditions of the lease are fully explained. In addition, the manager provides information about life in specific neighborhoods. Every attempt is made to match tenants to unit and area preferences. If there is a good match, an offer is made.

Applicants are given up to two offers in either conventional public housing or the Dispersed Housing Program. However, after two refusals, applicants are placed on an inactive list for six months and must reapply for future consideration. According to the DHA housing administrators we interviewed, this procedure generally has identified good tenants. Indeed, they stressed that fewer than 5 percent of their tenants would be considered "problematic." Further, they emphasized that when any problems occurred, their response was consistent and rapid. As a result, there has been a marked lessening of concern about DHA tenants on the part of community residents, they alleged.

Thus, the DHA since the 1989 controversy has initiated, and in some cases been forced to comply with, a concerted set of reforms related to facility siting, neighborhood outreach, and tenant screening. As we shall see in chapter 6, these reforms were, with rare exceptions, successful when measured by property value and crime impacts, and by the absence of worry expressed by homeowners near DHA units.

Supportive Housing Initiatives in Denver

A History of Rapid Expansion of a Fragmented Delivery System

Unlike the Denver Housing Authority's Dispersed Housing Program, supportive housing in Denver is delivered by a wide range of for-profit and nonprofit organizations. According to the Denver Community Development Agency's (n.d.) most recent *Housing Resource Directory*, 22 nonprofit and for-profit organizations provided "emergency/crisis/transitional" housing and another 21 provided "special needs" housing in the metropolitan area.

What constitutes "supportive housing" is clearly specified in Denver. Denver's Large

Residential Care Use Ordinance makes four distinctions within the general supportive housing rubric:[32]

- *Small Special Care Home:* a residential care facility that is the primary residence of fewer than nine unrelated persons who live as a single housekeeping unit and receive more than 12 hours per day of on-premises treatment, supervision, custodial care, or special care due to physical condition or illness, mental condition or illness, or behavioral or disciplinary problems.
- *Large Special Care Home:* a residential care facility as above, which is the primary residence of nine or more unrelated persons.
- *Community Corrections Facility:* a structure that provides residence to three or more persons who have been placed in a community corrections program requiring correctional supervision, including programs to facilitate transition to a less-structured residential arrangement.
- *Homeless Shelter:* a facility that primarily provides overnight accommodations for homeless people and is operated in a way that encourages short-term occupancy.

Between 1987 and 1997, 146 supportive housing sites were licensed or registered within Denver.[33] The locations of these sites are presented in map 2.7. It demonstrates a distinct clustering of sites in the Near South Side and East-Central areas of Denver, near the Downtown-Capitol district. Comparison with maps 2.1 and 2.2 suggests that supportive housing in Denver is disproportionately located in more predominantly minority census tracts. To be more precise, at the end of 1997, 41 percent of the 146 registered supportive housing facilities were located in census tracts having 20 percent or more Hispanic population in 1990. By contrast, 19 percent were located in tracts having 20 percent or more black population and only 8 percent in tracts with less than 5 percent each Hispanic and black populations.

If we compare the distribution of supportive housing facilities across neighborhood home value ranges (see map 2.5), we see that this distribution is considerably more uniform. Thirty-nine percent were located in tracts having values in the lowest third of the 1990 median home value distribution (sites located on the North Side and West Side areas of Denver), 24 percent were in the middle third, and 37 percent were in the highest third (near the Downtown-Capitol district).

The key characteristics of the supportive housing facilities in Denver are as follows:

- *Type:* Forty-two percent are classified as Small Special Care Homes, 44 percent as Large Special Care Homes, 9 percent as Adult Community Corrections Facilities (including 2 percent for Transitional Homes), 3 percent as Homeless Shelters, and 2 percent as combinations of the above.
- *Sponsor:* Sixty-three percent are operated by nonprofit agencies; 37 percent are operated by for-profit organizations; and three-fourths of the 12 sites developed in 1997 are for profit.
- *Scale:* Forty-two percent house fewer than 9 residents, 18 percent house between

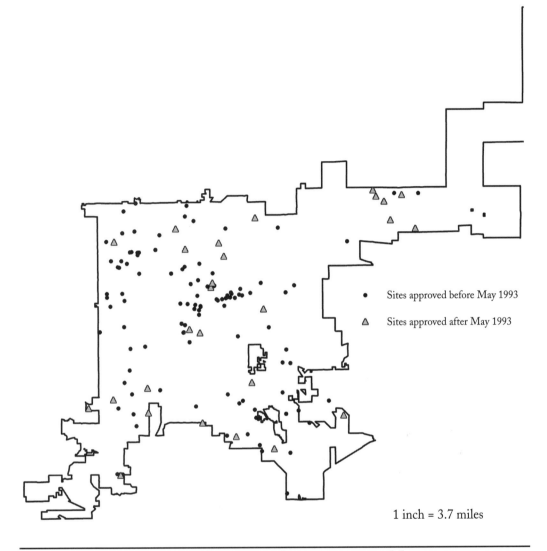

1 inch = 3.7 miles

- Sites approved before May 1993
- △ Sites approved after May 1993

Map 2.7. Denver supportive housing sites by zoning approval date

Source: City and County of Denver (1998b) *Bi-annual residential care use renewal*

10 and 19 residents, 30 percent house between 20 and 100 residents, 10 percent house more than 100 residents, and the smallest facility listed houses 3 and the largest 320.[34]

- *Age:* Only 22 percent (for the 95 percent of facilities listing opening dates) were developed prior to 1980, 41 percent from 1980 through 1989, and 37 percent since 1989 (through 1997).

From the above, it is clear that the pace of development of supportive housing sites in Denver intensified in the 1980s and 1990s. After low rates of production prior to 1980, the average annual rate of development rose from 4.7 sites during the 1980s to 5.3 during the 1990s. The level of Denver governmental financial support for these facilities grew concomitantly, registeringi $1.9 million for fiscal 1998.[35]

According to our Denver key informants, the most significant local event shaping the provision of supportive housing has been the *Goebel* case, in which chronically mentally ill plaintiffs sued governmental service providers for supplying inadequate care.[36] Public mental health services in Colorado are provided by state institutions and community mental health facilities, supervised by the Colorado Department of Institutions through its Division of Mental Health.

In 1981, due to insufficient funds and the failure of the state legislature to provide increased support, the Denver Department of Health and Hospitals, the care provider in the catchment area encompassing Downtown and the Capitol Hill areas, developed a plan to reduce mental health care services. Plaintiffs filed suit on behalf of themselves and up to 5,000 low-income, chronically mentally ill persons residing in this catchment area to enjoin the reduction of services. The suit alleged that the 1973 Colorado Act for the Care and Treatment of the Mentally Ill created broad statutory rights for certain identified chronically mentally ill persons to receive comprehensive care and treatment, and that the variety of participating state and local governmental bodies were denying this right. The trial court found for the plaintiffs in 1985, defined a plaintiff class, and ordered the defendants to submit a plan for delivery of appropriate community mental health services.

This plan was developed, but before it could be implemented in 1985 the state legislature amended the 1973 act to include the phrase "subject to available appropriations." The trial court concluded that it no longer had jurisdiction to order injunctive relief and dismissed all claims except for damages incurred between 1981 and 1985. Plaintiffs appealed on several grounds, and the case cycled between the state Supreme Court and the trial court until January 1994, when a settlement was finally reached, with 1,600 plaintiff class members certified (Pankratz 1998).

Under the terms of this settlement, Denver agreed to

- develop a follow-up and referral system for the chronically mentally ill who are treated on an emergency or inpatient basis at the (then) Denver General Hospital;
- provide $150,000 annually for supportive housing services from 1994 through 1996; and
- develop "affordable and appropriate" housing for 250 chronically mentally ill people, ranging from small group homes to independent apartments (Pankratz 1998; Lindsay 1998).

The DHA originally planned to develop the requisite 250 units, but it altered its policy with the advent of a new executive director in 1996 (Lindsay 1998). Instead, the DHA provided 100 Section 8 rental assistance certificates earmarked for chronically mentally ill tenants.[37] In response, the Community Development Agency devised a plan to use Denver funds to leverage state and other monies to contract with for-profit and non-profit developers to supply the required supportive housing units. The 250 mandated *Goebel* units were produced.[38]

In May 1998, however, a Denver judge ruled that Denver had failed to meet its third *Goebel* obligation (see above), inasmuch as the rents being charged in 7 supportive facilities were not "affordable" and 50 others did not meet other requirements for the chronically mentally ill people (Lindsay 1998; Pankratz 1998). The judge ordered Denver to contribute $2.8 million to buy down the mortgages on the 7 facilities to render them affordable and to develop 50 additional supportive units. Inasmuch as this is almost a million dollars more than Denver had planned to spend under its Consolidated Plan, the potential for continued rapid expansion of the supportive housing sector is apparent.

Legal Restrictions on the Siting of Supportive Housing in Denver

Thus, as in the case of the DHA's Dispersed Housing Program, supportive housing was expanded in Denver at an impressive pace during the 1980s and 1990s. There were different sources of public visibility and potential for conflict between the two programs, however. The DHA was faced with obtaining City Council approval of an intergovernmental agreement, specifying details of the Dispersed Housing Program expansion plans, whereas supportive housing developers had to operate within the context of an interminable, inflammatory court battle. Nevertheless, the outcomes of the ensuing debates were fundamentally similar: the passage by City Council of ordinances that strictly regulated numerous aspects of both affordable and supportive housing development.

Given the precedent set by the intergovernmental agreement ending the dispersed housing controversy, the siting patterns evident in map 2.7, and the above-mentioned acceleration in the pace of supportive housing facility development, the Large Residential Care Use Ordinance was passed by the Denver City Council on May 28, 1993. This law sought to ameliorate concerns related to the facilities of both supportive housing advocates and host neighborhoods (City and County of Denver 1998a, 1998c). For the former, the law affirmed the need for housing special care populations in noninstitutionalized, nonconcentrated residential settings, located throughout Denver in ways aiding their integration into the mainstream of society. For the latter, it affirmed the importance of maintaining viable neighborhoods and the potential validity of neighborhood concerns, specified minimum separation requirements among facilities, and established a mechanism of consultation between the developer and the host neighborhood, mediated by city officials.

As is plain from map 2.7, the 1993 ordinance made a difference in the location of supportive housing sites, though perhaps not so dramatic as in the case of the DHA Dispersed Housing Program. Considerable pre-1993 supportive housing was located in peripheral Denver neighborhoods and at large separations. The post-1993 vintage of sites clearly avoided areas near the core with preexisting concentrations.

Two key modifications in the ordinance have been made since 1993. In April 1997, the clause that forbade development of any new supportive facilities within a specified distance of an existing facility was amended to exclude small group homes. The consensus in the City Council was that the previous separation requirement would have ruled out so many potential sites, given the scale of Denver, that the supply of supportive housing would have been unfairly constrained.[39] In February 1998, the ordinance was further amended to expand the distance from proposed sites that defined which neighborhood organizations must be sent the development application as a form of prior notification.

As of late 1998, the Large Residential Care Uses Ordinance contained the following provisions of central interest here (City and County of Denver 1998a, 1998c):

- Developers of all supportive housing facilities (including Small Special Care Homes) must meet with a Zoning Department staff person prior to submitting an application, send a copy of the development application and their contact information to the neighborhood organization(s) whose boundaries encompass or are within 700 feet of the proposed site, designate a contact person who will be available to respond to community concerns on an ongoing basis, and be willing to participate in a meeting with the organization and city officials if requested.
- All proposed sites must have all necessary licenses, at least one staff person on-site, adequate parking, and exterior modifications that are harmonious with the existing neighborhood; the zoning for the site must conform with permissible zones specified for the particular supportive housing type.
- Large Residential Care Use Facilities must be located a minimum of 2,000 feet from another like facility, and no more than two other like facilities for that use can exist within a 4,000-foot radius. (A 10 percent exception to these spacing rules can be granted by the zoning administrator if it would not "substantially or permanently injure the surrounding neighborhood.")
- The proposed site must be at least 6,000 square feet and have a minimum width of 50 feet.
- Large Special Care Homes in most zones are restricted to being developed in structures existing on or before May 24, 1993, and are limited to a maximum of 40 residents.
- Community Corrections Facilities must be located more than 1,500 feet from a school and/or residential district, cannot exceed 1 resident per 200 square feet of gross floor area, and can house a maximum of 60 residents (40 in some zones).
- Homeless Shelters must be located more than 500 feet from a school and cannot have more than 200 beds.

The ordinance gives Denver's zoning administrator the power to approve, approve with conditions, or deny a permit for supportive housing. Permits are reviewed semiannually. Citizen complaints about a supportive care facility are investigated by the administrator and, if necessary, a conciliation meeting among the conflicting parties is arranged. The administrator is empowered to issue a cease-and-desist order and issue a summons and complaint into court.

The Persistence of Neighborhood Concerns Regarding Supportive Housing

It is instructive that the Large Residential Care Uses Ordinance requires an applicant for a supportive housing development to notify the nearby neighborhood associations, insofar as there remains a lively debate among scholars and practitioners about the wisdom of such (National Law Center on Homelessness and Poverty 1997; Cook 1997). Some advocate that developers adopt a "low-profile strategy," only informing the neighbors after a supportive facility has been put into operation. They argue that such notification needlessly intensifies opposition (Seltzer 1984; Pendall 1999), given evidence that neighbors' negative expectations about supportive housing far exceed their negative evaluations after the fact (Wahl 1993; Cook 1997). Others counter that failure to provide advance notification and a formal mechanism for neighborhood reaction and discussions with the developer merely erodes trust in the supportive housing industry and local government (Wenocur and Belcher 1990). Interestingly, a majority of our Denver key informants argued that the prime source of opposition was "misguided fears and ignorance about clients," which could only be assuaged through effective educational programs in neighborhoods prior to site development.

The experience during the post-1993 period in Denver has been one of continuing controversies over particular supportive housing proposals. This suggests either that the former position has merit or that the requisite neighborhood educational programs have not been adequately institutionalized. Although in principle the 1993 Large Residential Care Uses Ordinance should have allayed neighborhoods' potential concerns about the overconcentration of supportive housing, significant issues remained related to facility clientele and management. Four post-1993 controversies are illustrative.[40]

A site at 1125 Columbine Street was proposed for development by Atlantis, an agency providing health care and housing for people with physical disabilities. Eight units in the 34-unit complex were to be set aside for these clients. According to our informants, this proposed site generated intense controversy because media accounts erroneously characterized it as a "halfway house for criminals" and the site was located across from an elementary school. The political controversy was further complicated by the fact that the school simultaneously wanted to expand and use the proposed site for a parking lot. After numerous meetings with the community, during which the true characteristics of those living in the supportive facility were clarified and an alternative school parking arrangement was devised, opposition subsided and the facility went forward.

The 200 South Sherman Street site was a former single-family home to be converted for use by eight women with chronic mental illness and/or dual diagnosis with alcohol or substance addiction. The facility had previously been used as a group home, but in response to the *Goebel* case, it was converted by Denver Health to a facility for this mentally ill clientele. This change, according to an informant, made the neighborhood "go ballistic." Apparently, an anonymous flyer had been distributed in the neighborhood claiming that this was to be a group home for juvenile sex offenders. In concert, a nearby Catholic church, its schools, and residents vehemently protested, arguing that these new group home residents would pose a threat to school children walking past their facility.

Denver Health's meetings with the parties and attempts to inform them about the nature of the proposed mentally ill clientele failed to quell the protests. The church, however, ultimately ran afoul of the Office of Peace and Justice of the Archdiocese of Denver, which persuaded the church that it was inappropriate to deny housing to anyone. At this point, the negotiations between Denver Health, the church, and the neighborhood proceeded affirmatively. Several key results emanated from these negotiations. The clientele was limited to women, who were perceived as less dangerous by the neighborhood. The facility was repainted in a Victorian color scheme to better blend with the dominant neighborhood style. And Denver Health agreed to screen out any applicants if they had previous convictions as pedophiles.

The Colorado AIDS Project, in association with Del Norte Development, applied to rehabilitate an old, deteriorated mansion for use by 17 people with AIDS at Josephine and 14th Streets. According to our informants, the initial reaction of opponents in the neighborhood was not hysteria, but "solid reservations and good questions" whether the project would be badly managed, weakly supervised, and poorly maintained, thus blighting and endangering the area. The developers were able to counter effectively that their previous supportive housing facilities reflected none of the neighbors' legitimate worries. In addition, the facility was billed as "caring for our own neighbors," inasmuch as a high proportion of the residents in the neighborhood were gay. Final compromises included improving landscaping, adding parking, and neighborhood participation on the project's Board of Directors and the team designing an addition to the original structure. The project went forward nine months after the initial meeting with the neighborhood.

Inasmuch as the federal McKinney Act gives priority to nonprofit housing developers to acquire surplus military base property, several supportive housing providers in Denver proposed projects in the recently deactivated Lowry Air Force Base on the eastern edge of Denver. One was Catholic Charities, which wanted to develop 40 townhouses (amid 600 homes already on the former base) as transitional facilities for the homeless. Inasmuch as several private neighborhoods abut this area of the base, this proposal (and others) for supportive housing was met with considerable public outcry, with fears of crime, drugs, disease, and property-value decline aired verbally and through dissemination of flyers. Catholic Charities canvassed and distributed leaflets, and its president wrote letters to all members of Catholic parishes in the area in an attempt to build understanding and support, which eventually was forthcoming. So the project commenced.

The positions evinced by these cases correspond closely to public opinions of Denverites revealed by a series of focus groups and a written survey conducted by the Center for Human Investment Policy at the request of the Colorado Coalition for the Homeless (Gould and O'Brien 1997). The study was designed as a reconnaissance into the attitudes, values, and perceptions of residents in more than a dozen Denver neighborhoods toward the placement of supportive housing facilities. It revealed clear opinions on the part of prospective neighbors:

- Potential opposition was related not just to the presence of supportive facilities but also to their density and those aspects of other subsidized units already in the area.
- The facility should blend in well with homes in the area.
- Group homes for parolees should not be placed near a school.
- Group homes for the elderly and children were easier to incorporate into their neighborhoods than parolees and the mentally ill.
- The facility should be small and well maintained.
- Clients should be carefully managed by a responsible and responsive operator.

The study conceded that many Denver residents continue to worry that the placement of group homes nearby will lower their property values. But, to the researchers' surprise, they found that opposition to group homes came less from a bias against the clientele and more from a sense of anger, frustration, and powerlessness with the process for addressing their concerns about how supportive facilities were sited, approved, and managed. Respondents did not feel comfortable with the information provided by developers and did not expect these service providers to be responsive to their concerns. The study concluded that supportive housing providers and neighborhoods needed to establish bonds of trust so that they could thereby "recognize the benefits of strengthening the context in which they all coexist" (Gould and O'Brien 1997, 6).

By implication, the strong regulatory and public disclosure environment established by Denver may prove to be a necessary, but not sufficient, condition for assuaging public anxiety about the impacts of supportive housing. There needs to be more: a trust that the developer will be competent and responsible and that neighborhood concerns will be addressed promptly and fairly. This indeed raises a high bar for public policy performance, a topic we explore in depth in chapter 9.

Conclusion

Economic downturns, stagnant property values, and increased racial and class polarization in Denver during the 1980s produced conditions conducive to a heightened sense of vulnerability among residents in neighborhoods targeted for assisted housing units sponsored by the DHA and supportive housing developers. This perceived vulnerability, coupled with opportunism on the part of some local politicians, sparked massive neighborhood opposition against the efforts of these two long-established programs, which in turn substantially restricted in several ways future assisted units within the community. The public outcry against these programs took housing officials and developers by surprise; thereby contributing to public perceptions of governmental bodies that were insensitive and unwilling to address neighborhood concerns.

Were these restrictions needed and effective? As we shall see in chapters 6 and 7, there is strong empirical evidence that limitations on the concentration and scale of assisted housing facilities make sense for minimizing harmful impacts on the neighborhoods. Indeed, in retrospect, it appears that both in the cases of the DHA Dispersed Housing Program and the supportive housing programs, the Denver ordinances got it about right.

Whether all resident fears expressed during the Denver controversies were grounded or not, they pointed to concerns that providers of assisted housing need to be aware of and to address *before* units are developed in neighborhoods. The controversies underscored the need for extensive community outreach and public disclosure about any plans for additional assisted housing units, as well as ongoing sensitivity to neighbors' concerns arising from the operation of these units, to mollify resident fears and opposition.

Notes

1. Even though at this writing more recent demographic data are available, we provide data for the 1980s because that is the period relevant for our policy history.

2. Note that this low level of Hispanics' educational attainment in Denver is in marked contrast to that for Baltimore County; see chapter 3.

3. The 1980 and 1990 housing data were obtained from the U.S. Census. The 1990 to 1996 price changes were estimated from residential home sales extracted from tax assessor records; see chapter 5.

4. This information is based on interviews with four public housing administrators. For details on our methods for conducting archival research and key informant interviews in Denver, see Galster et al. 1999.

5. These homes' mortgages were originally insured under the FHA/VA programs. If owners defaulted on their mortgages, title to the home eventually passed to HUD.

6. *Minutes of the DHA Board of Commissioners*, 1960, various months.

7. *Minutes of the DHA Board of Commissioners*, October 19, 1960, p. 11; November 9–18, 1960, p. 4; December 14, 1960, p. 7.

8. *Minutes of the DHA Board of Commissioners*, March 21, 1961, p. 3.

9. *Minutes of the DHA Board of Commissioners*, May 7, 1963, p. 4.

10. *Minutes of the DHA Board of Commissioners*, February 15, 1967, p. 4.

11. See Gillies (1972, 36).

12. *Minutes of the DHA Board of Commissioners*, December 14, 1966, p. 3; January 25, 1967, p. 4); Johnston (1969, 37).

13. For further information, see *Minutes of the DHA Board of Commissioners*, May 22, 1968, p. 6; January 8, 1969, p. 3); Johnston (1969, 37).

14. *Minutes of the DHA Board of Commissioners*, July 22, 1970, p. 3.

15. *Minutes of the DHA Board of Commissioners*, December 30, 1970, p. 2.

16. This material is based on interviews with four public housing administrators.

17. This material is based on interviews with six public housing administrators.

18. The materials used in this section are derived primarily from a letter dated January 11,

1989, from Ron S. Paul, director of redevelopment, Denver Housing Authority, to Denver area brokers and realtors and from a February 1989 open letter to Denver realtors by Paul that was published in the *Denver Realtor News*, p. 12.

19. The information described in this section is based on interviews with four public housing administrators and six community leaders. In addition, the controversy was part of intense media coverage including the publication of dozens of articles chronicling the fate of the Dispersed Housing Program.

20. This information is based on interviews with four public housing administrators and five community leaders.

21. This information is from several community leaders.

22. This information is from a community leader.

23. This information is from a community leader.

24. This is based on several interviews with public housing administrators and community leaders, as well as from the *1990 Minutes of the Meetings of the Council of the City and County of Denver,* various months.

25. This information was obtained from interviews with nine public housing administrators.

26. This information is based on interviews with six public housing administrators and four community leaders, and from *Resolution No. 100, Series of 1989, Resolution Supporting an Intergovernmental Agreement between the City and County of Denver and Denver Housing Authority.*

27. This is based on an interview with one public housing administrator.

28. This discussion is based on the interviews of six public housing administrators.

29. K. Bailey (1990, 7).

30. The racial and ethnic profile of DHA residents reflects the overrepresentation of people of color, particularly Hispanics, in public housing. Fifty-one percent of DHA residents are Hispanic, 23 percent are black, and 14 percent are white. The Dispersed Housing Program contains about the same proportion of Hispanics as in DHA housing overall (52 percent), a higher proportion of blacks (31 percent), and a lower proportion of whites (7 percent). These statistics were derived from the DHA Client and Property Databases and provided by DHA administrators.

31. The information about the protocol followed was obtained from interviews with four public housing administrators.

32. The following is excerpted from City and County of Denver (1998a)

33. These data are City and County of Denver (1998b).

34. All community correctional facilities house between 40 and 84 residents; two transitional homes house 8 and 28 residents; three homeless shelters house 70, 110, and 250 persons.

35. According to the *City and County of Denver Consolidated Plan, 1998–2002*, $731,000 of this total is provided through the HOME program and another $650,000 through HOPWA.

36. *Goebel et al. v. Colorado Department of Institutions et al.,* 1981, (830 P.2d 1036) with several subsequent appeals and ancillary suits. The following section draws heavily from the Westlaw database's review of the case.

37. Interview with two DHA officials, February 1998.

38. Interview with Denver Community Development Agency official, February 1998.

39. Interview with a key informant, February 1998.

40. Inasmuch as all supportive housing sites are a matter of public record in Denver, we violate no confidentiality issues by using precise addresses below.

3

The Baltimore Controversies over the Section 8 and Moving to Opportunity Programs

Analogous to the case of the Dispersed Housing Program in Denver, the Section 8 program had operated in Baltimore County for nearly two decades with limited public awareness or opposition. Yet, with little warning, a controversy exploded in 1994 over the initiation of a new, experimental component of the Section 8 program: the Moving to Opportunity (MTO) demonstration. It would be the well-publicized MTO goal to move a relatively small number of low-income households from Baltimore City public housing developments into Baltimore County neighborhoods that would generate political fallout that transcended the local community. Indeed, the impact on the entire federal MTO demonstration proved devastating.

In this chapter, we begin with an overview of local area characteristics and trends that establish a context for local community response to the Section 8 program in general and the MTO demonstration in particular. Next, each of the components of the Section 8 program operative in the Baltimore metropolitan area is described. We then delineate the key facets of the controversy and the various types of opposition that emerged in response to the Section 8 and MTO programs. The chapter concludes with a brief summary of the lessons learned from Baltimore.

A Profile of Baltimore County

To place the policy history in its proper context, this section provides a general overview of the demographic and housing trends in Baltimore County for the years 1980 and 1990. Table 3.1 summarizes census data on population, education and employment, income and poverty, and housing characteristics for Baltimore County. Because the spatial distributions of these changes are vitally important to this project, we have also created a series of maps that highlight the geographic distributions of key indicators in census tracts throughout the county (maps 3.1–3.4).

Table 3.1

Selected Population and Housing Characteristics by Ethnicity, Baltimore County, 1980–90

Characteristic	1980				1990			
	All	*White*	*Black*	*Hispanic*	*All*	*White*	*Black*	*Hispanic*
Population								
Total population	655,615	586,204	53,598	5,394	692,134	582,397	84,648	8,131
Median age (in years)	32.3	33.1	26.7	27.1	35.2	36.4	29.4	29.2
Percentage of households headed by females	13.0	11.7	30.9	13.1	15.7	13.2	35.0	16.9
Percentage of foreign born	4.1	3.2	1.7	33.9	4.7	2.9	3.4	32.0
Education and employment								
Percentage with less than high school degree	31.7	32.3	27.7	23.8	21.6	21.9	20.1	21.1
Percentage college graduates	18.8	18.4	18.6	34.5	25.0	24.7	22.6	29.7
Labor force participation rate	66.3	65.5	75.2	69.7	68.6	67.1	78.3	75.0
Unemployment rate	5.0	4.8	7.5	4.5	3.7	3.2	7.0	4.3
Income and poverty status								
Median family income	24,413	24,683	20,436	25,313	44,502	45,394	37,463	41,935
Percentage of households receiving public assistance	4.0	3.6	8.9	3.6	4.1	3.7	7.8	3.8
Percentage of families living in poverty	4.1	3.5	10.6	5.9	3.8	3.3	9.2	4.4
Percentage of persons living in poverty	5.3	4.7	11.2	9.1	5.5	4.8	10.4	9.1
Percentage of female-headed families living in poverty	15.5	13.3	24.3	11.4	14.2	12.5	19.9	16.2
Housing								
Total year-round housing units	243,250				281,553			
Occupied housing units	237,371	215,875	18,336	1,612	268,280	230,692	30,413	2,593
Housing vacancy rate	2.4				4.7			
Percentage owner occupied	64.2	66.7	36.1	56.3	66.3	70.2	39.1	50.6
Percentage renter occupied	35.8	33.3	63.9	43.7	33.7	29.8	60.9	49.4
Percentage of housing units built prior to 1940	13.8	14.4	7.7	7.1	10.4	11.1	5.7	4.5
Percentage of housing units in 20+ unit structures	N/A	N/A	N/A	N/A	3.3	3.0	2.7	3.7
Median housing value	54,400	54,400	52,100	57,800	99,900	101,100	89,300	105,700
Median contract rent	232	233	227	238	458	460	449	46

Note: N/A means not available.

Sources: Various published tables were used from the following sources: U.S. Bureau of the Census (1983). *1980 Census of Population and Housing, Population and Housing Characteristics for Census Tracts: Baltimore, MD.* Washington, DC: U.S. Government Printing Office; U.S. Bureau of the Census (1993). *1990 Census of Population and Housing, Population Housing Characteristics for Census Tracts and Block Numbering Areas: Baltimore, MD.* Washington, DC: U.S. Government Printing Office.

Population Characteristics

In 1990, the population of Baltimore County was 692,134. Eighty-four percent of all county residents were white (i.e., non-Hispanic whites), 12 percent were non-Hispanic blacks, 1 percent were Hispanics, and the remaining 3 percent were of Asian or other ethnic ancestry. Nearly 5 percent of county residents were foreign born. During the 1980s, the population of Baltimore County increased by 6 percent. Nearly all of this increase can be attributed to the growth of black (58 percent growth) and Hispanic (51 percent growth) populations. The growth of the immigrant population during the 1980s played a slight role in the overall increase in the population. However, it warrants noting that nearly one-third of all Hispanic residents in the county were immigrants.

Baltimore County residents made up only 29 percent of the total metropolitan population of Baltimore in 1990—a slight decrease from 1980. An interesting pattern of geographic dispersion of ethnic groups is worth noting. Although 34 percent of whites and 27 percent of Hispanics resided in the county in 1990, only 14 percent of blacks lived there. During the 1980s, whites moved out of the county on net, while both blacks and Hispanics moved in, on net.

Map 3.1 shows the 1990 residential distribution of blacks in Baltimore County, the predominant minority group. We can see that out of the 194 census tracts in the county, 143 had less than 10 percent black population. Tracts with 20 percent and higher black population tended to be located in an area to the west of Baltimore City, following the Liberty Road corridor. These tracts also demonstrated the largest increase in the proportion of black population during the 1980s, with wholesale neighborhood racial transition often being evinced.

Education and Employment Characteristics

During the 1980s, the fraction of Baltimore County residents who had obtained college degrees had increased from 19 to 25 percent. At the same time, the percentage of residents who had not completed high school declined from 32 to 22 percent. There were marked differences in the educational attainment of whites, blacks, and Hispanics in Baltimore, particularly in terms of college completion. Nearly 30 percent of Hispanics had college degrees as compared with 25 percent of whites and 23 percent of blacks. Of interest, whites had the highest fraction of persons with less than a high school degree—22 percent—and blacks had the lowest fraction—20 percent.

In Baltimore County, minority residents had the highest rates of labor market participation, underscoring the youthfulness of these populations. In 1990, 78 percent of blacks and 75 percent of Hispanics were in the labor force, as compared with 67 percent of whites. The 1980s also witnessed an increase in the labor force participation rates of all groups, although the increase was the highest for Hispanics. In turn, unemployment rates declined in the 1980s, although the declines were negligible for blacks and Hispanics. Moreover, the black unemployment rate continued to be twice as high as that for whites; the Hispanic unemployment rate was approximately 1.3 times higher.

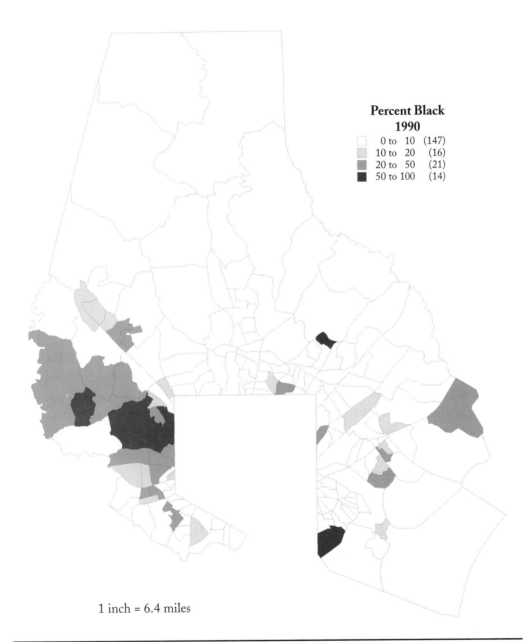

Percent Black
1990

0 to 10	(147)
10 to 20	(16)
20 to 50	(21)
50 to 100	(14)

1 inch = 6.4 miles

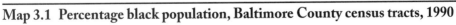

Map 3.1 Percentage black population, Baltimore County census tracts, 1990

Source: U.S. Bureau of the Census, *1990 Census of Population and Housing,* Summary file 3

Income and Poverty Status

In 1990, the median family income in Baltimore County was $44,502. This ranged from a low of $37,463 for blacks to a high of $45,394 for whites. Though the income gap between whites and blacks remained relatively stable during the 1980s, with black median family income about 83 percent of white median family income, the gap between white and Hispanic income increased. In 1980, median family income for Hispanics was 103 percent of white median family income. By 1990, Hispanic median family income had decreased to 93 percent of the white median family income.

During the 1980s, family poverty rates declined for all groups in the 1980s. By 1990, only 4 percent of Baltimore families were living in poverty. The black family poverty rate was 2.8 times higher than that for white families and 2.1 times higher than that for Hispanic families. When individual poverty rates are examined across ethnic groups, we see that poverty rates for both blacks and Hispanics were approximately twice as high as that for whites. One out of 10 blacks and 1 out of 11 Hispanics was poor in 1990; in contrast, only 1 out of 20 white residents was poor. During the 1980s, the individual poverty rate grew slightly for whites, remained the same for Hispanics, and actually declined for blacks.

Housing Characteristics

The housing stock in Baltimore is relatively new; only 1 out of 10 housing units was built before 1940. Whites were about twice as likely as blacks or Hispanics to live in these older housing units. Further, the 1980s witnessed a 16 percent increase in the housing stock. At the same time, vacancy rates increased from 2 percent in 1980 to 5 percent in 1990. Relatively few housing units were concentrated in sizable clusters; only 3 percent of the housing units were found in structures with 20 or more units.

Approximately two-thirds of all county residents were homeowners in 1990, although homeownership rates were 39 percent for blacks, 51 percent for Hispanics, and 70 percent for whites. During the 1980s, homeownership rates increased for whites and blacks but declined markedly for Hispanics. According to map 3.2, the percentage of renter-occupied housing varied substantially from tract to tract, with 59 tracts having more than 40 percent renter-occupied housing and 43 tracts having less than 10 percent renter housing. Further, one frequently could identify tracts with a high proportion of rental housing adjacent to tracts with high homeownership rates. Median rents essentially doubled in nominal terms in the 1980s. By 1990, the median rent in Baltimore County was $458 and ranged upward from a low of $449 for blacks and $464 for Hispanics. In 1990, the median housing value was $99,900 in the county, although this varied widely by ethnic group: $89,300 for blacks, $101,100 for whites, and $105,700 for Hispanics. Map 3.3 shows the median house values in Baltimore County census tracts. The area to the north of Baltimore City tends to have the most expensive housing, with most tracts having median house values of more than $150,000. Moreover, during the period from 1990 to 1996, property values declined or grew very slowly in most of the county. As shown in map 3.4, there were 63 tracts where property values did not grow at all and 96 tracts where values increased by 15 percent or less.

Summary: The Demographic Context of the Controversy

As described above, Baltimore County underwent significant demographic change in the 1980s. By 1990, a more diverse population lived in the county and the proportion of whites had decreased. A sizable black minority population had grown by 58 percent in the previous decade, with concomitant upsurges in neighborhood transition. Older whites and younger blacks and other minorities increasingly characterized the county. The income gap between blacks and whites remained virtually unchanged during the 1980s, however, despite increasing labor force participation and declining unemployment rates overall. Though poverty rates declined for all groups, minority poverty rates were still two times higher than that experienced by whites. The reality of racial and class changes in many county neighborhoods had begun.

Moreover, while there were overall patterns suggesting some modest degree of economic growth, marked variations appeared across the county. These differences are perhaps best signaled by declining or sluggish growth in property values. Slightly less than one-third of all tracts experienced declining values during the 1980s, and another half of the tracts showed negligible growth. Though these statistics alone do not necessarily paint an alarming future for Baltimore County, fears of an economic and social downturn festered. As the 1993 Baltimore County *Comprehensive Housing Affordability Strategy* (*CHAS*) stated, the county was "poised precariously between renewal and decline" (Baltimore County 1993, iii). A confluence of efforts by the public housing authority in Baltimore City to deconcentrate assisted housing into Baltimore County was about to threaten this precarious position.

The Section 8 Program and Deconcentration Initiatives in Baltimore City and County

To fully comprehend the Baltimore area's experience with the Section 8 program, and especially the political controversies that it has engendered, it is important to recognize that there are three distinct, though chronologically overlapping, variants of the program operating in different parts of the Baltimore metropolitan area. The first, which we shall refer to as the "basic Section 8" program, represents the standard local implementation of the national program that had already been operating for two decades at the time of major controversy, with independent administration by housing authorities in Baltimore City and Baltimore County. Under this standard Section 8 program, hundreds of Baltimore City residents moved to apartments in Baltimore County during the 1990s, using the cross-jurisdictional "portability" provisions of the subsidies.

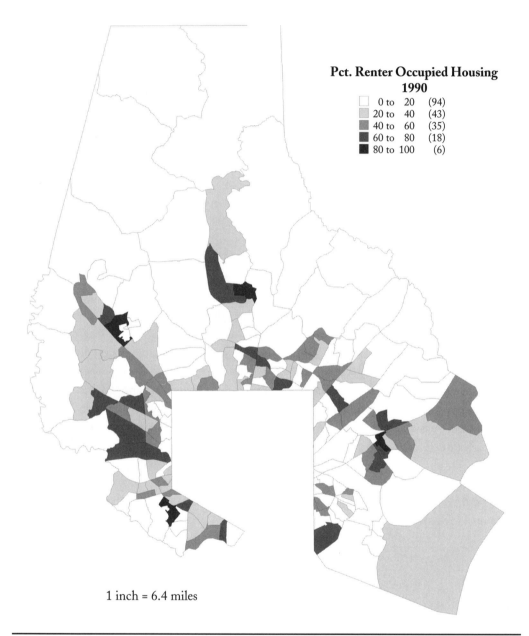

Pct. Renter Occupied Housing
1990

0 to 20	(94)
20 to 40	(43)
40 to 60	(35)
60 to 80	(18)
80 to 100	(6)

1 inch = 6.4 miles

Map 3.2.   Percentage renter-occupied housing, Baltimore County census tracts, 1990

Source: U.S. Bureau of the Census, *1990 Census of Population and Housing*, Summary file 3

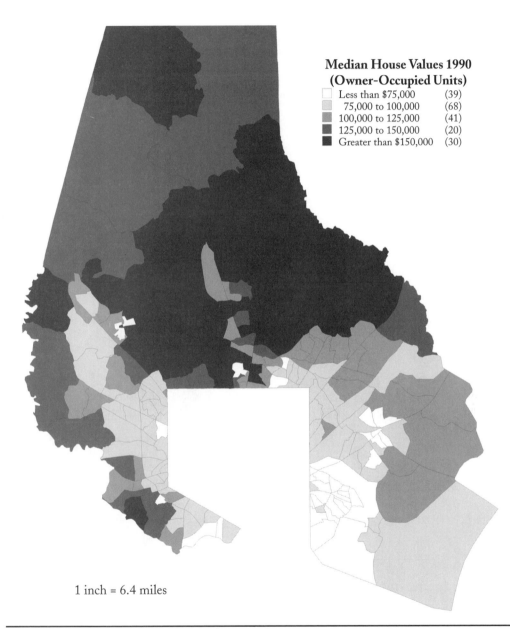

Median House Values 1990
(Owner-Occupied Units)
☐ Less than $75,000   (39)
   75,000 to 100,000   (68)
   100,000 to 125,000   (41)
   125,000 to 150,000   (20)
■ Greater than $150,000   (30)

1 inch = 6.4 miles

Map 3.3.   Median house value, Baltimore County census tracts, 1990

Source: U.S. Bureau of the Census, *1990 Census of Population and Housing,* Summary file 3

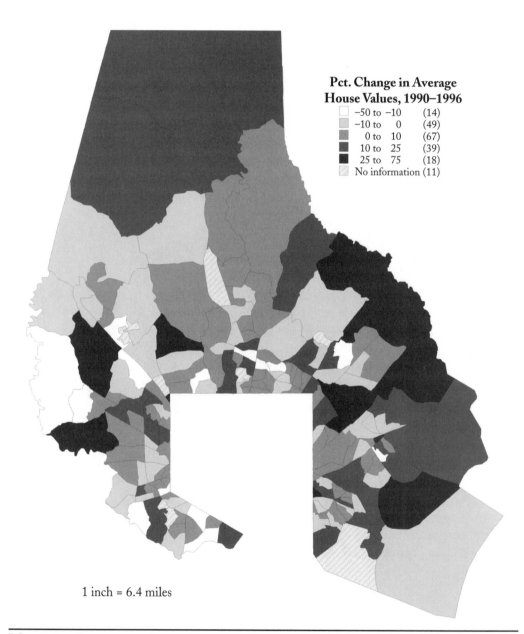

**Pct. Change in Average
House Values, 1990–1996**

☐	−50 to −10	(14)
	−10 to 0	(49)
	0 to 10	(67)
	10 to 25	(39)
	25 to 75	(18)
	No information	(11)

1 inch = 6.4 miles

**Map 3.4.   Percentage change in average house values, Baltimore County census
tracts, 1990–96**

Source: Authors' analysis of Experian home sales data

The second Section 8 variant, the one associated with the MTO demonstration, began in 1994 under the Housing Authority of Baltimore City (HABC) administration and finished placing its 143 tenants throughout the city and county by early 1997. The third variant, the "special Section 8" program, was agreed to in 1996 to comply with a Partial Consent Decree to settle a civil rights suit against the HABC. As part of this settlement, upward of 2,000 residents in HABC public housing were to be given opportunities for assisted housing of various sorts in the Baltimore suburbs.

Two key introductory points must be made regarding these three facets of the Section 8 program in the Baltimore region. First, all three components, to a greater or lesser degree, involved the actual or planned deconcentration of assisted tenants into suburban Baltimore County neighborhoods. Second, though the publicity surrounding MTO made it the lightning rod for opponents, in fact our work reveals that the term "MTO" was used more generically as a symbol of deconcentrated assisted housing in general. It is clear that it was the collective threat represented by all three Section 8 program variants that raised the political hackles of many in Baltimore County.

The Basic Section 8 Program

The Section 8 certificate program was initiated by the Housing Authority of Baltimore City in 1976. The voucher variant of the program began in 1985 (Ards 1991). The HABC operates by far the largest Section 8 program in the region (HUD 1996). According to 1995 statistics, the HABC administered 6,737 vouchers and certificates, Baltimore County administered 3,021, and the remaining six counties in the region administered 2,541.[1] The HABC Section 8 program has a waiting list of more than 22,000 households, with an approximately five-year expected waiting period.[2]

The most recent comprehensive study of the HABC Section 8 program (Ards 1991) revealed the following characteristics of participating households:

- In both certificate and voucher programs, the predominant household pattern was a single mother (mean age 35 years) with one or two children, with an average household size of roughly two-and-a-half persons.
- More than half of the participants in both certificate and voucher programs received some additional form of public assistance, with mean adjusted family incomes between $5,000 and $6,000, roughly half the mean income of all Baltimore City renters.
- Overall, 83 percent of voucher holders and 95 percent of certificate holders were black, compared with 55 percent for the city as a whole.

All of these statistics paint a portrait that would be used subsequently by Baltimore County opponents of the Section 8 program to foment fears of neighborhood racial and class transition, and the "invasion of the undeserving poor from the city."

As was typical of housing authorities prior to the deconcentration initiatives of the

Clinton administration beginning in 1993, the HABC did little to encourage or facilitate the mobility of its Section 8 certificate or voucher recipients outside of the city into the seven-county surrounding region.[3] At the orientation for new Section 8 participants, the HABC would merely hand out lists of landlords who had asked that they be so listed, and encouraged participants to check in the free apartment guides and Sunday newspapers. Large-scale landlords who had previously served Section 8 tenants were sometimes asked by the HABC to give presentations at these orientations.[4] Not surprisingly, there was little spatial dispersion of HABC Section 8 participants; Ards (1991) estimated that three-fourths resided in only 30 percent of the city's planning districts.

Subsequently, the HABC has strengthened its mobility counseling services, however. A new unit was formed, Tenant Readiness Training and Mobility Counseling, which new program participants may avail themselves of voluntarily. An HABC staff person assists in finding appropriate apartments in low-poverty areas and, if appropriate, links tenants with specialized counseling agencies providing credit, family mediation, employment training, and other services. As of the time of our study, March 1997, it was estimated that approximately 900 Baltimore residents had moved into Baltimore County with their Section 8 subsidy, representing roughly one of eight participants.

Recognizing that their increased deconcentration efforts may be greeted with opposition from recipient neighborhoods, however, beginning in 1997 the HABC instituted a variety of efforts to smooth community entry of its Section 8 program participants:

- *Maintenance checks:* If periodic building inspections and/or damage reports suggest that Section 8 tenants are responsible, they will be ticketed, with failure to respond being grounds for termination. The same procedure holds for landlords.
- *Neighborhood service centers:* In each of nine police districts in the county, the HABC established centers with staff who meet with community groups to deal with complaints and, if necessary, refer them to the HABC for resolution.
- *Tenant screening:* Although landlords are assumed to carry the major responsibility in this regard, the HABC tries to ascertain whether information about an applicant's criminal record can be obtained and forwarded to the landlord without violating confidentiality requirements.
- *Intensified lease violation reporting:* Instead of merely failing to renew a misbehaving tenant's lease at the first anniversary renewal option point (and thus creating no blot on the tenant's record), the HABC is encouraging landlords to immediately report any lease violations. In serious or repeated cases, the HABC will terminate assistance.

The MTO Program

The Housing Authority of Baltimore City was one of five local housing authorities (along with those of Boston, Chicago, Los Angeles, and New York) to win the competition to participate in the Moving to Opportunity Demonstration. This program was designed as an experiment to ascertain differences in mobility behavior and family outcomes for three groups: (1) a control group residing in public housing in concentrated poverty neighborhoods; (2) a group of former public housing residents who receive standard Section 8 assistance; and (3) a group of former public housing residents who may only use their Section 8 assistance in census tracts having 10 percent or lower poverty rates in 1990, but are given extensive mobility assistance by a nonprofit organization. It was expected that primarily members of the last, experimental group would end up moving to nonpoverty areas of the suburbs.

The HABC teamed with the Community Assistance Network (CAN) to carry out MTO in the Baltimore region.[5] CAN is a nonprofit organization based in Dundalk, Baltimore County, that, prior to MTO, had focused on assisting low-income people with child care, home weatherization, and self-sufficiency counseling.

The deconcentration efforts of the Baltimore MTO program were concentrated on the residents of eight HABC public housing developments located in five census tracts having, on average, two-thirds of their residents living in poverty. The chosen developments were home to 3,807 households. They had an average income of $6,880, with almost half receiving public assistance. More than 99 percent were black and 84 percent were female-headed households (HUD 1996).

CAN's effort to support the mobility of experimental group residents in these developments to low-poverty neighborhoods was distinguished by its emphasis on post-move contact. That is, CAN's principle was that counseling for at least a year following the move to a low-poverty area was needed to maximize the chances for self-sufficiency.[6] CAN augmented its capacity by subcontracting with other agencies for appropriate specialized services for MTO families.

The specific housing counseling services provided by CAN under MTO consisted of the following (HABC 1993):

- *Outreach:* This was designed to recruit apartment owners in low-poverty census tracts throughout the metropolitan area. The outreach effort included developing relationships with local realtors, landlord associations, and tenant associations, conducting windshield surveys to search for prospective buildings in appropriate neighborhoods, and creating informational and promotional materials. CAN provided landlords with rent payment records, references, family photographs, credit checks, and histories to attempt to personalize prospective tenants.
- *Written information:* CAN wrote and distributed literature to MTO families concerning tenant and landlord rights and responsibilities, housing and contract standards, and tenant–landlord and public housing laws. Baltimore Neighborhoods, Inc., a nonprofit fair housing group, provided information and counseling on identifying and remedying housing discrimination and harassment that participants might face.
- *Briefings:* CAN initiated seven required workshops for the MTO participant households that were required to move to low-poverty areas. Workshops presented

information about (1) the purposes and methodology of MTO; (2) effective housing search strategies; (3) advantages and disadvantages of living in low-poverty neighborhoods and what is involved in making the transition; (4) maps showing alternative low-poverty neighborhoods, with data on schools, shopping, transportation, demographics, health facilities, etc.; and (5) legal issues. Workshops also started the process of assessment of participants. The first MTO families who successfully moved to low-poverty areas were often used as resource persons in workshops for later participants.

- *Home visits:* All MTO families were visited in their current residences and had their credit history checked. The home visit was designed to show the counselor how the family was residing and behaving, to provide an opportunity to discuss confidential matters, and to build trust between the family and the counselor. The outcome of these visits was an assessment of which families were ready to begin the housing search and the obstacles to be overcome before other families were ready. Information provided was used to help recruit landlords to house the given family.
- *Supplemental assistance:* For families who were not ready for an immediate housing search, CAN provided referral to a variety of ancillary service providers. Among the services they provided were budget and credit counseling; employment counseling; food, clothing, and furniture; substance abuse counseling; day care; parenting skills; and home maintenance.
- *Tours of areas:* Heads of families judged ready for a home search were taken on small-group tours of neighborhoods in which they had expressed an interest. Community attributes were highlighted, such as schools, parks, stores, employment centers, hospitals, and day care facilities. CAN counselors averaged 10 hours per family.
- *Facilitation of lease-up:* CAN coordinated the discussion between the MTO family and the landlord and served as an agent or advocate on the family's behalf, contacted the HABC regarding the need for the Section 8 certificate or voucher, and informed the landlord about Section 8 rules and procedures, if necessary.
- *Post-occupancy follow-up:* Within 90 days of the lease date, CAN contacted the family to offer additional counseling and referrals. Special efforts were made to familiarize the families with local utility companies and service providers, so that prospective problems could be proactively avoided. Four months prior to each of the first two annual home inspections, CAN contacted each family to clarify what was expected of them. At any point during occupancy, CAN served as a liaison between the MTO family and the appropriate authority to report alleged cases of discrimination or harassment. Finally, contacts were also made with landlords of MTO families, offering CAN's help in resolving any difficulties and to inform them of additional services available to the families.

CAN and the HABC proved to be one of the more effective MTO administrators (HUD 1996). The HABC began to process applications for assignment to CAN in October 1994, and evinced the lowest startup costs of any MTO site (HUD 1999). By the end of February 1996, 222 families had been assigned to the MTO experimental group designated for deconcentration, and 98 had rented apartments in low-poverty areas by April

1996. By January 1997, the full quota of 143 families had successfully rented.[7] As of August 1997, the U.S. Department of Housing and Urban Development (HUD) reported that 57 percent (or 283) of the households that had been offered Section 8 subsidies were able to lease apartments and had actually moved. This compares favorably with the average 48 percent lease-up rate over all MTO sites (HUD 1999). Of this group, 69 percent moved to low-poverty neighborhoods in Baltimore City, whereas only 19 percent (47 households) relocated to areas in Baltimore County.[8]

Thus, while MTO in Baltimore was effective in aiding participants to utilize their Section 8 subsidies in low-poverty areas, only four dozen MTO households used the program to move from Baltimore City to Baltimore County. Indeed, even if all 143 MTO experimental group participants had moved into the county, the impact of MTO by the middle of 1997 would nevertheless have been dwarfed either by the interjurisdictional mobility evinced under the HABC's basic Section 8 program (approximately 900 households), or by the basic Section 8 program operated in and by Baltimore County itself (approximately 3,000 households). Nevertheless, perhaps because of its visibility and symbolic value, MTO became the lightning rod for opposition to all sorts of Section 8 deconcentration efforts, as we shall see below.

ACLU Suit Special Certificates

Soon before the announcement of MTO, the HABC announced plans to tear down, in stages, 2,728 units of decayed, high-rise public housing at Lafayette Court, Flag House Commons, Lexington Terrace, and Murphy Homes projects as part of its HOPE VI project. Initial plans called for replacement units to be supplied partially by Section 8 certificates and partially by low-density complexes constructed on the same inner-city sites as the demolished public housing. Thus, even before a final plan was approved, the HABC provided a well-publicized indication that its former public housing residents would be looking for housing elsewhere.

The American Civil Liberties Union (ACLU) objected to the on-site replacement units and filed suit in January 1995 on behalf of blacks who were current and future residents of HABC housing.[9] They alleged that the mayor and City Council of Baltimore, the HABC, and HUD had created and maintained over many years a system of de jure segregation in public housing, which the HABC's proposed redevelopment scheme would merely perpetuate. The plaintiffs sought relief to restore to class members the positions they would have enjoyed had housing assistance been provided in a nondiscriminatory manner. A partial consent decree was approved on June 25, 1996. It contained three components for deconcentrating low-income housing opportunities (Evans 1996; Hendren 1996):

- *Special Section 8 certificates.* More than 1,300 certificates were to be awarded to residents of demolished HABC developments. Certificates could be used only in census tracts having poverty rates below 10 percent and in complexes having fewer than 20 percent of residents who were certificate holders. HUD was to provide $2.5 million to the HABC to subcontract with a nonprofit provider of mobility counseling services to assist families in finding affordable housing in nonimpacted areas.[10]

- *Homeownership Section 8 program.* A set of both site-based and tenant-based certificates were to be provided to be used to accumulate equity in apartments with an ultimate goal of purchase. The HABC was to use more than $18 million from its Urban Revitalization Demonstration (HOPE VI) grant for Lafayette Courts to fund at least 168 tenant-based certificates, and HUD was to allocate 496 site-based Section 8 certificates for this purpose.
- *Scattered-site replacement units.* The HABC was to join with private developers and the Maryland State Partnership Rental Program to develop 188 public housing units within larger, market-rate apartment complexes. Although privately owned and managed, these units would receive public housing operating subsidies. These units would replace some of the units demolished at Lexington Terrace.

In sum, the HABC's announced plans for public housing redevelopment (even before details were finalized in the ACLU consent decree) unleashed the prospect that more than 2,100 low-income, black, female-headed households would be relocated into low-poverty neighborhoods. In scale, this initiative dwarfed the deconcentration efforts of the HABC's basic Section 8 and MTO programs combined. Although no one could know for certain where these households would locate, an expectation on the part of Baltimore County residents was reinforced that many would soon become their neighbors.

Section 8 in Baltimore County

Independent of any inflows of Section 8 households originally subsidized through the Housing Authority of Baltimore City, the Baltimore County Housing Office (BCHO) administered during our study period a substantial Section 8 program in its own right. During the first half of the 1990s, roughly 3,000 BCHO certificates and vouchers were in use in any given year.[11] Thus, even with several hundred certificates and vouchers administered by the HABC being used by households moving into Baltimore County, it must be emphasized that during the period of major controversy (and of our study), the vast majority of the Section 8 program impact was "home grown." Nevertheless, as we shall see below, it was the rhetoric labeling Section 8, and MTO in particular, a tool of "invasion" by undesirables living *outside* the county that proved most potent in the ensuing controversy.

The Geopolitical Context of the 1994 Section 8 / MTO Controversy

Neighborhood reaction in Baltimore County to the Section 8 and MTO programs in 1994 was an expression and extension of deep-rooted community concerns and the nexus of several specific community events. The geopolitical context of reactions to these programs grounds the perceived relationships we observed in the county between deconcentrated assisted housing policy and neighborhood racial and class change.

As the statistical profile above made clear, by the early 1990s Baltimore County had experienced a long period of increasing population diversification and widespread property-value stagnation. Despite understandable misgivings over the tenuous future of the county, it nevertheless was increasingly portrayed by the media as a place of opportunity, and the city as a place of decay (McDougall 1993).[12] The Baltimore County *CHAS* echoed the concern that "more and more of the City's poor will seek in the County the decent, safe, and affordable housing that they feel the City can no longer provide" (Baltimore County 1993). As conditions seemed to worsen rapidly in the city, county residents braced for an influx of former city citizens who they feared would strain public services, stir up social ills, and lower neighborhood standards, thereby upsetting the precarious stability of their communities.[13]

The race and class distinctions between city and county indeed were dramatic, and have been highlighted in several reports. For example, the 1993 MTO application submitted by Baltimore City emphasizes the difference between the city's poverty population (21.9 percent) and the county's (5.5 percent).[14] The Baltimore metropolitan statistical area was pictured as a black center with a white outer ring (McDougall 1993; Rusk 1995; Goering et al. 2003).

Not surprisingly, therefore, race and class played fundamental roles throughout the Baltimore County debate on deconcentrated assisted housing policy. The popularly perceived vehicle of this unwanted demographic "invasion" was the city's Section 8 program, in all its variants. Of course, for many county residents, the city's Section 8 program was synonymous with "poor and black."[15] Perhaps nowhere else in the county did these issues come as starkly to the fore as in Dundalk and Essex.

The Dundalk and Essex Epicenter

The Baltimore County communities of Dundalk and Essex, which abut the southeastern edge of Baltimore City, proved the epicenter for opposition to MTO.[16] These older, blue collar, ethnic suburbs house an aging population with long-standing ties to the community. Once home to large contingents of employees from Bethlehem Steel, Martin Aircraft, Western Electric, and other manufacturing firms, the area steadily declined as employers left or downsized and neighborhoods where former workers lived became depressed (Baltimore County 1993, ii).

Though Dundalk and Essex still had a strong sense of neighborhood identity, homeownership rates were declining and rental housing markets were increasingly weak and becoming "housing of last resort" as quality lessened.[17] The communities contained expanding pockets of highly concentrated rental housing.[18] Although house values increased modestly between 1980 and 1990, housing in the communities was substantially less expensive than other Baltimore County neighborhoods, which made it more affordable for lower-income buyers.[19] By the late 1980s, the economic indicators for most of the census tracts in these communities were low enough that they, ironically, disqualified them as destinations for MTO families.[20] They were, however, home to substantial concentrations of standard Section 8–assisted households.[21]

Despite the ineligibility of most neighborhoods within Dundalk and Essex from MTO, local opposition to the program was fierce. Community meetings, parades, and editorial pages throughout the summer and fall of 1994 bore witness to the slogan plastered on billboards and placards across the area: "Say No to MTO." Across the board, our key informants suggested that the reaction to MTO was fundamentally not, however, about a specific housing demonstration program. Rather, MTO became a primal, symbolic "battle cry."[22] It crystallized the pent-up anxiety and rage of area residents to the general decline of their community over several decades—abetted if not caused by past assisted housing policy—and offered up a visible scapegoat.

This anxiety was manifested in the ongoing racial strife in Dundalk and Essex. In 1989, a federal grand jury indicted two white men for firebombing the home of an African-American woman in Dundalk. One of the men lived two blocks away from the woman (McDougall 1993). One county official familiar with the Dundalk area suggested an explanation: "These are the people that fled the City in their youth to get away from blacks. Now they are too old to move. [With the in-moving of low-income blacks] they see erosion of their primary asset."[23] Moreover, Dundalk and Essex residents saw in the City of Baltimore an area plagued by crime[24] and other social maladies that were "contagious" and could easily "infect" their communities if they were not vigilant. Their perceptions were epitomized by the city's public housing developments. In an effort to lessen the downward slide of their community, Dundalk and Essex residents thus thought it crucial to oppose MTO, Section 8, or any other assisted housing program that helped public housing residents move in.

There appear to be five strands of argument that were articulated regarding the connection between deconcentrated assisted housing and neighborhood decline: (1) the uncivil behavior of subsidized tenants; (2) racial and class prejudices against subsidized tenants; (3) subsidized tenants as a precursor to poverty concentration; (4) mismanagement by the housing authority; and (5) housing subsidies leading to poorly managed properties. Similar issues around Section 8 have emerged in other communities across the nation (HUD 2001). Let us consider each in more detail.

Uncivil Behavior of Subsidized Tenants

During the public debate over Section 8 and MTO, allegations were made about the prospective behavior of participating tenants. Baltimore County residents were concerned that the city was "exporting" its problems.[25] Tenants were seen as "unskilled," "unclean," and "undisciplined." The much-publicized problems of HABC public housing as havens for crime, drugs, and welfare mothers fueled county resident concerns about an increase in crime in receiving neighborhoods.[26] Public housing residents (and, by association, Section 8 and MTO tenants) would bring unwanted behavior to Baltimore County neighborhoods, thus eroding community standards and the quality of life. Such concerns were illustrated by a 1994 letter from the Democratic candidate for the Maryland House of Delegates to constituents. In the letter, she pledged "to lead community effort(s) against any infringement of nuisance laws, health standards, or housing standards which may have been brought by MTO."[27]

Racial and Class Prejudice against Subsidized Tenants

Assumptions about the behavior of Section 8 and MTO in-movers included stereotypes about race and class. But even beyond their expected behaviors, minorities and lower-income tenants likely were opposed in their own right (Simpson and Yinger 1972). Racial and class prejudice may result in an out-migration of white residents and reduce housing demand by prospective white, nonpoor in-migrants when a neighborhood is seen as becoming "integrated" (Bradburn, Sudman, and Gockel 1971; Galster 1990b). Thus, not only is the residential quality of life eroded for those who are prejudiced, but this erosion may be capitalized into declining property values.

Subsidized Tenants as a Precursor to Poverty Concentration

There was a fear that "opening the door" to one subsidized tenant would inevitably lead to the concentration of low-income tenants in the neighborhood because of a perceived tendency for Section 8 households to cluster.[28] Several of our interviewees from both the city and the county indicated that there were some legitimate grounds for this worry. As was noted above, until recently the HABC had not actively encouraged the dispersal of Section 8 recipients, and had been seen as concentrating such tenants in transitional neighborhoods within the city.[29] Clustering of rental properties at fair-market rent levels and recruitment of Section 8 tenants to a location by word-of-mouth from peers were cited as additional causes of Section 8 clustering.

Mismanagement by the Local Housing Authority

County residents' lack of faith in the Housing Authority of Baltimore City's ability to screen tenants heightened anxiety about the number and type of residents sent to receiving communities. Distrust of the HABC also bred insecurity about its ability to monitor housing quality standards. It was believed that both forces could cause property values to decrease in Baltimore County neighborhoods affected by MTO and Section 8, as standards for assisted residents and their properties declined.

Housing Subsidies Leading to Poorly Managed Properties

There was a widespread sentiment among all categories of our respondents that the Section 8 program often created perverse incentives for property management that adversely affected surrounding neighborhoods. Some landlords were seen as becoming lax with screening tenants, enforcing lease provisions, and adequately maintaining their properties because they believed that they had a "captive Section 8 market" that would continue to provide them with a steady stream of income regardless of their management practices. Thus, the public's perception about the association between deteriorated, badly run buildings and Section 8 tenantry is partly grounded in fact, it was argued.[30]

However, there was a recognition among a substantial number of our key informants that assisted housing programs may not, indeed, be as much a cause of neighborhood decline as its result.[31] In soft local real estate markets, owners may be forced to reduce vacancies and thus become more lax on screening of Section 8 tenants and/or actively seek more such tenants, inasmuch as they may be able to receive more rent from the housing authority than they could on the open market.[32] Even an opponent of MTO volunteered that the macro forces leading to population loss from eastern Baltimore County were fundamentally responsible for neighborhood decline, because under those circumstances more dwellings would be converted to renter occupancy and rents would more likely fall below fair-market rent levels.[33] Unfortunately, the idea that the increased presence of assisted housing may be the result rather than a cause of neighborhood decline did not seem to enter into the public debate in any meaningful way.

The Undeserving Poor

Yet one more argument was consistently raised that, though not alleging deleterious neighborhood impacts, sets an important contextual tone. The working-class nature of Dundalk and Essex brought out significant angst regarding what residents viewed as "welfare-like handouts" to the "undeserving poor" that provided them the same sort of housing that "they [Dundalk residents] worked hard for."[34] This theme was especially resonant with the audience of older, blue collar workers who had built equity over time in their homes and had long-standing roots in the neighborhoods. Community residents saw "the American Dream" they had worked decades for—home, school, and community—being given to "freeloading outsiders."[35] Moreover, because the projected in-movers were African Americans, Section 8 and MTO stoked fires of revulsion in its symbolizing of "forced integration"[36] and "social engineering" (Waldron 1994).

A Confluence of Unfortunate Coincidences

Even though it could be argued that the Dundalk and Essex communities were ripe for an upsurge in public opposition to Section 8 and MTO, the exceptional vehemence of local sentiment there and elsewhere in Baltimore County was the result of a confluence of unfortunate coincidences. These incidents included[37]

- a hotly contested county–council political race that included the board president of CAN (the organization contracted to provide MTO counseling);
- Baltimore City's plan to demolish thousands of public housing units under the auspices of HOPE VI, to be replaced with substantial numbers of Section 8 certificates and vouchers for the original poor, black residents;
- local and federal candidates vying for voters in areas of "Reagan Democrats," like Dundalk and Essex;
- tensions between the city and county, with deep-seated distrust of city government on the part of county citizens;
- HUD delays in issuing regulations implementing MTO in Baltimore; and
- Senator Barbara Mikulski of Maryland, a native of Dundalk, as chair of the Senate Appropriations Subcommittee for HUD.

The summer of 1994 saw former Maryland State Legislature delegate Lou DePazzo and CAN board president Jean Jung running for the Seventh District County Council seat, which included Dundalk. As president of CAN's Board, Jung could easily be excoriated as encouraging the movement of Baltimore City low-income blacks to Baltimore County through MTO. Although the Seventh District seat did not include significant areas targeted for MTO moves because they already exceeded a 10 percent poverty rate, the DePazzo campaign continually linked Jung with CAN and MTO, thereby implicitly keeping the focus on Dundalk as the reputed receiver of poor families from Baltimore City.

Thanks to the timing of the HABC's HOPE VI plan, there was little doubt in the minds of many Baltimore County residents as to who these in-movers would be. As was noted above, the HABC had recently announced the impending demolition of 2,728 units of public housing under HOPE VI. Some of these units were originally to be replaced on-site, but providing residents with Section 8 and encouraging their moves to Baltimore County was also part of the announced long-term plan.

Though proponents of MTO might cite the fact that the program was targeted to fewer than 150 families, the specter of thousands of displaced public housing residents loomed as more frightening. Indeed, even prior to MTO, County planners were figuring Baltimore City's public housing plight into estimating the county's affordable housing needs. They wrote that Baltimore County could "reasonably expect" an increase in the "poor and marginally skilled" population because of the city's public housing woes (Baltimore County 1993, 16).

Thus, when MTO was announced it seemed to some as the "straw that broke the camel's back." MTO became a convenient symbol around which to mobilize opposition to deconcentrated assisted housing strategies in general.

The symbol was brandished with particular visibility in communities that were not solidly in the camp of either party. Areas like Dundalk had been important sources of traditional Democratic power but more recently could not be relied upon. In an effort to appeal to this uncommitted constituency, candidates from both parties took up the issue of MTO. From state delegate candidates Michael Davis (Republican) and Diane DeCarlo (Democrat) to Republican gubernatorial hopefuls Ellen Sauerbrey and Helen Bentley, MTO became an issue around which to rally partisan support. Continued media and campaign attention further heightened public awareness about all sorts of programs to deconcentrate assisted housing.

An early inquiry about MTO appeared as a letter to the editor in the May 12, 1994, *Dundalk Eagle* from a community leader questioning the details of the program and asking for a public presentation.[38] Responsive letters from the executive director of CAN and another from a housing administrator in a nearby county, described the broad goals of the program but explained that a contract was still in negotiation and details were not finalized. Without regulations in place to answer questions quickly and definitively, MTO opponents could (and did) portray HUD as stonewalling.[39] Worst-case scenarios were put forth for public consumption by MTO opponents without compelling arguments offered to rebut them being forwarded. Therefore, the MTO administrators' inability to communicate clearly and effectively the goals and details of the program only exacerbated the public's feelings of mistrust and anxiety.

Pairing distrust of the city government with a belief in the incompetence of the HABC, opponents to MTO rhetorically painted an exceedingly bleak picture (Carson 1994a, 1994b). In some cases, weak neighborhood housing markets had indeed given rise to concentrations of Section 8 households, and some notoriously "bad" developments were connected to HUD through financing, insurance, or project-based Section 8.[40] But the realities of HUD program shortcomings were exaggerated to the maximum extent possible by those who sought to exploit MTO for their own political benefit. For them, the more appropriate meaning of MTO seemed to be "Moving toward Opportunism."

Opposition continued to mount in a series of community meetings held throughout the summer. Attendance and tempers were high as community leaders, residents, advocates, and opponents were brought out by the MTO issue. Invited to speak on the goals of the program at a community meeting at a local high school, representatives from HUD headquarters in Washington and local housing officials were peppered with hostile questions and statements.[41] After contentious public meetings abated, community organizations, local landlords, and politicians kept the issue in the news. As the November elections approached, politicians repeatedly used MTO as a symbol for a variety of social and economic issues. Lou DePazzo and other leaders in the anti-MTO fight won election handily.

Thus, what started as a purely local concern ended in changed national policy because of political serendipity. Senator Mikulski happened at the time to be chair of the Senate Appropriations Subcommittee for HUD, and thus was in a position of power over the future of MTO. Citing concerns forwarded by her constituents about program oversight, she successfully led the effort in late August 1994 to halt further MTO funding (Mariano 1994).

Yet local anxiety did not end with the discontinued financing of MTO. When Baltimore mayor Kurt Schmoke and HABC commissioner Daniel Henson III met with HUD secretary Henry Cisneros in late September 1994 to discuss the program, Baltimore County opponents viewed the meeting as further evidence of a "secret deal" between the city and HUD.[42] No "secret deal" emerged, but the settlement of the ACLU case against the HABC's HOPE VI plans did in 1996. As was noted above, the settlement reified the worst fears of opponents to deconcentrating assisted housing, for it required Section 8 participants to use their assistance in low-poverty neighborhoods. Not surprisingly, at this writing unrest still ferments over efforts to deconcentrate assisted housing in Baltimore County.[43]

Conclusion

By the early 1990s, neighborhoods across Baltimore County, like Denver, had experienced an influx of minority residents while at the same time witnessing declining or negligible growth in property values. These trends produced a heightened sense of vulnerability among local residents that only intensified with the announcement of the proposed addition of low-income housing units in the county through a confluence of deconcentration policies. As in the case of Denver, fears about the negative impacts of assisted housing on property values and crime rates fueled massive public protests, which local politicians further incited out of political opportunism. Section 8 assisted housing in the suburbs became the convenient scapegoat for a complex mix of resentments and frustrations about neighborhood changes that played themselves out in a number of local, state, and national campaigns. The political resistance in Baltimore County ultimately proved so fierce that all but the first wave of participation in the national MTO demonstration program were discontinued.

The controversies in Baltimore County, much like those in Denver, provide clear demonstrations of how potential opposition to deconcentrated assisted housing is contingent on the conditions prevailing in the affected neighborhoods and the local political and institutional context. Residents who are already uneasy about changes under way in their community are more likely to perceive these programs as severe threats, and react accordingly (HUD 2001). As we shall show in forthcoming chapters, in certain circumstances some of this unease appears to be justified. The issue becomes even more polarizing where there are widespread sentiments that administrators of deconcentrated assisted housing programs are incompetent, local government cannot be trusted to oversee them effectively, communication of program policies and goals is poor, and there is a perception that neighborhood concerns are not being taken seriously (HUD 2001). Our two policy histories thus provide clear goals for how policy reforms must create a new geographic and perceptual context if expanded deconcentration efforts are to proceed appropriately.

Notes

1. Personal correspondence from Bob Gajdys, executive director of the Community Assistance Network, Inc. (January 13, 1997). The primary difference between vouchers and certificate versions of Section 8 is that the latter limits recipients to pay "fair market rent" for their apartment, whereas voucher holders have more flexibility in rents they pay, though subsidy amounts do not differ.

2. Interview with local housing program administrator.

3. The effort was described as "very minimal" by one local housing program administrator. Another called it "not real counseling."

4. Parts of this section are based on an interview with a local housing program administrator.

5. This section is based on information presented in HUD (1996) and HABC (1993).

6. Interview with local housing program administrator; HABC 1993. See also Edkins 1996 and Goering et al. 2003.

7. Interview with local housing program administrators.

8. Lucas (1997, 18). HUD's database contained information on only 253 of the 283 "mover" households, which included both the restricted and the nonrestricted MTO groups.

9. *Thompson v. HUD.*

10. When first proposed, this component of the settlement drew fire from Baltimore County Executive C. A. "Dutch" Ruppersberger, and 1,600 county residents attended a public forum to discuss the issue (Mercurio 1995; Hendren 1996).

11. We provide additional spatial information about the Section 8 program in Baltimore County in chapter 5.

12. Also confirmed by interviews with local housing program administrators and nonprofit leaders.

13. Interviews with local housing program administrators, elected officials, and nonprofit leaders.

14. This quote is based on information presented in Edkins 1996.

15. Interview with local housing program administrator.

16. The focus of opposition to housing mobility in Baltimore was MTO. While Section 8 is implicated, "MTO" was the catch phrase referring to any publicly assisted mobility program. It will be used here to refer to the opposition in 1994 to the MTO program and the broader meaning conferred on it as described in the text.

17. Baltimore County 1993, 14; Goering et al. 2003. This was confirmed in interviews with housing administrators and nonprofit leaders.

18. See map 3.2.

19. See map 3.3.

20. MTO required receiving census tracts to have less than 10 percent of the population below the poverty line in 1989.

21. Our data did not permit us to distinguish between households receiving assistance from HABC or BCHO.

22. Interview with an elected official.

23. Ibid.

24. According to the 1993 Baltimore County *CHAS*, the Baltimore County Police Department receives about 400,000 calls a year compared to twice that number for Baltimore City.

25. A local public official expressed this as "dumping the worst of the worst." This widespread sentiment was confirmed in four other Baltimore County interviews.

26. Baltimore County interviews; see also similar concerns of community residents discussed in Goetz, Lam, and Heitlinger 1996.

27. This document presented in Edkins 1996.

28. This was confirmed in numerous interviews in Baltimore County. For scholarly discussion of these issues, consult Cox 1982; Rohe and Stegman 1994; and Pendall 2000.

29. Interview with nonprofit leader.

30. Interviews with local housing program administrators, elected officials, and nonprofit organization leaders.

31. Other anecdotal evidence about landlords who specialize in the "Section 8 submarket" is presented in Peterson and Williams 1995.

32. Interviews with elected public official and local housing program administrators.

33. Interview with elected public official.

34. Interview with housing program administrator. See also Montgomery 1994; Edkins 1996.

35. Ibid.

36. Interview with elected official.

37. Interviews with elected officials, nonprofit leaders, and local housing program administrators. See also Goering et al. 2003.

38. Reported in Edkins 1996; also see Hersl 1994.

39. Interview with housing program official.

40. Interview with housing program administrator.

41. Conversations with Baltimore County housing official, 2000; also see Goering et al. 2003.

42. Interview with elected official. See also Carson 1994a.

43. See Pollock and Rutkowski 1998; Goering et al. 2003.

4

Deciphering the Neighborhood Impacts of Assisted Housing: Methodological Issues

Investigators of the neighborhood impacts of deconcentrated assisted housing face two challenges. First, the analyst must carefully identify the magnitude of the effect and, to the greatest degree possible, identify assisted housing as the cause of any measured effect. Second, the analyst must then interpret why this effect may have manifested itself and what it might mean for reshaping public policy. The former challenge is addressed with quantitative research methods, the latter with qualitative methods. This chapter describes how we have tried to meet these challenges with statistical modeling and focus group discussions.

The Statistical Modeling Approach: A Nontechnical Overview

In this overview, we aim to give a comprehensible (albeit somewhat superficial) description of what our statistical models of neighborhood impact are trying to accomplish and how they go about doing so. Readers for whom this proves a sufficiently detailed explanation can then skip to the description of the focus group sites and methods at the end of this chapter. This will provide a sufficiently detailed explanation to understand the results presented in chapter 5. Those wishing to probe methodological subtleties and technical details of our model are referred to subsequent sections and to the appendix.

Our impact models build upon the work of numerous researchers who have investigated the degree to which a variety of factors associated with a neighborhood affect the sales prices of single-family homes and the reports of crimes. The heart of these investigations consists of a statistical model that attempts to explain the variation in sales prices or crime reporting rates in different neighborhoods according to characteristics of the neighborhood, the larger community, and (in the case of the property-value model) the particular house being sold.

To use the property-value model to illustrate, we want to decompose the selling price of a single-family home into implicit prices paid for the home's myriad attributes—such as rooms, yard size, fireplaces, maintenance levels, year of construction—as well as attributes associated with the home's surroundings. This latter set can include the quality of local public schools; the condition of nearby properties; proximity to shopping; the socioeconomic and racial characteristics of neighbors; and of particular interest here, the presence of assisted housing. The idea is that homes with a different bundle of attributes will sell for different prices, and that a home's sales price can be predicted by measuring the amount of each attribute present and multiplying that amount by its implicit price. By adding up the implicit values of the different attributes of a house, one can arrive at its total sales price.

The method for decomposing home sales prices into implicit prices of attributes is an econometric technique known as *multiple regression analysis*. In this technique, a sample of home sales is drawn and as many attributes of each home and its environs as feasible are measured. The home sales price becomes the "dependent" variable in the regression model, and the attributes become the "independent" (or explanatory) variables. The multiple regression computer algorithm estimates coefficients for each attribute variable, finding the coefficients that provide the "best fit" between the observed house prices and those that would be predicted by the model. These estimated coefficients can then be interpreted as the implicit prices of these attributes.

Thus, if a regression of home sales prices on the properties' housing and neighborhood attributes were to produce, for example, a negative coefficient for the attribute "age of the home," we would interpret this to mean that the market does not value older homes as much as newer ones, all else being equal. Similarly, if our regression were to estimate a positive coefficient for the attribute "a park is within two blocks," it would signify that the market valued proximity to parks.

It is important to realize that a coefficient of an individual variable is estimated independent of the effects of all the other attribute variables specified in the regression model. That is, one can interpret these coefficients as the additional impact on price that is contributed by the given attribute, controlling for the effects of all the other attributes. A crucial implication is that the accuracy of results is greater if one can control for as many attributes as possible in the multiple regression.

For the purposes of our study, we focus attention on a particular attribute: "proximity to an *assisted housing site*" or, alternatively, "proximity to a *number of assisted households*."[1] We define "proximity" in terms of three distance "rings": within 500 feet, 501–1,000 feet, and 1,001–2,000 feet. What we specify as "assisted housing" will vary depending on the application of our model: a Denver Housing Authority dispersed housing site, a supportive housing site in Denver, or a Section 8 household in Baltimore County. Our goal is to ascertain the degree to which proximity to assisted housing affects sales prices and (in Denver) crime report rates, statistically controlling for a wide variety of attributes. These attributes include the home's structural characteristics; characteristics of the surrounding neighborhood, measured at both the census tract scale and the "microneighborhood" scale of 2,000 feet around an assisted site; and measures to adjust for seasonal and business-cycle influences.

To do this, we structure our multiple regression, what we call our "econometric pre/post model," to create the equivalent of a controlled "pre/post" experiment. In effect, we compare the *level and trend* of home prices or crime in a neighborhood before and after a site within the given area is occupied by an assisted household, while statistically control-ling for trends in other areas where no assisted housing is located. For the price-impact models, level and trend are estimated on the basis of sales of identical homes in the neigh-borhood or, more accurately, homes whose differences in prices have been adjusted so as to make them comparable. For both the price- and the crime-impact models, the level and trend are adjusted for changing patterns in areas of the city where no assisted housing is located. This ensures that areawide intertemporal trends in home prices or crimes were not confounding our tests. Were it to prove the case that either the level or the trend in prices or crimes was different after occupancy by an assisted household nearby, that would signal to us that such was producing an independent effect.[2]

This pre/post econometric approach is central to the power of our method and, in-deed, represents a significant methodological advance in the analysis of neighborhood im-pacts. It therefore warrants some additional explanation. Our model takes the locations of assisted housing sites that opened between the late 1980s and mid-1990s.[3] For each site, we circumscribe a circle with a 2,000-foot radius and take every home sale (or crime re-port) within this circle that occurred up to the time that the assisted housing site opened. Then, for each of the three distance rings noted above, we use a regression model to cal-culate the level and trend in prices (crime), adjusting for any differences in attributes that may affect a home's price. We do the same for several years' worth of sales (crime reports), beginning with the quarter after an assisted site was opened. Finally, we compare the two levels and trends and draw conclusions about whether there was any impact.

This approach addresses a key weakness in previous analytical attempts to measure the impacts of introducing assisted housing into a neighborhood: that of determining the direction of causation. Because they do not control for the quality and market strength of the microneighborhood into which assisted housing is placed, other models are not able to determine, for instance, whether assisted sites lead to neighborhood decline or whether such sites are systematically located in areas having low property values and quality of life to begin with. There are several reasons why the latter explanation is possible, including the fact that property acquisition and rehabilitation costs are lower in undervalued areas and that landlords in such neighborhoods may be more likely to participate in programs like Section 8.

To more clearly see how we make these comparisons and draw conclusions regard-ing the impact of assisted housing sites, consider the following illustrative (and hypotheti-cal) examples of potential home price impacts:

1. Prior to the opening of an assisted site, the surrounding neighborhood's prices are holding constant, with the average home selling for $80,000. After the assisted housing site begins to operate, prices remain at $80,000. Conclusion: no impact from the assisted housing site.
2. As in example 1, but in the quarter after the assisted housing site opens, prices drop to $70,000 and remain constant thereafter. Conclusion: negative impact from the assisted site.
3. As in example 1, but in the quarter after the assisted housing site opens, prices remain at $80,000 but decline thereafter. Conclusion: negative impact from the assisted housing site.
4. As in example 1, but in the quarter after the assisted housing site opens, prices either rise to $90,000 or rise thereafter. Conclusion: positive impact from the assisted housing site.
5. Prior to occupancy of an assisted housing site, the surrounding neighborhood's prices are rising 5 percent annually, and, just before the opening date, the average home sells for $80,000. The quarter after the assisted housing site opens, prices remain at $80,000, but thereafter prices rise only 2 percent annually. Conclusion: negative impact from the assisted housing site.
6. As in example 5, but in the quarter after the assisted housing site opens, prices drop to $70,000 but thereafter continue to rise 5 percent annually. Conclusion: negative impact from the assisted housing site.
7. As in example 5, but in the quarter after the assisted housing site opens, prices either rise to $90,000 or thereafter prices rise 10 percent annually. Conclusion: positive impact from the assisted housing site.

One can easily extend the logic above to cover the situation of a neighborhood initially in decline before the assisted housing site was occupied. But what is trickier is the situation where post-occupancy there is *both* a change in the *level* of prices and in the *trend* of prices, and the two work in opposite directions.

For example, take a situation where prior to the occupancy of an assisted housing site, the surrounding neighborhood's prices are rising 5 percent annually. Just before the opening date, the average home in the area sells for $80,000. In the quarter after the assisted housing site opens, prices rise to $90,000 (a positive impact in the short term), but thereafter prices rise only 2 percent annually (a negative impact in the long term). One can see that at some future time the initial $10,000 price increase will be eroded by the slower appreciation rate, such that the level of prices in the neighborhood will be exactly what it would have been had the initial $80,000 value continued to appreciate at the original 5 percent rate. Prior to this date, the impact on the neighborhood would have been positive. Past this point into the future, however, this hypothetical neighborhood may have lower prices than would have occurred in the absence of the assisted housing site.

The crime-impact model works analogously to the property-value model. We have again used a pre/post econometric design to measure the possible impact of assisted housing sites on crime rates in nearby areas. To do this, we calculated annual crime rates in areas defined by rings of 0–500, 501–1000, and 1,001–2,000 feet around selected assisted housing sites. By including in our models observations of crime rates both before and after the opening of the site, and by controlling for general trends in crime rates in parts of Denver not near any assisted housing, we are able to estimate the effect the site may have had on crime in nearby areas.

The general set of models described above, when estimated over either the entire set of house sales or reported crimes and for all assisted housing sites, allows us to determine the average impacts of assisted housing for either Denver or Baltimore County. This assumes, however, that the impacts are similar in all areas of the city or county and for all types of sites. To determine whether the housing programs we were studying might have different impacts in different types of neighborhoods or for different types of sites, we estimated our models on various groups of neighborhoods and subsets of assisted housing sites.

The next two sections of this chapter set our model in the context of methodological history and provide more technical detail. Readers who do not require this level of explanation may skip to the discussion of our focus group sites and procedures at the end of this chapter. In chapter 6, we will present our results in the context of graphs that portray situations analogous to those described hypothetically above. Our assessment of impacts relies on the logic illustrated here, so readers who do not read the technical description of the models below will still be able to understand the results derived from our empirical analysis.

Previous Quantitative Studies of the Impacts of Assisted Housing: Ambiguous Results and Methodological Shortcomings

Property Value Impacts of Housing for Low-Income Households

Through the 1980s, at least a dozen scholarly studies had investigated the question of whether subsidized housing for low-income households generates a negative impact on neighboring single-family property values.[4] The preponderant conclusion reached by these studies was that there was no sizable or statistically significant impact, whereas a few studies even concluded that there was a positive impact. For example, Nourse (1963) found that prices rose faster in Saint Louis neighborhoods surrounding newly built public housing than in control neighborhoods. De Salvo (1974) concluded that developing Mitchell-Lama apartment complexes led to much faster rates of appreciation in the low—and moderate-quality submarkets in which they were located compared with control areas. Warren, Aduddell, and Tatalovich (1983) claimed that positive externalities associated with privately owned, federally subsidized apartment complexes resulted in higher median property values in the Chicago census tracts where they were located.

Only two studies of this period even hinted at dissension, and both could be convincingly discounted on methodological grounds. Warren, Aduddell, and Tatalovich (1983) found that in Chicago census tracts having more than one-third poor households and two-thirds minority households, the presence of 30 percent or more of the housing stock consisting of public housing units proved detrimental to values. Unfortunately, this study suffers from serious omitted-variables bias and aggregation bias (inasmuch as census tract median property values are employed as the dependent variable). Guy, Hysom, and Ruth (1985) found that new, Fairfax County, Virginia, townhouse clusters' prices were directly related to distance from two privately owned, mixed-income apartment complexes subsidized by the federal Below-Market Interest Rate (BMIR) program. These conclusions can be challenged because there is no way to distinguish the effects of low-income neighbors from those of a large-scale apartment building nearby (because the two are perfectly collinear), and there is a strong association between the distance from the BMIR developments and the median income of the census tract.

Recently, however, the conventional wisdom of no impact has been shaken by four more sophisticated statistical studies that have emphasized the contextuality of impacts. These studies have concluded that, with certain circumstances and certain kinds of developments, subsidized housing for low-income households can create severe effects on nearby property values. Cummings and Landis (1993) studied six developments built by BRIDGE, a nonprofit organization in the San Francisco Bay area. Although they found no impacts from three developments and positive impacts from two, one was observed having sales prices within a half-mile that were lower by $49,519.

Goetz, Lam, and Heitlinger (1996) studied property values near several types of subsidized rental housing developments in Minneapolis. They concluded that each 100 feet closer proximity to a Minneapolis Community Development Corporation's subsidized rental development raised home sales prices by $86 a dwelling, but each 100 feet closer to a subsidized rental development run by a private, for-profit owner (such as site-based Section 8) reduced sales prices by $82 per dwelling.

Lyons and Loveridge (1993) investigated the impacts of 120 locations where federally subsidized tenants resided in Saint Paul. They found that each subsidized tenant residing within one-quarter mile of a single-family home reduced the assessed value of that home by a statistically significant $21; each such tenant within 2 miles reduced it by $5. Adding an additional proximate site where one or more subsidized tenants lived reduced assessed property values $1,585 if they were located within one-quarter mile. Moreover, this reduction in assessed value fell with the distance from subsidized site until it reached $609 if the sites were within 2 miles.

Lyons and Loveridge also disaggregated the number of subsidized units by program type at various distances from the property being assessed and found that the statistically significant impacts ranged from negative to positive. Specifically, within a quarter mile, each additional Section 8 site-based assisted unit reduced values by $50 per dwelling; the comparable reduction for Section 202 elderly units was $200. Within a half-mile, each Section 221d(3) unit raised assessed values by $603 per dwelling and, surprisingly, public

housing units did so by $19. The authors found no statistically significant relationship be-
tween the locations of 39 Section 8 certificate- or voucher-holding tenants in the sample
and assessed values at any distance from them ranging from 300 feet to 2 miles. All the
statistically significant coefficients for subsidized units or tenant-based assistance sites
showed monotonically decreasing magnitudes at progressively larger radii measured from
the given assessed value. Moreover, coefficients for the squared values of the number of
subsidized units or sites consistently showed diminishing marginal impacts.

Finally, Lee, Culhane, and Wachter (1999) examined various kinds of assisted housing in Philadelphia and single-family homes sales occurring within one-eighth and one-
fourth mile of them during the 1989–91 period. Results indicated a remarkable variation
in apparent impact according to subsidized housing program. Specifically, controlling for
neighborhood conditions, sales within one-eighth mile of (1) any conventional public housing site were 9.4 percent lower; (2) each additional scattered-site public housing unit were
0.8 percent lower; (3) each additional Federal Housing Authority–assisted unit were 0.2
percent higher; (4) each additional new or rehabilitated Section 8 site-assisted unit were
0.1 percent higher; (5) each additional Section 8 certificate or voucher household were
0.5 percent lower; and (6) each additional low-income tax credit unit were 0.1 percent
lower. When proximity was measured at a quarter-mile distance, the magnitude of the coefficients given above consistently dropped by roughly half.

Property Value Impacts of Supportive Housing for Special Needs Households

The intellectual history of research on property-value impacts from supportive housing
offers remarkable parallels to that related to low-income housing in general. Through the
1980s, numerous scholarly studies had reached a common conclusion: There was no impact of supportive housing on neighboring single-family property values. After reviewing
"every available study," the Mental Health Law Project concluded that "[they] conclusively
establish that a group home as community residential facility for mentally disabled people
does not adversely affect neighbors' property values or destabilize a neighborhood" (1988,
abstract)." A few studies even concluded that there was a positive property value impact,
especially in lower-valued neighborhoods (Dear 1977; Wagner and Mitchell 1980; Gabriel
and Wolch 1984; Farber 1986; Boydell, Trainor, and Pierri 1989; Hargreaves, Callanan,
and Maskell 1998).

Only one study of this period provided dissension, and it could be challenged on methodological grounds. Gabriel and Wolch (1984) studied the relationship between the number of human service facilities per 1,000 residents of census tracts in Oakland and median
home sales prices in the tract, using multiple regression analysis. When all tracts were included in the regression, larger numbers of residential facilities for both adults and children proved inversely related to median prices. When regressions were disaggregated by
predominant race of occupancy, however, the only adverse impacts appeared to be from
adult residential facilities located in predominantly black tracts. In any event, the lack of

variables controlling for other aspects of census tracts that could affect prices besides human service facilities renders all conclusions from this study suspect.

Recently, however, the conventional wisdom of no impact has been shaken by several statistical studies that have concluded that, with certain circumstances and kinds of developments, supportive housing can create severe effects on proximate property values. Galster and Williams (1994) investigated the effects of dwellings occupied exclusively by severely mentally disabled tenants on the sales prices of nearby homes in two small Ohio towns. Controlling for features of the dwelling and the neighborhood, proximity within two blocks of two small, newly constructed apartment buildings for the mentally ill resulted in a 40 percent decrease in sales prices. However, proximity to three similar, new apartment complexes or to three rehabilitated apartment buildings for the mentally ill had no impact on prices. The authors interpreted the results as suggesting that siting, building type, and tenant allocation procedures mattered more for potential neighborhood spillover effects than occupancy by mentally ill tenants.

Lyons and Loveridge (1993) investigated the impacts of four locations where federally assisted buildings housed handicapped tenants in Saint Paul. The apartment complexes ranged in size from 10 to 103 units. Surprisingly, they found a negative impact from each handicapped unit, but the size of the negative impact diminished with marginal increases in the number of units. For example, an apartment with 10 handicapped units within one-half mile of a single-family home reduced the assessed value of that home by a statistically significant $1,670; within 1 mile, it reduced it by $682. But an apartment with 100 handicapped units within one-half mile of a single-family home was estimated to *increase* the assessed value of that home by $1,300; although within 1 mile it reduced it by $1,600. The authors offered no explanation for these results.

Colwell, Dehring, and Lash (2000) analyzed seven group homes that opened during the 1987–94 period in seven communities in suburban Chicago. Each site housed between four and eight handicapped tenants. Controlling for neighborhood-specific housing price trends and levels, they considered whether there were any noticeable aggregate shifts in the overall home sales price gradients across these seven areas after a nearby group home was announced. They found no post-announcement impact within 750 feet, but a reduction in sales prices of 13 percent if the sales were within sight of the group home. Moreover, if a community protest arose after the announcement, an additional 7.7 percent price decline occurred, which the authors attributed to the negative "signaling" effect that such a protest had for the market evaluation of the area.

Crime Impacts of Assisted Housing

With one notable exception, previous studies of the relationship between assisted housing and crime rates have focused on conventional public housing developments. Despite this focus, extant research on crime in and around public housing may be characterized as dated, fragmented, and controversial. Holzman's (1996) review of criminological research on public housing in the United States describes the knowledge gap that currently exists. Holzman states that "investigators seeking background material on crime in public housing have had to chiefly rely on a small number of studies done prior to 1981" and "most of this research amounts to only snapshots of a relatively few densely populated localities" (p. 362).

Although several studies have found higher crime rates in public housing and neighborhoods with public housing (O. Newman 1972; Brill and Associates 1975, 1976, 1977a, 1977b, 1977c; Holzman, Hyatt, and Dempster 2001), others found evidence that levels of crime in and around public housing were exaggerated (Farley 1982). Perhaps the strongest evidence for a causal relationship was provided by Roncek, Bell, and Francik (1981), who studied public housing sites in Cleveland. They concluded that public housing, especially larger sites, had a positive impact on crime rates in surrounding blocks. More recent research, much of which concentrates on drug trafficking and public housing (Dunworth and Saiger 1993; Harrell and Gouvis 1994), has helped to rekindle the debate on public housing and crime by challenging the direction of causality. No consensus has yet emerged about the degree to which public housing acts as an independent factor tending to increase the level of crime in the neighborhoods where it is located.

The impact of other forms of subsidized housing on crime has previously been analyzed only by Goetz, Lam, and Heitlinger (1996). This exceptional study analyzed the effect on monthly rates of reported crime emanating from 14 multifamily low-income housing projects that were purchased and rehabilitated by community development corporations in central neighborhoods of Minneapolis from 1986 to 1994. This represents the only extant study employing a regression analysis roughly analogous to the one in our study (though with a different unit of observation and measurement of crime). They tested for each site individually, as well as in the aggregate, the degree to which both the level and the trend in crime differed pre- and post-rehabilitation.

Overall, they found that in the aggregate there was a significantly lower level of crime calls to police (both for total and violent crime) from these properties after their conversion to subsidized housing, though there was a slightly higher trend in crime afterward. When analyzed individually, 8 developments showed no change, 5 showed a decrease, and 2 showed a slight increase in calls. Only 1 of the 14 projects evaluated, however, represented supportive housing: a 25-unit, single-room-occupancy hotel with a homeless transitional facility; its development had no measurable impact on crime. Clearly, no generalizations can be made from the Goetz, Lam, and Heitlinger study, nor from previous research on conventional public housing, about the impacts of developing assisted housing sites on crime rates in surrounding areas.

Why the Eroding Research Consensus?

One possible explanation for why the analyses given above have come to such variant, nongeneralizable conclusions is that they employ different methodologies, each of which suffers from serious, if somewhat different, shortcomings. The three alternative approaches can be termed control area, pre/post, and econometric.

The *control area approach*[5] selects neighborhoods that are otherwise comparable to one(s) that have assisted housing located within them and then compares property value levels or trends in both sets. The fundamental challenge here is identifying areas that indeed are identical in all respects save for assisted housing and that have no other forces or land developments that differentially affect them subsequent to the assisted housing development. Indeed, this challenge may be insurmountable, inasmuch as developers and occupants of assisted dwellings may choose certain neighborhoods precisely because they have attributes that are particularly attractive for their purposes.

The *pre/post approach*[6] compares levels and/or trends in property values in the same neighborhood(s) between periods preceding and then succeeding the introduction of an assisted development.[7] The difficulty here is ensuring that there are no additional forces that may affect values in the target neighborhood, such as macroeconomic or local housing submarket pressures, and are coincident with the assisted development. For example, the entire metropolitan area's housing market may be in an area of deflationary prices, whereupon there will be a tendency for any pre/post comparison of values in any neighborhood to show a secular trend of decline, regardless of the presence of an assisted housing site.

The *econometric approach* has many variants,[8] but typically it tries to ascertain whether there is an independent, cross-sectional variation in housing prices that can be associated with proximity to an assisted site. Although not an inherent flaw in the approach, virtually all previous econometric studies have failed to control for the idiosyncratic characteristics of the microneighborhood environment that surrounds (say, within a radius of a quarter-mile) but is unrelated to the assisted housing site. Instead, most settle for variables that measure characteristics of the encompassing census tract, which may be poor proxies for conditions in the area near the assisted site. Thus, if these omitted, microneighborhood variables were correlated with the location of assisted housing, apparently statistically significant proximity effects might erroneously be attributed to the latter instead of the former. One candidate for such an important omitted variable is the presence of a (possibly large) apartment building in the area, into which some special-needs households or low-income households are placed at a later date after the building is rehabilitated. In such a case, the statistics could not distinguish between the impacts of proximity to an apartment building and proximity to an assisted housing development.

The Problem of Sorting Out Direction of Causation

The criticism given above takes on additional importance when considering a major flaw that all three approaches share: They cannot convincingly distinguish the direction of causation between trends in neighborhood property values or crime and the siting of assisted housing.[9] Put differently, because they do not control for the quality and market strength of the microneighborhood where assisted housing is placed relative to the larger universe of potential sites, they cannot ascertain, for instance, whether assisted sites lead to neighborhood decline or whether assisted sites are systematically located in areas having low property values and quality of life to begin with and/or expected to depreciate further in the future.

There are several reasons why the latter causal pattern is possible, although the reasons are somewhat different depending on the particular assisted housing program in question. In the case of supportive housing, the reasons are related to behaviors of the public agency developers and owners of the facility and the nature of the local real estate market. First, the public authority or nonprofit organization developing a supportive housing facility will be encouraged to husband its scare resources by acquiring the least-expensive properties (vacant land or existing structures) available; these may also be associated with above-average crime rates. Second, if new construction of supportive housing is contemplated, the location of vacant, appropriately zoned parcels will likely be constraining on choices. Third, if rehabilitation of structures for use as supportive housing is contemplated, minimization of expected lifetime development costs of the structure implies choices of certain (smaller, low-rise) building types that likely are concentrated in certain types of neighborhoods (Harkness et al. 1997).

There also are several reasons to suspect that developers of assisted housing for general low-income populations, and even subsidized tenants themselves, may choose neighborhoods with low property values (Turner, Popkin, and Cunningham 2000). First, if the site involves a subsidized structure, the developer would be encouraged to conserve scarce resources by acquiring the least-expensive properties available. Second, private landlords may be more willing to participate in the Section 8 program, and even actively recruit Section 8 tenants, if their properties are in weak housing submarkets and they cannot otherwise obtain fair-market rents for their apartments (Goering, Stebbins, and Siewert 1995; Pollock and Rutkowski 1998). Neighborhoods with high crime rates may be especially prone to this sort of selection bias. Third, Section 8 households that use vouchers may try to move into modest-value neighborhoods so as to free up more of their income for nonhousing consumption, inasmuch as the value of their voucher is fixed.

All these reasons imply that the particular microneighborhoods where assisted housing or subsidized households are located are not likely to be representative. Indeed, their levels or trends in housing prices and crime rates are likely to be systematically inferior. Thus, to precisely answer the question, "Does assisted housing lead to more crime and lower values in the neighborhood, or vice versa?" one must carefully measure these characteristics in the vicinity of where assisted housing *eventually* will be located.

Three price-impact studies come close to achieving the appropriate level of control, but they ultimately fall short. Galster and Williams (1994); Colwell, Dehring, and Lash (2000); and Briggs, Darden, and Aidala (1999) employ a "spatial fixed effects" specification, wherein dummy variables denote the idiosyncratic *level* of home prices associated with the microneighborhood within a certain distance from an assisted housing site (either future or current). A corresponding set of dummy variables denotes whether these price *levels* differ significantly after the assisted housing is announced or begins operation.

This econometric version of a pre/post method fails, however, to control for the *trend* in sales prices extant in this microneighborhood prior to the introduction of the subsidized housing. For example, if the given area were to be on a trajectory of steep depreciation prior to the introduction of assisted housing, it would likely manifest a lower level of prices after the opening of the assisted site than before. This, however, would not be due to the assisted site, but rather to a continuation of preexisting trends in this microneighborhood. Thus, only an econometric specification that controls for pre-/post-occupancy deviations in *both* price *levels and trends* in the microneighborhood near the assisted site can yield unambiguous implications about the causal impact of the assisted housing site.

Our approach overcomes the shortcomings of earlier approaches by devising an econometric specification that grafts on a pre/post design. By measuring both level and trend of prices and crimes in a neighborhood before an assisted household is present, it controls for fixed, microneighborhood characteristics causally unrelated to assisted housing, yet spuriously correlated with it. By relating post-assisted housing property value and crime trends and levels in the affected neighborhood to those in larger geographic areas, it controls for intertemporal forces affecting all areas. By doing both, the model distinguishes the self-selection of assisted housing into weak neighborhood submarkets from the ultimate consequences of such housing on these neighborhoods.

Problems of Spatial Patterns in the Data

A second, overarching shortcoming of the literature is a failure to test for and, if necessary, adjust for spatial patterns in the data. *Spatial dependence*, sometimes known as *spatial autocorrelation*, refers to the possibility that, in the example of the property-value model, the observed price of one home is not independent of the prices of other homes nearby in geographic space. If left uncorrected, such spatial dependence would lead to biased coefficient estimates and misleading tests for their statistical significance. The severity of this potential problem in house price regressions has been demonstrated by Can and Megbolugbe (1997).

Spatial heterogeneity, sometimes known as spatial submarket segmentation, refers to the systematic variation in the behavior of a given process across space. Here, the issue is whether the coefficients produced by the regression equation are invariant across space or whether they assume different values according to the local socioeconomic, demographic, and/or physical contexts of the various neighborhoods in a metropolitan area. If such were the case, coefficient estimates and statistical tests again would be misleading.

All extant empirical work related to the property-value impacts of assisted housing has failed to account for spatial econometric issues. Several researchers have explored the use of spatial statistics to analyze crime data (Griffith 1987; Anselin 1992; T. C. Bailey and Gatrell 1995). However, no studies to date on subsidized housing and crime have employed spatial statistical techniques to diagnose spatial dependence or heterogeneity and to control for them appropriately in constructing a predictive model. Our approach involves testing for both these spatial patterns and, where necessary, correcting for them. The details of our procedures are found in the appendix.

Detailed Specifications of the Statistical Models

Property-Value-Impact Model Specification

Our basic property-value-impact model may be expressed symbolically as

$$LnP = c + [Struct][b] + [Quarter][n] + [Tract][m] + [SpaceH][p] +$$
$$d{\cdot}DAll_{500} + e{\cdot}DAll_{1k} + f DAll_{2k} + g{\cdot}DPost_{500} + h{\cdot}DPost_{1k} + j{\cdot}DPost_{2k} + q{\cdot}Time_{500}$$
$$+ r{\cdot}Time_{1k} + s{\cdot}Time_{2k} + t{\cdot}TrPost_{500} + u{\cdot}TrPost_{1k} + v{\cdot}TrPost_{2k} + e \qquad (1)$$

Where the components of the models are defined as follows:

LnP	Log of the single-family home sales price
c	Constant term
$[Struct]$	Vector of structural characteristics of home, including home and lot size, age, building materials and type, and numerous amenities
$[Quarter]$	Vector of dummies indicating the time (year and quarter) of sale; seasonal and intertemporal trend measure
$[Tract]$	Vector of census tract dummies indicating the location of home; tract fixed-effect measure; census tracts are locally determined geographic units, ranging in size from 2,500 to 8,000 persons, used by the U.S. Bureau of the Census to collect and tabulate data. Tracts are meant to approximate "neighborhoods" by capturing a group of residents with similar population characteristics, economic status, and living conditions
$[SpaceH]$	Vector of X, Y, XY, X^2, and Y^2 spatial heterogeneity correction variables; see the appendix
$DPost_x$	Post-occupancy dummy for distance ring x; equals 1 if sale occurs within x feet of one or more assisted housing sites; zero otherwise; see the appendix for details
$DAll_x$	Dummy for distance ring x; equals 1 if sale occurs within x feet of current or future assisted housing site; zero otherwise
$TrPost_x$	Post-occupancy trend variable for distance ring x; equals 0 if sale is pre-occupancy for all sites in distance ring; if sale is post-occupancy of a site in ring x, then equals 1 if sale occurs in first quarter after site was occu-

pied, equals 2 if sale occurs in second quarter after site was occupied, etc.; see the appendix for details

$Time_x$ Trend variable for distance ring x; equals 0 if no sites are in distance ring x of the sale; otherwise, equals 1 if sale occurs in first quarter of study period (the first quarter of 1987), equals 2 if sale occurs in second quarter of study period, and sale is in distance ring x, etc.

e   A random error term; see the appendix for discussion of its statistical properties

All lowercase letters in the equations (b, c, d, etc.) represent coefficients to be estimated.

The model tests for both price level shift and price trend slope alteration effects in impact areas near assisted housing sites, and thus makes relatively few assumptions about what form any impact might take. Below, we summarize how the various trend and fixed effects are being controlled for in the model in a way that permits us to identify unambiguously the impact of proximity to an assisted housing site:[10]

[*Quarter*]   Measures quarterly changes in the overall county house price levels associated with seasonality and general market trends

[*Tract*]   Measures the fixed effect on house prices due to location in the area defined by the census tract

$DAll_x$ Measures the fixed effect throughout the county of being in the area defined as within distance x of one or more assisted housing site(s), regardless of whether occupied yet

$DPost_x$ Measures the fixed effect throughout the county of being in the area defined as within distance x of one or more assisted housing site(s) after occupancy

$Time_x$ Measures the trend in house prices during the study period in the area throughout the county defined as within distance x of one or more assisted housing site(s), regardless of whether occupied yet

$TrPost_x$ Measures the trend in house prices during the study period in the area throughout the county defined as within distance x of one or more assisted housing site(s) after occupancy

The test for statistical significance of the post-occupancy shift coefficients (g, h, j) of the $DPost_x$ variables is equivalent to testing that there is a discontinuous change in the price levels in the neighborhoods (defined by a particular distance ring) around assisted housing sites post-occupancy. The test for statistical significance of the post-occupancy trend coefficients (t, u, v) of $TrPost_x$ is equivalent to testing that there is a change in the price trends in the neighborhoods around assisted housing sites post-occupancy. If both the shift and trend post-occupancy coefficients prove to not be significantly different from zero, it would reject the hypothesis of impact.

If one or both are statistically significant, however, the magnitude of assisted housing impact across all sites involves assessing whether $(d + qTime^*) - (g + tTrPost)$, $(e + rTime^*)$ $- (h + uTrPost)$, and/or $(f + sTime^*) - (j + vTrPost) \neq 0$, where $Time^*$ represents the latest quarter prior to the opening of the assisted housing program. If the alterations in shift and trend terms yield contrary implications (such as a downward shift but increased slope in the price gradient), it will be necessary to calculate net effects at different quarters post-occupancy.

Note that our basic model implicitly assumes that the measured impact of proximity to any assisted site(s) is invariant to the number of such proximate sites. We also report our estimates of a variant of our model that relaxes this assumption and allows the post-occupancy shift variable to assume the number of assisted housing sites (distinct addresses) at the given distance at the time of sale. Yet another variant does the same, but uses the number of assisted units or households (measured as beds, in the case of supportive housing) instead of sites. These variants also test for the possible effects of the number of sites or units on the post-occupancy price trends by use of multiplicative interaction variables with the *TrPost* variables. That is, these models measure whether the intertemporal decline (or appreciation) in house prices is magnified by the number of assisted housing sites or units present within the given range.

As table 4.1 shows, there was considerable variation in the number of assisted sites and units across our sample. This variation occurred because sometimes after the opening of the initial assisted site being analyzed it was soon followed by another nearby. This means, for example, that a home sale occurring in the period after the occupancy of the initial assisted site in the vicinity may also have been near one or more additional sites that opened subsequent to the initial site. This variation allowed us, through the interactive model specifications above, to explore threshold effects: whether there was a critical value for concentration of assisted sites or units within a particular range that created negative impacts.

Crime-Impact Model Specifications

Our econometric approach for investigating the crime impacts of assisted housing relies on the same intuition that guided the home price impact modeling effort described above. In particular, we again utilize the "pre/post development" approach for three geographic areas centered on each of our analysis sites: a circular area with a 500-foot radius and two concentric rings with widths defined by distances of 501–1,000 feet and 1,001–2,000 feet from the assisted housing site. We measure both the rate (reported crimes divided by the resident population) and change in rate of crimes in each of these areas both before and after the assisted housing facility begins operation; any pre/post difference signifies an impact from the facility. Of course, this comparison is made controlling for factors that likely affect reported crime trends throughout Denver. These are estimated on the basis of crime rates measured for the portions of census tracts across the city that do not have assisted housing sites within 2,000 feet.[11] In symbolic terms, our crime-impact model specification may be expressed:[12]

Table 4.1

Maximum Numbers of Assisted Sites and Units (Beds) Observed at Time of
Home Sale, by Proximity

		Proximity (feet)		
		0–500	*501–1,000*	*1,001–2,000*
Denver				
Supportive housing	Sites	2	2	6
	Beds	116	151	167
Dispersed DHA housing	Sites	6	11	16
	Units	26	34	55
Baltimore County				
Section 8	Sites	46	84	154
	Units	206	303	467

Note: "DHA" is Denver Housing Authority.

Sources: Authors' analysis of unpublished dispersed and Section 8 data from the Denver Housing Authority and the Baltimore County Housing Office, respectively; supportive housing data obtained from City and County of Denver (1998b) *Bi-annual residential care use renewal.*

$$Crime_{it} = c + [Year_t][n] + [Tract_j][m] + [Site_s][n] + [SpaceL][p] +$$
$$d \cdot CRAll_{500} + e \cdot CRAll_{1K} + f \cdot CRAll_{2K} + g \cdot CPost_{500} + h \cdot CPost_{1K} + j \cdot CPost_{2K} +$$
$$q \cdot Time_{500} + r \cdot Time_{1k} + s \cdot Time_{2k} + t \cdot TrPost_{500} + u \cdot TrPost_{1k} + v \cdot TrPost_{2k} + e \qquad (2)$$

where the components of the models not previously defined in equation 1 above are defined as follows:

$Crime_{it}$	Annual rate of reported crimes of type i per 100 residents during year t
$[Year_t]$	Vector of dummy variables indicating the year t; a temporal trend site measure for all areas within census tracts not within 2,000 feet of a supportive site
$[Tract_j]$	Vector of dummy variables denoting each of j census tracts; a tract fixed-effect measure
$[Site_s]$	Vector of dummy variables denoting each of s sites; a site fixed-effect measure to correct for autocorrelation and heteroskedasticity
$[SpaceL]$	A spatial lag variable with a distance cutoff of 15,000 feet to correct for spatial autocorrelation; see the appendix for details
$CRAll_x$	Dummy variable for distance ring x; equals 1 if observed crime rate is for area within x feet of current or future assisted housing site, whether operating or not; zero otherwise
$CPost_x$	Post-opening dummy variable for distance ring x; equals 1 if observed crime rate is for area within x feet of currently operating assisted housing site; zero otherwise. If the site opened in the same year as the crime rate

observation, then $CPost_x$ equals 1 if the site opened in the first half of the year, and zero otherwise.

$TrPost_x$ Post-occupancy trend variable for distance ring x; equals 0 if crime is pre-occupancy for all sites in distance ring; if crime is post-occupancy of a site in ring x, then equals 1 if crime occurs in first year after site was occupied, equals 2 if crime occurs in second year after site was occupied, etc.

$Time_x$ Trend variable for distance ring x; equals 0 if no sites are in distance ring x of the crime; otherwise, equals 1 if crime occurs in first year of study period (1990), equals 2 if crime occurs in second year of study period, and crime is in distance ring x, etc.

The control variables specified above work in analogous fashion to those discussed in the context of price-impact equation 1 above. Should the coefficients of any of the $CPost_x$ or $TrPost_x$ variables prove statistically significant, it would suggest that the presence of an assisted housing site had a consistent impact on the level or trend, respectively, of the type of crime being measured in the distance range x. We also test variants of equation 2 that allow impacts to vary by number of sites in the range.

Alternative Stratifications of Regressions

The issue of aggregation poses an additional methodological challenge to the analyst. At one extreme, one can assume that all assisted housing has identical impacts across all housing submarkets and thereby gain maximum sample sizes, statistical power, and generality. Such an assumption may obscure important contextual variations, however. At the other extreme, one can permit variations in impact across many neighborhood submarkets, but the price will be less precision and statistical power in estimating impacts in each.

To explore whether the assisted housing programs we were studying might have different impacts in different types of neighborhoods, we estimated our models on various strata, where sample sizes proved adequate to do so. The different strata were defined according to the characteristics of census tracts, such as racial and ethnic composition, median property values, and changes in average house prices. Though these stratified estimations did not always yield useful or interesting results (because of sample size problems), in many cases they provided decisive indications that impacts are highly contextualized. We report these selected results from stratified models in chapters 6 through 8.

Qualitative Analysis of Impacts with Homeowner Focus Groups

The use of focus groups has a long-standing history in the social sciences as a tool to provide in-depth information for evaluative purposes.[13] The main purpose for using focus groups here was to determine the extent to which homeowners living near assisted housing perceived any impacts and whether their perceptions matched and might help explain the statistical results of the crime- and property-value impact models. They also potentially gave us an opportunity to probe causal mechanisms of assisted housing's neighborhood impacts.

Through the use of focus groups, we engaged in an in-depth discussion with homeowners living near assisted housing about what makes a good neighborhood, what affects quality of life in their neighborhood, what are the characteristics of community residents, and how they perceive changes in the quality of life and the composition of their community. The focus groups also provided a more contextual understanding of the relative importance homeowners place on different factors, such as changes in crime, property values, and the presence of assisted housing or tenants, that may affect the quality of life in their neighborhoods. To understand how the focus group participants formed their views on these topics, we probed them on their perceptions, sources of information, and local social networks.

Although the focus groups allowed us to capture any comments made by homeowners about assisted housing sites or clients, it is important to note that these topics emerged in the discussion only if they were brought up by focus group participants themselves. The discussion guide was designed not to beg the question about the presence of assisted housing programs. In fact, the lack of awareness about such sites may be part of the explanation for the lack of an observed impact in some areas. We were therefore reluctant to trigger a socially destructive "experimenter effect" by revealing the presence of assisted housing sites in the neighborhood. Three sets of focus groups, totaling 19 discussions in all, were conducted: one each for homeowners near Denver Housing Authority (DHA) dispersed housing in Denver (6 groups), supportive housing in Denver (9 groups), and Section 8 households in Baltimore County (4 groups). The first and third sets of discussions were conducted in 1998, the second set in 1999. This qualitative methods section of the chapter first describes each of the neighborhoods in which these focus groups were conducted and the assisted housing site within each. The remainder of the chapter gives an overview of the procedures we followed to recruit focus group participants and conduct the discussions.

Description of Denver Dispersed Housing Sites and Corresponding Focus Group Neighborhoods

The location of each of the six focus group sites near DHA dispersed housing sites in Denver is shown on map 4.1, and the descriptive characteristics of the sites and encompassing census tracts are presented in table 4.2.[14] We refer to the sites in the text and the table by their neighborhood name. A number after the name indicates that multiple sites included in our analysis are located in the same neighborhood. In all cases, the named neighborhoods consist of more than one census tract. In the neighborhood descriptions below, our data refer to these multitract areas.[15] The focus group sites were selected from among those DHA dispersed sites that began operation between 1991 and 1995; homeowner responses to them thus reflect their long-term presence in the neighborhood. They represent a cross section of neighborhoods where such sites are located.

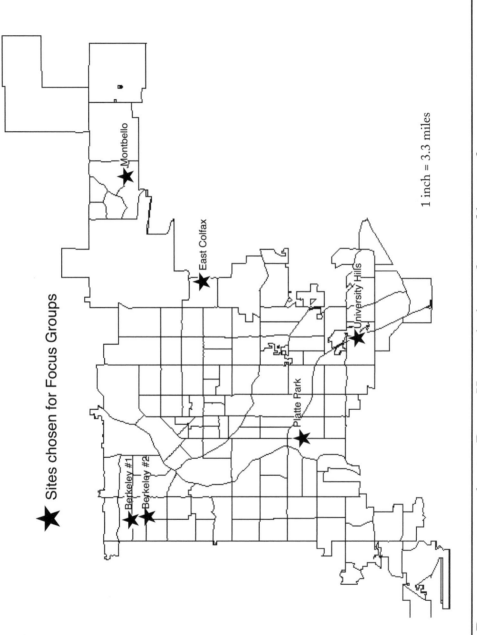

Map 4.1. Denver census tracts, showing Denver Housing Authority dispersed housing focus group sites

Source: Unpublished data from the Denver Housing Authority

Table 4.2

Characteristics of Denver Dispersed Housing Focus Group Sites and Encompassing Census Tracts

Site	Move-in Year	HHs at Site	Other DHA Units within 2,000 feet	Census Tract Population, 1990	Percentage Black		Percentage Hispanic		Percentage Renters, 1990	Median House Value, 1990	Percentage Change in House Values	
					1980	1990	1980	1990	1990	1990	1980–90	1990–96
Montbello	1992	1	1	4,371	40.1	54.7	12.9	13.3	19.1	63,900	3.3	78.4
East Colfax	1994	1	14	7,172	22.4	32.6	7.6	10.6	60.5	55,200	16.6	101.8
Berkeley #1	1994	1	8	3,269	0.0	0.5	17.2	27.6	34.3	65,800	28.2	73.7
Berkeley #2	1995	2	7	5,257	0.4	0.6	19.0	29.3	40.8	64,900	22.8	86.1
Platte Park	1994	5	2	5,236	0.4	0.6	6.7	9.0	40.3	80,200	40.7	92.2
University Hills	1991	1	2	4,235	0.8	1.7	2.9	3.4	25.7	75,400	21.4	61.8

Note: "DHA" is Denver Housing Authority. HHs refers to the number of dispersed housing units located within the site.
Source: Data for these site descriptions were obtained from the DHA, Experian home price data, and the U.S. Census.

Montbello, located in Northeast Denver, had a population of 19,093 in 1996. Often perceived as being a primarily black neighborhood, Montbello's resident population was considerably more diverse. Approximately 58 percent of the residents were black, 24 percent were white, and 14 percent were Hispanic. Homeowners occupied nearly 71 percent of all housing units in the area. The housing was relatively new; there were no housing units constructed before 1940. The average sale price for homes in Montbello was estimated at $83,890. Among renters, nearly half would have been considered rent burdened, paying more than 30 percent of their income for housing. Four percent of the units in the neighborhood were publicly subsidized. Focus group participants were drawn from the area near a single-family home that was converted by DHA and occupied by a low-income household in 1992.

East Colfax is located in East Denver, adjacent to the recently closed Stapleton Airport and Lowry Air Base. In 1996, this neighborhood had a population of 7,736. Nearly 54 percent of the population were white, nearly one-third were black, and 11 percent were Hispanic. Approximately 40 percent of the housing units were occupied by owners. Only 10 percent of the units were constructed before 1940. In 1995, the average sale price for homes in East Colfax was $63,221. Approximately 44 percent of all renters were rent burdened. Five percent of the units in the neighborhood were publicly subsidized. Here, the focus group was drawn from an area having a cluster of 15 DHA dispersed units.

Two dispersed housing focus group sites were located in the West Denver neighborhood of *Berkeley*. This neighborhood had a population of 8,601 in 1996. Nearly 70 percent of all residents were white, 29 percent were Hispanic, and less than 1 percent were black. Homeowners occupied 62 percent of all housing units in the neighborhood. Sixty percent of all housing units were built before 1940. The average sale price for homes located in Berkeley was $92,912. Slightly less than half of all renters paid more than 30 percent of their income for rent. About 6 percent of the housing units were publicly subsidized. One Berkeley group was drawn from an area adjacent to a DHA single-family dispersed unit; the other group had a DHA duplex nearby. In both cases, a total of nine dispersed units were in the vicinity.

Platte Park is in Southwest Denver and had a resident population of 5,299 in 1996. Nearly 90 percent of the neighborhood residents were white and 9 percent were Hispanic. Homeowners occupied 60 percent of the housing units in the area. This is a neighborhood of very old homes: 73 percent of the housing units were built before 1940. The average sale price of homes located in Platte Park was $125,404 in 1995. Approximately 36 percent of all renters were rent burdened. Less than 3 percent of the housing units in the neighborhood were publicly subsidized. The focus group was recruited from nearby a dispersed apartment building having five low-income households.

University Hills is in Southeast Denver and is one of the most racially and ethnically homogeneous neighborhoods in the city. University Hills had a population of 5,752 in 1996, of whom 93 percent were white. Only 3.3 percent were Hispanic and 1.3 percent were black. Two-thirds of the housing units were occupied by homeowners. Slightly more than 1 percent of the units were built before 1940. The average home sale price in the area was $110,276. Approximately 37 percent of all renters paid more than 30 percent of their incomes on rent in this neighborhood. Only 2 percent of the housing units in the area received public subsidies. A DHA single-family dispersed unit was in the midst of our focus group participants' homes.

Description of Denver Supportive Housing Sites and Corresponding Focus Group Neighborhoods

The location of each of the nine supportive housing focus group sites is shown on map 4.2 and the descriptive characteristics of the sites and surrounding census tracts are presented in tables 4.3 and 4.4. We refer to the sites in the text and the table by their neighborhood name. The focus group sites were selected from among those that began operation between 1989 and 1995 and represent a cross section of neighborhoods where supportive housing sites are located.[16]

Clayton, located in North Denver, had a population of 3,863 in 1998. Nearly 70 percent of neighborhood residents were black, 17 percent were Hispanic, and 11 percent were white. Almost 59 percent of the housing units were owner occupied. More than 60 percent of all renters in the neighborhood were rent burdened. Slightly more than one-third of the homes in Clayton were built before 1940. The average sales price for homes in Clayton was $53,784. More than 14 percent of the housing in the neighborhood was publicly subsidized. Clayton had the highest crime rate among the study areas, at 114.1 per 1,000 people. The focus group was recruited from the vicinity of a former single-family home that had been converted into an eight-bed hospice.

Congress Park is a middle-class neighborhood located close to downtown Denver. In 1998, Congress Park had 9,441 residents. Nearly 80 percent of the residents were white, about 12 percent were black, and another 7 percent were Hispanic. Approximately 37 percent of the housing units were owner occupied. Among renters, almost one-third were rent burdened. Slightly fewer than two-thirds of the housing units were built before 1940. In 1995, the average home sales price was $176,121. Approximately 4 percent of the units were publicly subsidized. In 1997, the overall crime rate was 75 per 1,000 population. The relevant supportive facility was a seven-bed apartment building used for the care of children with developmental disabilities. The vicinity had the greatest concentration of other supportive sites—eight, containing 132 beds—of any of our focus group areas.

Harvey Park, located in Southwest Denver, had a resident population of 10,349 in 1998. Approximately 69 percent of the residents were white and 25.5 percent were Hispanic. The neighborhood has a growing Asian presence as well. Seven out of 10 housing units in Harvey Park are owner occupied. Nearly half of the renters were rent burdened. This neighborhood is made up of newer homes; only 1 percent of the units was built before 1940. In 1995, the average sale price of homes in the neighborhood was $100,983. Fewer than 2 percent of the units were publicly subsidized. The overall crime rate in Harvey

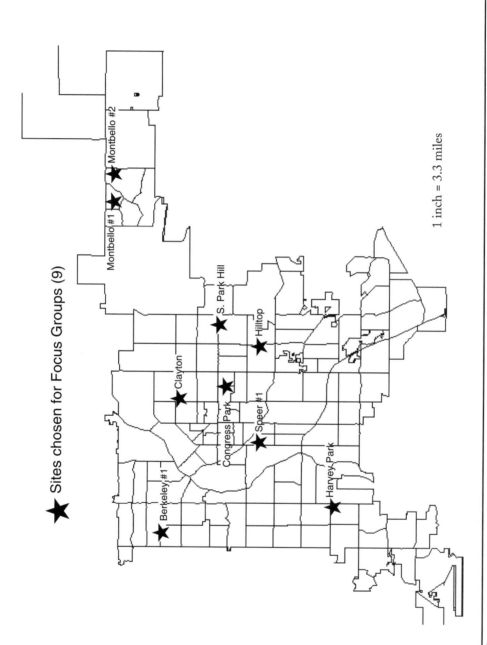

★ Sites chosen for Focus Groups (9)

Montbello #1

Montbello #2

S. Park Hill

Hilltop

Clayton

Congress Park

Speer #1

Berkeley #1

Harvey Park

1 inch = 3.3 miles

Map 4.2. Denver census tracts, showing location of focus group sites

Source: Tabulations from the *Bi-annual residential care use renewal.* City and County of Denver, 1998b.

Table 4.3

Characteristics of Supportive Housing Sites in Denver Focus Group Areas

Neighborhood	Program Type	Zoning	Starting Year	Number of Residents	Other Supportive Housing within 2,000 feet	
					Sites	Units
Berkeley	Senior special care	R2	1989	8	1	116
Clayton	Hospice	R2	1993	8	1	8
Congress Park	Children with developmental disabilities	R3	1984	7	8	132
Harvey Park	Mental health	R1	1989	8	0	0
Hilltop	Development disabilities	R0	1992	8	0	0
Montbello #1	Development disabilities	R1	1990	4	1	12
Montbello #2	Children's home	R1	1992	8	0	0
S. Park Hill	Mental health	R1	1990	8	0	0
Speer	Mental health	R3	1993	6	5	66

Source: City and County of Denver. (1998b) *Bi-annual residential care use renewal.*

Park was 57 per 1,000 people in 1997. Here, the supportive housing consisted of a single-family home converted into a group home for the mentally ill; no other supportive housing sites were within 2,000 feet.

Hilltop, one of the most exclusive neighborhoods in Denver, is highly segregated by class and ethnicity. Of the 8,415 residents living in Hilltop in 1998, nearly 93 percent were white. The largest minority group in the neighborhood is Latinos, who make up 3.6 percent of the population. Three-quarters of all housing units in Hilltop are owner occupied. Among renters, nearly 40 percent are rent burdened. One of Denver's newer neighborhoods, only 15 percent of the housing stock was built before 1940. The average home sale price was $281,173 in 1995. Publicly subsidized housing units made up only 0.1 percent of the neighborhood housing stock. This neighborhood had one of the lowest crime rates in Denver, at 25.6 per 1,000 people. A single-family house converted for use as a group home for eight individuals with developmental disabilities was the locus for recruiting focus group participants; no other supportive facilities were nearby.

Montbello was described above. The supportive housing facility in question for one of our two focus groups here was a home for 4 people with developmental disabilities, and another, 12-bed supportive facility nearby. The second group in Montbello was recruited from the environs of an 8-bed home for children, with no other supportive housing sites in the vicinity.

South Park Hill, located in East Denver, is adjacent to the old Stapleton Airport. In 1998, this neighborhood had a population of 8,975. Approximately three-quarters of the

Table 4.4

Characteristics of Neighborhoods (Census Tracts) Surrounding Denver Supportive Housing Focus Group Sites

Neighborhood	Population, 1990	Percentage Black		Percentage Hispanic		Percentage Renters, 1990	Median House Value, 1990	Percentage Change in House Values	
		1980	1990	1980	1990	1990	1990	1980–90	1990–96
Berkeley	5,257	0.4	0.6	19.0	29.3	40.8	64,900	–22.5	56.5
Clayton	2,916	89.4	87.1	2.8	7.8	34.3	60,600	–20.7	71.2
Congress Park	3,962	10.5	11.8	4.3	10.7	81.6	97,400	–17.5	60.2
Harvey Park	5,623	1.8	3.1	27.0	36.8	48.9	63,400	–27.5	42.4
Hilltop	3,809	2.9	0.8	0.6	1.6	6.1	194,500	3.8	7.8
Montbello #1	3,004	33.0	48.7	22.4	16.8	32.7	55,100	–31.2	81.5
Montbello #2	4,371	40.1	54.7	12.9	13.3	19.1	63,900	–34.8	50.0
S. Park Hill	4,048	20.4	22.3	4.0	4.1	23.0	105,300	–16.1	35.4
Speer	3,882	3.7	3.6	16.6	23.8	81.0	83,100	–7.3	93.7

Source: Data for these site descriptions were obtained from the Experian home price data as well as from the U.S. census.

residents were white, 17 percent were black, and about 5 percent were Hispanic. Three out of four housing units were owner occupied. Four out of 10 renters paid 30 percent or more of their income on housing. Nearly two-thirds of the housing stock was built before 1940. In 1995, the average sale price for homes in South Park Hill was $183,284. Only 2.2 percent of the housing units in the neighborhood were publicly subsidized. The overall crime rate in 1997 was 63 per 1,000 people. Here, our group resided near a single-family home converted into an eight-bed facility for people with mental illness; no other supportive facilities were nearby.

Speer, located just southwest of downtown Denver, experienced considerable gentrification during the 1990s. The community, home to 10,275 residents in 1998, was predominantly white (77 percent), with a smaller black population (3.5 percent) and a growing Hispanic one (16 percent). The neighborhood has a mix of architecturally significant, turn-of-the-century homes and newer construction (39 percent of the units were built before 1940). This neighborhood was primarily renter occupied; fewer than one out of five residents owned their homes. Among renters, one-third paid more than 30 percent of their income for housing. The average home sale price in 1995 was $135,813. Only 1.2 percent of the housing units in Speer were publicly subsidized. The overall crime rate in the neighborhood was 92 per 1,000 people in 1997. The focus group here was recruited from the area around a home converted into a six-bed facility for the care of the mentally ill. The environs were heavily affected by other supportive facilities—five sites containing a total of 66 beds.

Description of Baltimore County Section 8 Sites and Corresponding Focus Group Neighborhoods

The four neighborhoods in which we conducted focus groups in Baltimore County were chosen to reflect as wide a variety of racial composition, property values, and intensities of Section 8 residence as available resources permitted. Map 4.3 shows the locations of these sites; table 4.5 provides descriptive information.

Dundalk can be characterized as a once-thriving blue-collar community outside Baltimore City's southeastern edge. The area declined as industrial employers left or downsized, and neighborhoods where former workers lived became depressed. The median house value in 1990 of $72,900 was the lowest of any in our focus group neighborhoods and was substantially lower than other Baltimore County neighborhoods, which made it more affordable for lower-income buyers and renters. Respondents in the Dundalk focus group lived in brick rowhouses that were built more than 50 years ago during the community's heyday. The area was highly owner occupied; 85 percent of the residents were homeowners in 1990. As was explained in chapter 3, Dundalk was the epicenter for protest over the Moving to Opportunity program in 1994. Our focus group was recruited from the area around a rowhouse that had been occupied since 1994 by a household receiving Section 8 assistance; 12 other such households lived within 2,000 feet of this site at the time of the focus group.

Millbrook abuts the northern edge of Baltimore City. Focus group respondents noted that this area is home to residents from a variety of racial, cultural, and religious backgrounds, with a significant Jewish population and an influx of recent Russian immigrants. From 1980 to 1990, the census tract saw a growth in the share of black residents from 0.3 percent to 5.5 percent. More than half of the residents in this census tract were renters. Focus group respondents were owners of rowhouses; the median house value in 1990 was $88,000. They noted the presence of large rental complexes adjoining their community. Here, our focus group was recruited from the vicinity of an apartment building where three households receiving Section 8 assistance resided. The environs also contained the highest concentration of other Section 8 households (188) among our groups.

Rodgers Forge is a neighborhood near the large suburb of Towson in Baltimore County. This community of rowhouses had the highest median house value of any of the census tracts represented in the Baltimore County focus groups, at $115,900. The area was predominantly white, with renters making up almost half of the residents in the census tract. The Rodgers Forge focus group resided near a rental property housing one household receiving Section 8 assistance. At that time, there were no other Section 8 subsidies within 2,000 feet of this site.

The Village of Twelve Trees is in the Randallstown area of Baltimore County and is the farthest of any of the focus group neighborhoods from Baltimore City. Twelve Trees is a secluded community of rowhouses surrounded by trees and serviced by good neighborhood amenities, including a pool and play areas. The larger Randallstown area underwent significant racial change during the 1980s, with the black population more than doubling during that time. The Twelve Trees community also saw similar racial changes. However, the census tract that includes Twelve Trees evinced the most significant appreciation in housing values of any of the focus group neighborhoods in Baltimore County. Here, the focus group came from the area surrounding a single household using Section 8, though three others were within the immediate vicinity.

Recruitment of Focus Group Participants

Because one of the core research questions posed in the focus groups concerns property-value change, we limited focus group participation to homeowners who had resided in the neighborhood for two or more years. A targeted mailing was used to identify and screen potential focus group participants. Using a mailing list generated from property tax roll records, a recruitment letter (written in both English and Spanish in Denver) was sent to all homeowners living within 1,000 to 1,400 feet of the selected assisted housing site.[17]

The recruitment letter described the project as a study on the quality of life in American neighborhoods. To conform to informed consent requirements, the letter indicated that the study was being sponsored by the U.S. Department of Housing and Urban Development. Participants were not, however, told that assisted housing was the focus of our research. When necessary, we used a screening form returned by prospective participants

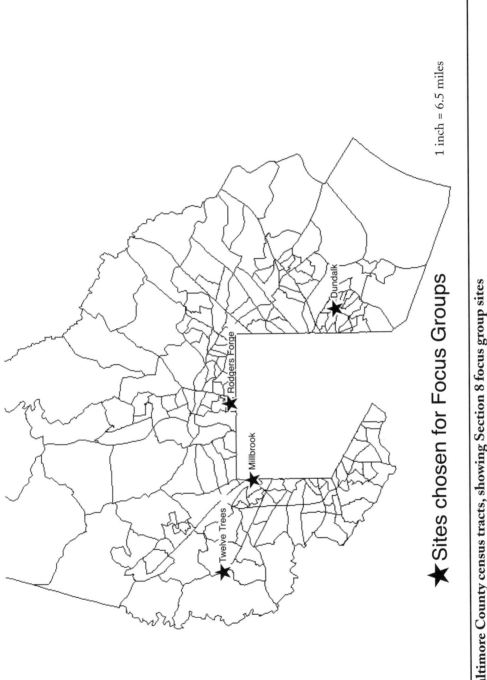

★ Sites chosen for Focus Groups

Map 4.3.   Baltimore County census tracts, showing Section 8 focus group sites

Source: Unpublished data from Baltimore County Housing Office.

Table 4.5

Characteristics of Baltimore County Focus Group Sites and Surrounding Neighborhoods

| Site | Move-in Date | Section 8 Households at Site | Other Section 8 Households within 2,000 ft. | Census Tract Population 1990 | Percentage Black | | Percentage Renters, 1990 | Median House Value, 1990 | Percentage Change in House Values | |
					1980	1990			1980–90	1990–96
Dundalk	1994	1	12	3,680	1.5	0.3	14.9	72,900	82.5	0.3
Millbrook	1994	3	188	6,030	0.3	5.5	51.6	88,000	72.6	8.2
Rodgers Forge	1991	1	0	2,755	0.3	1.0	45.2	115,900	89.6	5.8
Twelve Trees	1995	1	3	8,841	15.4	35.7	37.6	97,800	63.6	37.8

Source: Data for these site descriptions were obtained from the Experian home price data and the Baltimore County Office of Community Conservation and from the U.S. Census.

to form focus groups that were representative of the demographic characteristics of the neighborhood.

Composition of the Focus Groups

The six *dispersed housing focus groups in Denver* ranged from 4 to 10 participants with an average size of 6 participants across all sites. On average, participants had resided in their homes for 12 years and in their neighborhoods for 15 years. The longest average tenure was found in the East Colfax and Berkeley #1 sites (17 and 16 years, respectively); the shortest average tenure was 4 years in University Hills. Nearly one-third of the participating households had children under 18 years of age. Nearly 30 percent of the participants were employed in professional or managerial positions. Another 16 percent were employed in administrative support occupations. About 1 in 5 of the participants was retired, and almost 14 percent identified themselves as homemakers.

In ethnic composition, 73 percent of the Denver participants were white, 14 percent were black, 8 percent were Hispanic, and 5 percent were of another race. About 1 in 5 were high school graduates, whereas another 6 out of 10 had college degrees. Approximately 1 of 5 participants was aged 34 years or younger, and nearly one-third were over 50. Nearly 3 out of every 4 participants were female.

The nine *supportive housing focus groups in Denver* ranged from 5 to 16 participants, with an average size of 9 participants across all sites. On average, the participants had resided in their current neighborhoods for 19.1 years and in Denver for 34.7 years. The longest average tenure was found in Clayton (30.2 years) and the shortest average tenure was 10 years in the Speer neighborhood. Only 29 percent of the participating households had children under 18 years of age, with the highest percentages found in the Montbello neighborhood. On average, nearly one-third of the participants were retirees. However, more than half of the participants from Harvey Park, Clayton, and Hilltop were retired.

The racial and ethnic composition of the groups reflected both the demographics of the neighborhoods and the self-selection of residents in response to our invitation to participate. On average across the groups, 73 percent of the Denver participants were white, 12 percent were black, and another 12 percent were Hispanic. Nonetheless, the focus group in Clayton was 100 percent black and the focus groups in South Park Hill, Hilltop, and Speer were 100 percent white. Eighty percent of the respondents had attended college, with nearly half holding undergraduate or graduate degrees. Approximately 62 percent of the respondents were women.

The four *Section 8 focus groups in Baltimore County* ranged from 5 to 11 participants, with an average of 8 participants across groups. Of the four groups, three were made up entirely of white homeowners (Dundalk, Millbrook, and Rodgers Forge), and one was made up entirely of black homeowners (Twelve Trees). The racial composition of the groups reflected both the demographics of the neighborhoods and the self-selection of residents in response to our invitation to participate. Participants in the white groups, on average, were older, more likely to be retired, and more likely to have children. Participants in the black group were more likely to be women and to be highly educated.

Across all the Baltimore County groups, most participants were longtime residents, with an average of 17 years at their current address. Variation between groups in length of neighborhood residency was understandably linked to the age of the neighborhood. In the newest community, the Village of Twelve Trees, participants had resided an average of 9 years in the neighborhood. The older communities, like Dundalk, fielded focus groups with older participants. In Dundalk and Rodgers Forge, between 40 and 45 percent of the participants were retired, with half of the group in their late 50s or above. Focus group participants from these neighborhoods also included more households composed of only one adult and were more likely to represent a household with children. Across the groups, almost half of the participants came from households that included children. Most participants were well educated, with three out of five having at least a four-year college degree.

Topic Areas Addressed in Focus Groups

Four main topic areas were addressed in the discussion guide. The first area concerned general questions on what makes for a good place to live and residents' feelings regarding how their neighborhood reflected this definition. The second set of questions elicited participant opinions regarding neighborhood residents, existing social networks, and respondent perceptions regarding the presence or absence of community cohesion.

The third area included questions on perceived changes in the neighborhood during the past five years, including changes in property values. Participants were asked to identify the changes that had occurred and to provide explanations as to why they thought these changes had occurred. If assisted housing of any kind was mentioned in the discussion, additional probes were utilized to further identify how it affected property values.

Fourth, participants were asked to describe any perceived changes in neighborhood residents. These questions were used to assess any perceived changes in both the characteristics of neighborhood residents as well as the tenor of neighborhood interaction. Facilitators did not independently suggest housing programs as a topic of discussion, nor did they confirm or deny the presence of such programs or the location of particular assisted sites in a neighborhood.

Focus Group Facilitation

Each focus group was conducted by a two-member interviewing team consisting of a facilitator and a recorder. The facilitator led the group discussion, ensuring that all participants joined in the discussion, saw that all issues were satisfactorily discussed, and guided the conversation in an efficient and effective manner. Facilitators and recorders were assigned to mirror the racial and ethnic composition of the focus group.

During the facilitator's introductory remarks, verbal and written assurances of respondent anonymity were provided. Each participant reviewed and signed an informed consent form prior to the group discussion.

As a safeguard against bias, neither the facilitator nor the recorder was informed about the results of the quantitative impact analyses prior to the focus group sessions. In this manner, researchers were less likely to prejudge responses or lead participants based on this prior information.

Data Analysis Strategies

During each focus group session, the recorder was asked to keep detailed notes regarding the content of the discussion. Upon completion of the focus group, both the facilitator and the recorder were asked to write up their notes and impressions of the session. When possible, these notes were written up prior to a debriefing session between members of the research staff to check for inter-rater reliability. With few exceptions, facilitator and recorder notes were comparable.

The notes and the initial write-ups completed by the facilitator and recorder were integrated into a two-page summary of findings for each focus group. The focus group comments were analyzed to identify key themes that emerged in the discussion. Analytical files based on these key themes were then created identifying relevant materials from the group discussion. Using content analysis, these thematic files also were analyzed to identify any contextual information that would facilitate interpretation of the quantitative results.

Conclusion

Statistical analysis of the relationship between assisted housing and either property values or crime rates is fundamentally complicated by selection biases. Owing to the actions of landlords, assisted housing developers, and assisted tenants, there will be a tendency for assisted sites to gravitate toward neighborhoods with lower-priced, slowly appreciating housing and higher rates and trends in crime. Whether such assisted housing generates an additional impact on property values or crime rates in these neighborhoods subsequently is obscured by the fact that values were lower and growing more slowly and crime was higher and growing faster in the first place, on average, than in neighborhoods where such housing was absent.

We provide a strategy that overcomes this challenge. Our statistical model provides the basis for comparing both the level and trend in property values and crime rates before assisted housing opened in a neighborhood to the level and trend afterward, controlling for a variety of other causal influences and the spatial patterns in the data. This pre/post comparison yields unambiguous evidence of the impacts independently caused by assisted housing.

To complement and enrich the statistical results, we structure focus group discussions among homeowners in the vicinity of assisted housing sites. By probing their perceptions about neighborhood quality of life issues we can gain a deeper understanding of how assisted housing may affect neighborhoods.

Notes

1. We use "beds" as a measure of the household capacity of a supportive housing site. Providers must specify the number of beds in the proposed assisted site when registering it with the City and County of Denver. The city database, from which our data come, contains this information but does not track the actual occupancy of the site over time.

2. The price or crime levels and trends, as well as the other coefficients in our models, are *estimates* and therefore have uncertainty associated with their values. Although an estimated coefficient may be positive or negative, the uncertainty associated with this estimate may be large enough that one cannot say reliably that this attribute has an effect. In reporting our results, we generally use a standard of "95 percent confidence," meaning that we only show impacts that we are confident would appear in at least 95 out of every 100 samples drawn.

3. Data limitations make the years slightly different, depending on the model. Price series for testing Denver dispersed housing and assisted housing impacts run for the period 1987–97; for Baltimore County Section 8 impacts they run 1989–97. Crime data in Denver neighborhoods are available only for 1990–97. In order to get clean pre- and post-observations, we impose a minimum of two years' worth of data on prices and crime both before and after the occupancy of a site.

4. See Matulef (1988), Martinez (1988), and Puryear (1989) for reviews. A related strand of literature, the impacts of group residences for handicapped individuals, is not considered here. For a review, see Galster and Williams (1994).

5. Studies of supportive housing impacts employing the control area approach include Dear (1977); Wolpert (1978); Boeckh, Dear, and Taylor (1980); Lauber (1986); Iglhaut (1988); and Boydell, Trainor, and Pierri (1989). Studies of low-income housing impacts using this method include Nourse (1963), Schafer (1972), De Salvo (1974), and William L. Berry & Company (1988).

6. Studies of supportive housing impacts employing the control area approach include Wagner and Mitchell (1980); Lindauer, Tung, and O'Donnell (1980); Ryne and Coyne (1985); District of Columbia Association for Retarded Citizens (1987); Iglhaut (1988); and Boydell, Trainor, and Pierri (1989). Studies of low-income housing impacts using this method include: Rabiega, Lin, and Robinson (1984); Puryear (1989); and Briggs, Darden, and Aidala (1999).

7. The comparison often is accomplished with the aid of multivariate statistical procedures to control for differences in the properties being sold pre- and post-occupancy of the site.

8. Cf. Warren, Aduddell, and Tatalovich (1983); Guy, Hysom, and Ruth (1985); Cummings and Landis (1993); Lyons and Loveridge (1993); Goetz, Lam, and Heitlinger (1996); and Briggs, Darden, and Aidala (1999).

9. Lyons and Loveridge (1993) also discuss this problem.

10. A site refers to a unique street address for a single or multifamily property.

11. We used MapInfo mapping software to create separate geographic boundaries for the three distance rings and for areas within a census tract not within 2,000 feet of an assisted housing site. Each of these distinct geographic areas was treated as an individual observation in our regressions. To determine crime reporting rates for each observation, we divided the total crimes reported

in the area by a population total calculated from 1990 Census block group-level data. Because these areas varied greatly in size, we weighted them in the crime-impact regressions by a variable proportional to the total 1990 Census population in the area for which the crime reporting rate was calculated (i.e., a weighted least-squares approach). This gave more influence in the regression estimations to areas with larger population than to those with smaller population.

12. Unlike the property-value model, the crime model does not have a "proximity to number of assisted sites" model. In the crime model, each distance ring is only near one analysis site, and therefore the "number of sites" model would be identical to the "any site" model. The number of beds does vary from site to site, however, so it is possible to estimate a separate "number of supportive beds" model.

13. For an extensive discussion on the appropriate methodology and use of focus group interview data for evaluation purposes, see Hayes and Tatham (1989), Stewart and Shamdasani (1990), and Krueger (1994).

14. Data for these census tract descriptions were obtained from the DHA, Experian home price data, and the U.S. Census.

15. These data are 1996 estimates obtained from the Piton Foundation, a Denver-based non-profit organization (http://www.piton.org; accessed July 1998).

16. Data for the neighborhood descriptions are 1998 estimates obtained from the Piton Foundation (http://www.piton.org; accessed May 1999).

17. Because property-tax rolls were used to identify addresses of potential participants, only homeowners could be selected. The Urban Institute subcontracted with the Latin American Research and Service Agency (LARASA) in Denver to conduct the focus group recruitment process. LARASA staff also organized and helped facilitate the focus-group sessions there.

5

Patterns of Assisted Housing, Property Values, and Crime Rates

Discerning quantitatively the impact of assisted housing programs on single-family property values and reported crime rates places great demands on the quantity and quality of statistical data obtained. For the former impact, we needed data on residential property sales, including the street address of the house (so that the sale could be fixed in space); the amount and date of the sale; and the characteristics of the house, such as square footage, lot size, number of rooms, age, and type of construction, that also affect the price of sale. Furthermore, we needed data for a range of sales starting at least two years prior to the opening date of the particular housing program sites in question. For the crime-impact model, we needed a list of the dates, types, and locations of reported crimes, and the population of various geographic areas so standardized crime rates could be calculated.

For both models, we required the locations and opening dates of the Section 8 households in Baltimore County and the Denver Housing Authority (DHA) dispersed and supportive housing sites in Denver. Again, to identify the location of these sites, we needed their addresses. In addition, some basic characteristics of the sites, such as number of beds (residents) and type of services provided, proved useful for explaining the nature of these programs and for interpreting some of the empirical results.

This chapter describes the sources, character, and quality of the aforementioned data we obtained. It paints a quantitative portrait of assisted housing programs, home prices, and crime rates in Denver and Baltimore County. First, we describe the single-family home sale data and the distinctive patterns of home price trends evinced during the 1990s in Baltimore County and Denver. Next, we describe the data on property crimes, violent crimes, and other types of crimes reported on a geographic basis in Denver, and present statistical and map profiles of crime there during the 1990s. Finally, we convey information on the number and location of the three assisted housing programs being analyzed: Section 8 in Baltimore County, DHA dispersed housing, and supportive housing in Denver. We call special attention to our "analysis sites," the subsets of assisted housing program locations that were selected for impact analysis because they fulfilled the criteria for putting into operation our pre/post design for the statistical model described in chapter 4. In particular, we have sites that went into operation prior to the imposition of program limitations in Denver that exceeded these limitations. This allows us to test the efficacy of these limitations.

Home Sales

The most complete source for home sale data is the property tax rolls maintained by local property tax assessment offices. Because all property sales must be registered with the assessor, these records contain a complete set of the most recent sales transactions for every residential property. Furthermore, because the sales price legally must be reported to the assessor, the data are considered to be quite accurate. The assessor's records also contain data on the physical attributes of the property, as well as information on the buyer and seller. Tax roll records are in the public domain and can be obtained directly from some tax assessment offices or through private data vendors.

We purchased a complete set of property tax roll records for Baltimore County and Denver from the private data vendor Experian. Experian obtains tax roll data directly from tax assessment offices throughout the country and then reformats and resells the data to private users. The Experian data contain all of the information available from the tax rolls on the property itself (including address, number of rooms, square footage, and type of construction), as well as the dates and amounts of the last two sales for each property.

The tax roll data may not be sufficient to obtain a complete sales history for each property, however. If a property was sold more than two times during the period of interest, then the sales record will not be complete, because only the two most recent sales will be recorded. Therefore, we supplemented the tax roll data with a sales history data file, also obtained from Experian, that had a listing of the dates and amounts of every sale of the properties in the county, though no property characteristics. This sales history file allowed us to have a complete record of sales going back to 1989 for Baltimore County and back to 1987 for Denver. By matching the sales history file with property characteristics, we were able to add to our sample 86 percent of the properties with more than two sales in the past decade in Denver and 70 percent of such properties in Baltimore County.

Both the tax roll and sales history files were geocoded to match street addresses with latitude and longitude coordinates, census geographic identifiers (i.e., state, county, tract, and block), and U.S. Postal Service ZIP+4 codes.[1] The geocoding rates were very successful for both study locations. We were able to geocode 92 percent of property addresses in Baltimore County and 98 percent of property addresses in Denver to an exact street address or to a ZIP+4 centroid.[2] Sales records that could not be geocoded to at least this level of precision were excluded from the analysis.

From the final set of sales data, we selected only sales of single-family homes. Table 5.1 summarizes the sales prices and the numbers of sales of single-family homes per year from the cleaned sales file.[3] The average sales price in Baltimore County during the 1989–97 period was $122,000, ranging from $10,000 to $390,000. The average sales price for Denver during the 1987–97 period was $87,000, ranging from $9,000 to $344,000. The total volume of sales is fairly even from year to year, with the exception of 1997, for which we only have partial data.

To get a sense of how house prices changed in our study areas in the 1990s, figure 5.1 shows trend lines for prices of single-family homes from 1990 through the second quarter of 1997. Each point on the graph represents the total percentage change in average house prices from the first quarter of 1990. These trend lines were derived from our regression models, and thus incorporate adjustments for the quality and location of the home. To deemphasize seasonal fluctuations, the trend lines have also been smoothed by taking one-year moving averages.

The difference in price trends is quite striking. Whereas house prices in Baltimore County were stagnant, in Denver there was a dramatic increase in property values throughout most of the 1990s. House prices in Baltimore County fluctuated a little, but on average did not increase by more than 7 percent after 1990. In contrast, in Denver house prices

Table 5.1

Single-Family Home Sales in Denver and Baltimore County

	Denver, 1987–97	Baltimore County, 1989–97
Sales price ($)		
Mean	86,853	122,134
Standard deviation	50,515	60,133
Minimum	9,000	10,000
Maximum	344,000	390,000
Number of sales		
Total	74,569	77,797
1987	4,517	—
1988	6,533	—
1989	7,083	8,789
1990	7,665	9,717
1991	7,615	8,755
1992	8,644	9,832
1993	8,781	9,624
1994	8,626	9,280
1995	7,599	8,577
1996	7,285	8,894
1997	221	4,329

Note: "Cleaned" sales of single-family homes with top and bottom 2 percent of sales by price and land area removed.
Source: Authors' analysis of Experian home sales data.

Percentage change in Prices

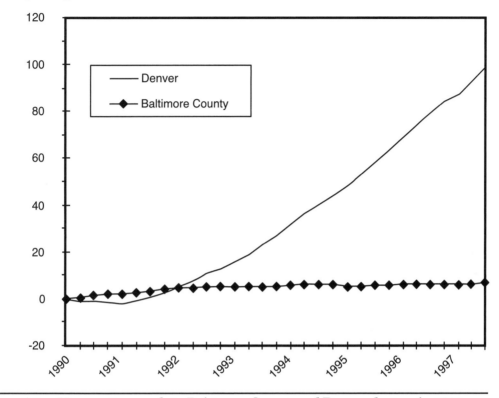

Figure 5.1. Home price trends in Baltimore County and Denver during the 1990s (Percentage change in single-family sales prices)

Source: Authors' analysis of Experian home sales data.

dropped slightly in 1991 but soon began a sharp rise that continued throughout the rest of the period, ending at almost a 100 percent average increase by mid-1997.

Crime Rates

The Denver Police Department provided databases of crimes reported to the police from 1990 to 1997. Each annual database of 45,000—54,000 records included the date and type of crime, and the "state plane coordinates" where the crime took place. We converted the state plane coordinates to latitude and longitude for our mapping and distance calculations. The rates were based on 1990 block group population. Major categories were assigned to groupings of crimes for the analysis.[4]

Maps 5.1 and 5.2 show the variation across census tracts that is masked by the citywide figures. Violent crime reached 6.7 crimes per 100 residents in the highest crime area, and did not occur at all in some southern tracts. One tract experienced 59 property crimes per 100 residents, whereas other neighborhoods only had 1. Violent and property crimes reveal the same pattern of higher crime along the northern edge and the center toward the west, following the general pattern of the poorer and higher minority areas.[5]

The total rate of reported crime in Denver rose from 10 crimes per 100 residents in 1990 to 11.6 crimes in 1993 and then declined for the next four years to 9.6 crimes in 1997 (table 5.2). Property crime, which makes up the majority of all crimes, also followed this pattern. Criminal mischief, which describes low-level property damage, also peaked in 1993. The downward trend in violent crime did not begin until 1995, two years after the property crime shift. The level of disorderly conduct, which includes disturbing the peace and emitting loud noise on public property, remained steady at 0.2 crimes per 100 residents for the eight years of analysis.

Baltimore County Section 8 Program Participants

The Baltimore County Housing Office (BCHO) provided data on the location and tenure of households receiving Section 8 certificates and vouchers in Baltimore County. The BCHO is responsible for administering all Section 8 certificates and vouchers that are used within the county, including those for people who move from other jurisdictions, such as for the Moving to Opportunity program.

The BCHO maintains a database of all Section 8 households for whom it is responsible. These data include identification numbers for the landlords and tenants, the current address of the Section 8 household, the date when the household moved to this address, the number of household members, the number of bedrooms in the unit, the household's income, and the sex, race, and ethnicity (Hispanic or non-Hispanic) of the household head.[6]

The data do not include a specific move-out date, but records for households who move out of their unit are coded as "inactive." Because we needed to know the period of

Table 5.2

Denver Crime Rate per 100 Residents, by Year and Type

Type	1990	1991	1992	1993	1994	1995	1996	1997
Total Crimes	10.0	10.3	11.5	11.6	10.8	10.5	10.5	9.6
Property	6.6	6.5	7.5	7.5	6.8	6.7	6.6	5.9
Violent	0.8	1.0	1.0	1.0	1.0	0.9	0.8	0.7
Criminal Mischief	1.2	1.3	1.4	1.4	1.3	1.2	1.2	1.1
Disorderly Conduct	0.2	0.2	0.2	0.2	0.2	0.2	0.2	0.2
Other	1.1	1.2	1.3	1.4	1.5	1.6	1.8	1.7

Source: Authors' analysis of unpublished data obtained from the Police Dept., City and County of Denver.

**Violent Crimes
per 100 residents, 1997**

◻ 0
0.1 to 0.5
0.5 to 1.0
■ 1.0 to 7.0

Outliers
No information

1 inch = 4.0 miles

Map 5.1.   Violent crimes, Denver census tracts, 1997 (crime, per 100 residents)

Source: Authors' analysis of unpublished data obtained from the Police Dept., City and County of Denver.

**Property Crimes
per 100 residents, 1997**

0 to 1
1 to 5
5 to 6
6 to 60
Outliers
No information

1 inch = 3.9 miles

Map 5.2.   Property crimes, Denver census tracts, 1997 (crime, per 100 residents)

Source: Authors' analysis of unpublished data obtained from the Police Dept., City and County of Denver.

occupancy for each Section 8 location to ascertain continuously occupied sites during our impact analysis, we had to determine when the household moved out. The BCHO was able to provide us with a series of monthly "snapshot" files from February 1991 through August 1997. These files contained records for all households that were receiving a Section 8 subsidy in that month. By tracing the tenant identification numbers in this series of files, we could determine when someone moved out by identifying the month when the record for that household disappeared from the active file.

The BCHO files contained information on approximately 11,000 Section 8 households that lived in the county sometime between February 1991 and August 1997. The addresses of each of these households were geocoded to allow us to identify unique locations where Section 8 tenants lived. We were able to geocode 96 percent of the records to an exact street address and an additional 2 percent to a ZIP+4 centroid. By aggregating these records by their geographic coordinates (latitude and longitude), we identified a total of 4,969 unique Section 8 sites in Baltimore County.[7]

The locations of the Section 8 sites are shown in maps 5.3 through 5.7. Each dot on these maps represents a single Section 8 site (unique address), which may contain more than one subsidized household. Map 5.3 gives an overview of the entire county, and the next four maps zoom in on the regions with the highest numbers of Section 8 sites. One can see that almost all of the sites are located in the southern part of the county, closer to Baltimore City. There also appear to be definite clusters of Section 8 households, such as in the southeast corner of map 5.4, where Dundalk is located.

Map 5.3 can be compared with the maps in chapter 3 to get a pictorial sense of how the distribution of Section 8 households is related to several demographic and housing market characteristics of Baltimore County census tracts. Not surprisingly, there is an obvious correspondence between the distributions of Section 8 and rental housing (cf. maps 5.3 and 3.2). The Section 8 households also appear to live primarily in census tracts with single-family homes of more modest values; these tracts tended to have values that appreciated the least during the study period (cf. maps 5.3, 3.3, and 3.4). The analyses reported in chapter 8 indicate that this pattern continues down to smaller geographic scales. There are many reasons for this phenomenon, which has important implications for policy, as is discussed in chapter 9. There are a few exceptions to this generalization, however, and this motivated the choice of one of our focus groups.

One other pattern is noteworthy. Baltimore County Section 8 holders clearly did not concentrate in predominantly black census tracts (cf. maps 5.3 and 3.1). Of course, given that blacks and whites represent roughly equal numbers of the Section 8 certificate holders in the county, there is likely some racial self-selection occurring such that many Section 8 in-movers match the predominant race of other residents. The significance of racial self-selection in understanding the property-value impacts of Section 8 will be explored in chapter 8.

Table 5.3 provides some statistics on occupancy of the Section 8 sites. Of the Section 8 sites occupied sometime during the period 1991 through 1997, the average move-

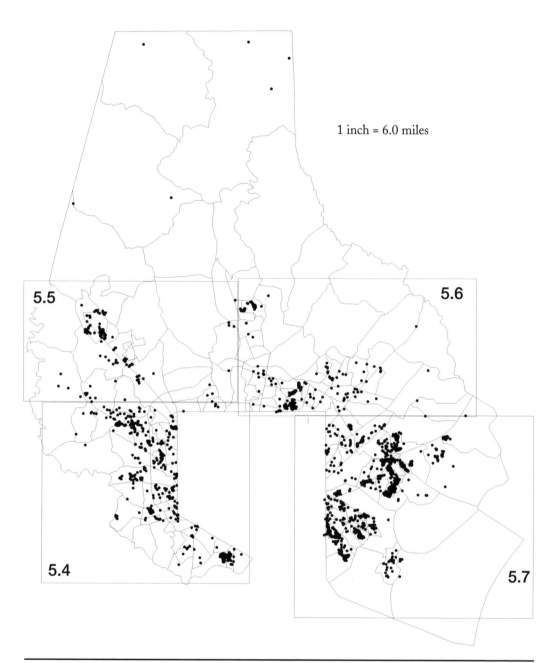

1 inch = 6.0 miles

5.5

5.6

5.4

5.7

Map 5.3.   Locations of Section 8 households, Baltimore County, 1991–1997

Source: Unpublished data from Baltimore County Housing Office.
Note: Lines are census tract boundaries.

Table 5.3

Occupancy Statistics for Section 8 Sites in Baltimore County, 1991–97

Statistic	
Number of sites	4,969
Sites with Moving to Opportunity households	29
Maximum number of Section 8 households at a site	Sites
1	3,649
2	695
3	253
4	130
5	69
6–10	159
11–20	14
Average move-in date for first household at site	First Quarter of 1992
Average percentage of period that site was occupied	47
Average number of Section 8 households per site	
1991	1.48
1997	1.54

Source: Authors' analysis of unpublished data from Baltimore County Housing Office.

in date for the first household to occupy a site was the first quarter of 1992. The average site was occupied just under half of this time period. The average number of households per site did not change much from 1991 through 1997, varying between 1.39 and 1.54.

Dispersed Public Housing Program in Denver

As with Baltimore County Section 8, we needed data on the location and tenure of households for DHA public housing sites. We were able to obtain these data from the DHA. The DHA maintains a complete database of all its public housing projects. The database consists of a property data file, with information on the buildings and housing units, and a tenant data file, which tracks occupancy dates and household characteristics, such as income and the race, sex, and ethnicity of household head. The property data include the project address, the year the property was built, the acquisition date, and the number of units. Unlike the Baltimore County data, the DHA tenant files have both move-in and move-out dates, so we were able to know exactly when each tenant occupied the unit.

The DHA files contained information on 541 public housing sites, all of which were occupied at some time between 1980 and 1997. The addresses of these sites were geocoded to allow us to identify the locations where tenants lived. We were able to geocode 97 per-

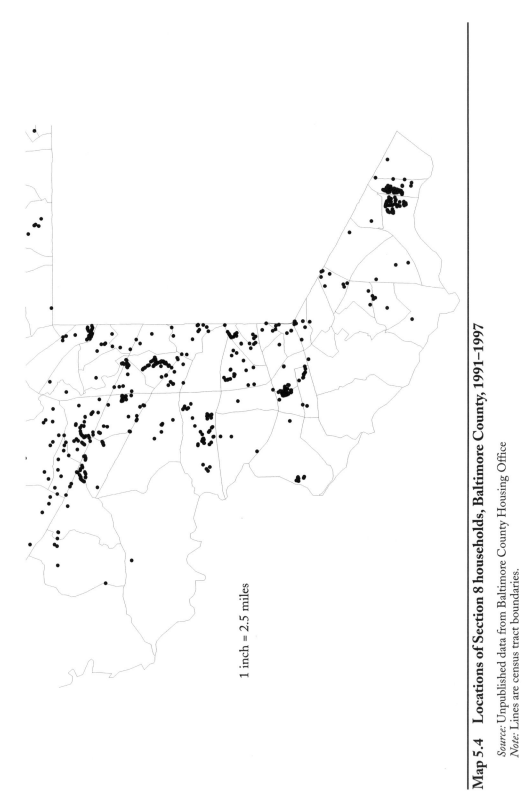

1 inch = 2.5 miles

Map 5.4 Locations of Section 8 households, Baltimore County, 1991–1997

Source: Unpublished data from Baltimore County Housing Office
Note: Lines are census tract boundaries.

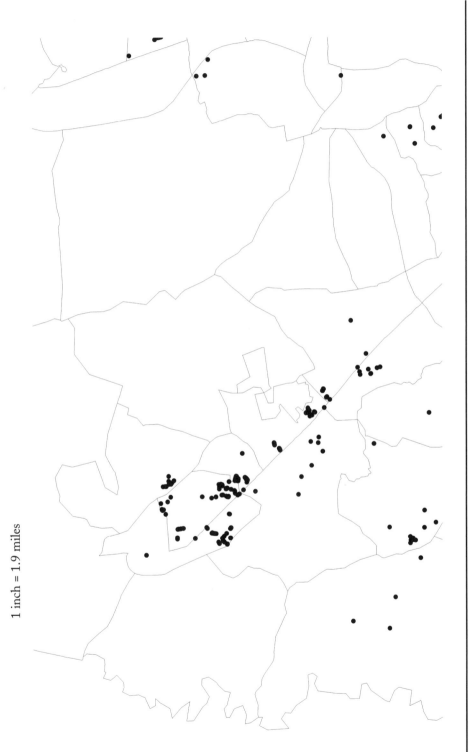

1 inch = 1.9 miles

Map 5.5   Locations of Section 8 households, Baltimore County, 1991–1997

Source: Unpublished data from Baltimore County Housing Office.
Note: Lines are census tract boundaries.

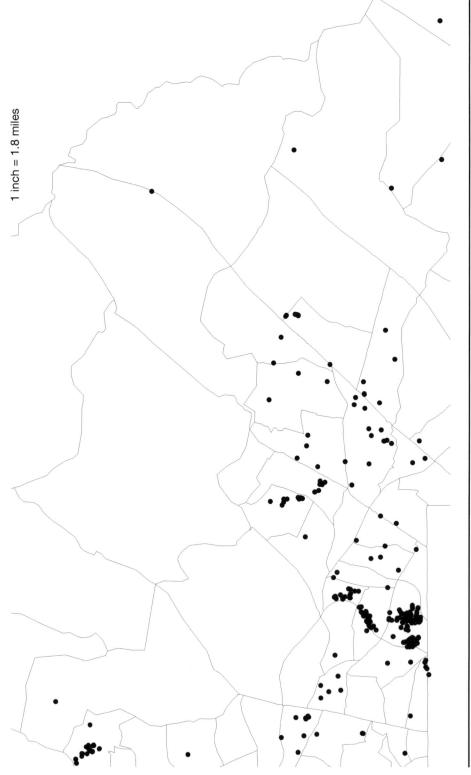

1 inch = 1.8 miles

Map 5.6   Locations of Section 8 households, Baltimore County, 1991–1997

Source: Unpublished data from Baltimore County Housing Office.
Note: Lines are census tract boundaries.

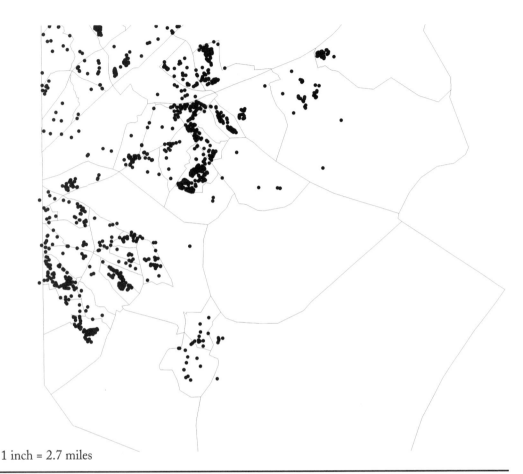

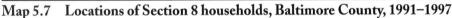

1 inch = 2.7 miles

Map 5.7   Locations of Section 8 households, Baltimore County, 1991–1997

Source: Unpublished data from Baltimore County Housing Office.
Note: Lines are census tract boundaries.

cent of the records to an exact street address and an additional 1 percent to a ZIP+4 centroid. The locations of the DHA public housing sites were shown in map 2.6. To recapitulate the central point, although the northeastern and southwestern quadrants of the city contain the largest numbers of public housing sites, in general they are fairly evenly spread throughout the city, with some small clusters in a few locations.

As was explained in chapter 2, this deconcentrated pattern is the result of a combination of DHA choices and clustering restrictions imposed by the Denver City Council after 1989. The result is that Denver now evinces a remarkably uniform distribution of dispersed public housing units across the majority of census tracts. Although the primary exceptions to the uniform pattern are the highest-value, predominantly white areas in the south-central and eastern portions of Denver (cf. maps 2.6 and 2.1, and 2.2 and 2.4), these also correspond to areas with little rental housing (map 2.3). Moreover, it is clear that dispersed units were

Table 5.4
Occupancy Statistics for Public Housing Sites in Denver, 1980–97

Statistic	All Housing Sites	Dispersed Housing Sites
Average move-in date for first household at site	Second Quarter of 1981	Fourth Quarter of 1980
Average percentage of period that site was occupied	69	74
Number of occupied sites		
1980	315	273
1985	329	286
1990	334	287
1995	498	426
1997	539	432
Average number of households per site		
1980	8.3	2.2
1985	9.9	2.6
1990	10.2	2.8
1995	7.0	2.3
1997	7.0	2.3
Total households		
1980	2,609	601
1997	3,753	1,005

Source: Authors' analysis of unpublished data from Denver Housing Authority.

located not only in many of the highest-value tracts in 1990, but also in ones that appreciated the most during the housing boom of the 1990s (cf. maps 2.6 and 2.5).

Table 5.4 provides some statistics on the public housing developments. The average move-in date for the first household to occupy a site was the second quarter of 1981. The average site was occupied 69 percent of the time from 1980 through 1997. As a result of the DHA's efforts to move to smaller-scale, more dispersed housing projects, the number of occupied sites increased from 315 in 1980 to 539 in 1997, whereas the average number of households per site dropped from a high of 10.2 in 1990 to 7.0 in 1997.

As is shown in table 5.5, the vast majority of public housing sites had five or fewer housing units, whereas 90 percent of the sites had no more than 10 units. This reflects the more recent acquisition of smaller housing projects by the DHA. Table 5.6 shows how the size of the public housing projects acquired or built by the DHA have changed over the years. In the 1950s, the average public housing site had 42 units, but by the 1990s the DHA was acquiring projects with an average of only 2 housing units. This reduction of facility scale likely yielded important consequences, as we shall explore in chapter 6.

Table 5.5

Public Housing Sites in Denver by Number of Units, 1997

	All Sites		Dispersed Sites	
Number of Housing Units	*Number*	*Percent*	*Number*	*Percent*
Total	541	100.0	433	100.0
1	272	50.3	250	57.7
2	134	24.8	107	24.7
3–5	62	11.5	50	11.5
6–10	20	3.7	17	3.9
11–20	17	3.1	9	2.1
21–30	9	1.7	0	0
31–40	2	0.4	0	0
41–50	7	1.3	0	0
51+	18	3.3	0	0

Source: Authors' analysis of unpublished data from Denver Housing Authority.

Table 5.6

Denver Public Housing Sites,
Average Year Built and Number of Housing Units, by Year of Acquisition

			Number of Housing Units	
Year of Acquisition	*Number of Sites*	*Average Year Built*	*Mean*	*Largest*
Non-dispersed sites				
Total	108	1961	27	260
1950–59	15	1958	70	260
1960–69	16	1960	57	207
1970–79	12	1959	39	160
1980–89	4	1971	66	127
1990–97	61	1961	4	67
Dispersed sites				
Total	433	1958	2	20
1950–59	11	1955	4	14
1960–69	44	1966	3	20
1970–79	194	1960	2	11
1980–89	41	1956	1	3
1990–97	143	1955	2	19

Source: Authors' analysis of unpublished data from Denver Housing Authority.

Supportive Housing Facilities in Denver

Data on the location and characteristics of the supportive housing sites were obtained from the combined lists obtained from the Denver Zoning Commission and the Colorado Department of Health and Environment. The resulting supportive housing database consisted of 146 supportive housing sites, which were occupied at some time between 1987 and 1997 (table 5.7). The databases included information on the program's address, the year the program started, the type of program, and the number of beds (residents). The sites varied widely in age, resident population, and size.

We identified the supportive housing locations by geocoding the addresses of the sites. We were able to geocode 90 percent of the records to an exact street address and an additional 10 percent to a ZIP+4 centroid. The locations of all of the supportive housing sites are shown in map 2.7. The sites were scattered throughout the city, with a higher concentration in the center and northwestern corner.

More than half of the sites were opened in the 1980s and 1990s, as is shown in table 5.7. We were unable to ascertain the opening dates of 20 percent of the sites. Some of the sites with missing dates had closed by the time of our analysis, whereas others had merged or been folded into a larger organization.

The sites covered a wide array of programs, with about three-quarters housing adults and one-quarter children (table 5.8). Almost one-third of the sites provided personal care, the most frequent program type for adults. Unspecified children's homes represented the largest group for children. Another one-quarter of the programs served mentally ill or developmentally disabled adults and children. Adult Correctional Facilities and Substance Abuse programs each represented 10 percent of the total sites.

The size of the supportive housing facilities ranged from 3 to 320 beds, with an av-

Table 5.7

Opening Dates of Supportive Housing Sites in Denver

Year of Opening	Number of Sites
Total	146
Before 1970	9
1970–74	4
1975–79	21
1980–84	19
1985–89	27
1990–94	20
1995–97	16
Unknown	30

Source: Authors' analysis of City and County of Denver (1998b)
Bi-annual residential care use renewal.

Table 5.8

Supportive Housing in Denver, by Program Type

Program Type	Number of Sites
Total	146
Adult clients	107
Personal care—unspecified	41
Mental health	17
Developmentally disabled	17
Correctional facilities	14
Substance abuse	13
Personal care—senior housing	3
Hospice	1
Convent	1
Child clients	27
Children's home—unspecified	17
Correctional facilities	7
Developmentally disabled	3
Unknown	12

Source: Authors' analysis of City and County of Denver (1998b) *Biannual residential care use renewal.*

erage of 40 beds per site (table 5.9). Approximately 40 percent of the sites had fewer than 10 beds, and an additional 40 percent held 10 to 50 beds. The remaining 20 percent were larger facilities, ranging from 50 to 320 beds. As we shall see in chapter 8, the scale of the facility appears to have important consequences.

Analysis Samples of Assisted Housing Sites

The above sections of this chapter described a variety of characteristics of the assisted housing program sites under study in Baltimore County and Denver. All were not utilized in our quantitative analysis, however. Rather, we could only conduct our econometric analysis of property-value impacts and crime impacts on subsets of assisted housing sites, which we will refer to as "analysis sites."

To operationalize our pre/post econometric specification described in chapter 4, we necessarily were restricted to those assisted housing locations that met three criteria: (1) sufficient observations of single-family home sales or crime rates within various distances over at least two years both prior to first occupancy of the site and then subsequently; (2) no confounding effects of other nearby assisted housing sites during the pre-period; and (3) a site that had been continuously occupied by a subsidized household (though not necessarily the same one), so that we could measure a consistent "post-occupancy" impact.

Table 5.9

Supportive Housing Sites in Denver, by Number of Units

Number of Units	Number of Sites
Total	146
3–4	9
5–9	47
10–19	29
20–50	28
50–99	15
100–149	8
150–320	10

Source: Authors' analysis of City and County of Denver (1998b) *Bi-annual residential care use renewal.*

These criteria were operationalized somewhat differently due to data differences among programs and impacts being analyzed.

Analysis Sites for the Property-Value-Impact Model

Given that our home sales data spanned the period from 1987 (for Denver) or 1989 (for Baltimore County) to mid-1997, we confined our property-value-impact analysis sites in all three programs to those that were first occupied between the first quarter of 1989 (Denver) or 1991 (Baltimore County) and the third quarter of 1995. Moreover, only those sites that also had an average annual rate of single-family homes sales of at least 2.0 in each of the ranges 0–500 feet, 501–1,000 feet, and 1,001–2,000 feet qualified as property-value-impact analysis sites, to ensure minimum sample sizes for calculating trends pre- and post-occupancy. These criteria limited our property-value-impact analysis sites to 72 Section 8 sites in Baltimore County, 92 dispersed housing sites in Denver, and 11 supportive housing sites in Denver. Inasmuch as the last group was quite heterogeneous, their characteristics are presented in table 5.10.[8]

It is essential for the interpretation of property-value-impact results to note that 10 of the supportive housing analysis sites are Small Special Care facilities and one is a Large Special Care Facility (but houses only 12 residents). None of the property-value analysis sites are Community Corrections or Homeless Facilities. The specific Special Care program types span a wide range, including senior care, substance abuse rehabilitation, mental health, developmental disabilities, children with disabilities, and hospice. Thus, the property-value-impact model results should be interpreted as stemming from a set of small-scale facilities engaged in a wide range of supportive activities, but not qualifying as community corrections or homeless shelters and transitional facilities.

Table 5.10

Characteristics of Supportive Housing Sites for Property-Value-Impact Analysis

Neighborhood	Program Type	Zoning	Starting Year	Number of Beds	Other Supportive Housing (within 2,000 feet) Sites	Units
Berkeley #1	Senior special care	R2	1989	8	1	116
Clayton	Hospice	R2	1993	8	1	8
Hilltop	Developmental disabilities	R0	1992	8	0	0
Montbello #1	Developmental disabilities	R1	1990	4	1	12
Montbello #2	Children's home	R1	1992	8	0	0
Montbello #3	Substance rehabilitation	R1	1995	12	1	4
Montbello #4	Unknown	R1	1995	5	0	0
South Park Hill	Mental health	R1	1990	8	0	0
Speer #1	Mental health	R3	1993	6	5	66
Virginia Village	Personal care boarding home	R1	1992	4	0	0
Washington Virginia Vale	Substance rehabilitation	R1	1989	8	1	151

Source: Authors' analysis of City and County of Denver (1998b) *Bi-annual residential care use renewal.*

The limitation of property-value statistical modeling to the analysis sites above implies a corresponding limitation to the home sales observations employed. Our subset of sales to be used in the econometric analysis was chosen in the following manner. We used all sales that either were (1) not within 2,000 feet of any occupied assisted housing site or (2) within 2,000 feet of one (or more) of our analysis sites after it was occupied. We omitted sales that were within 2,000 feet of any other occupied assisted housing site(s) but did not qualify as an analysis site(s).

This exclusion allowed us to conduct unambiguous tests based on our pre/post principles of deciphering impacts. That is, we limited our property-value-impact analyses to home sales in areas where either (1) the first assisted housing would be developed within 2,000 feet or (2) no assisted housing had been or would be developed during the study period within 2,000 feet. The resulting sample sizes of sales observations were 37,169 for the Section 8 impact model in Baltimore County, 43,361 for the dispersed housing impact model in Denver, and 45,601 for the supportive housing impact model in Denver.

Analysis Sites for the Reported-Crime-Impact Model

For the reported-crime-impact model, we limited ourselves to the dispersed housing and supportive housing sites opening from 1992 through 1995 in Denver, so as to have at least two years of crime data available both pre- and post-year of opening. Three of these sites were then excluded because they were within 1,000 feet of preexisting supportive sites. We therefore employed 38 dispersed housing and 14 supportive housing analysis sites in our crime-impact analysis.

Table 5.11

Characteristics of Supportive Housing Sites for Crime-Impact Analysis

Neighborhood	Program Type	Zoning	Starting Year	Number of Beds	Other Supportive Housing (within 2,000 feet) Sites	Units
Berkeley #2	Personal care boarding home	R2	1993	116	1	8
Clayton	Hospice	R2	1993	8	1	8
Cole	Personal care boarding home	R2	1994	4	0	0
College View	Personal care boarding home	R1	1994	7	0	0
Globeville	Community correctional facility for adults	I2	1993	60	0	0
Hampden	Personal care boarding home	R2	1993	60	0	0
Hilltop	Developmental disabilities	R0	1992	8	0	0
Montbello #2	Children's home	R1	1992	8	0	0
Montbello #3	Substance rehabilitation	R1	1995	12	1	4
Montbello #4	Unknown	R1	1995	5	0	0
Rosedale	Personal care boarding home	R5	1993	164	0	0
Speer #1	Mental health	R3	1993	6	5	66
Speer #2	Personal care boarding home	R3	1993	53	0	0
Virginia Village	Personal care boarding home	R1	1992	4	0	0
Wellshire	Mental health	R1	1995	4	1	8

Source: Authors' analysis of City and County of Denver (1998b) *Bi-annual residential care use renewal.*

Again, the heterogeneity of the supportive housing crime impact analysis sites warrant further discussion; see table 5.11. Note that nine of these sites were Small Special Care facilities, five were Large Special Care Facilities (with two housing more than 100 residents), and one was a large Community Corrections Facility; none were Homeless Facilities. Thus, the supportive housing crime-impact model results should be interpreted as stemming from a diverse set of small- and large-scale facilities engaged in a wide range of supportive activities, but not qualifying as homeless shelters or transitional facilities.

It is important to recognize that the supportive housing analysis samples for property-value impacts and crime impacts only have six sites in common, all Small Special Care Facilities. This lack of correspondence in the two samples occurs for two reasons. First, because we had a longer panel of data for home sales than crime reports, some sites opening in the 1989–91 period could qualify for the former analysis but not the latter. However, we imposed a minimum number of proximate sales in the vicinity of sites for them to qualify for the property-value analysis; no such restriction was necessary for the crime analysis.

There was no minimum level of crimes used to qualify a geographic area (i.e., a census tract or any of the concentric rings around supportive sites) for inclusion in the sample, because zero crime represented a valid observation. However, we did eliminate geographic areas as units of observation following the same principles applied to home sales above. We used all geographic areas (i.e., their measured crime rates) that either were (1) not within 2,000 feet of any occupied supportive site (or one for which we had no opening date) or (2) within 2,000 feet of one (or more) of our analysis sites after occupancy.

We omitted site areas that were within 1,000 feet of any other occupied supportive site(s) but did not qualify as an analysis site(s). One additional area was excluded because it did not have a nonzero spatial lag variable. Finally, we excluded any area with a 1990 population less than 40 persons because the small denominator resulted in extremely high crime rates. This yielded a sample of 896 geographic areas for the dispersed housing crime-impact analysis and 1,304 geographic areas for the supportive housing crime-impact analysis.

Analysis Sites Not Conforming to the Denver Ordinances

Chapter 2 discussed the two important sets of limitations that were imposed on assisted housing in Denver in the wake of a public controversy. Both the late 1989 regulations for the DHA Dispersed Housing Program and the 1993 ordinance for supportive housing imposed impaction standards on facility concentration and scale. Our analysis samples allow us to test the extent to which the parameters of these limitations were reasonable guidelines for avoiding negative neighborhood impacts.

In the property-value impact analysis, we had observations of both dispersed and supportive facilities that were developed *before* their respective limitations were put into place *and* which would have violated these limitations had they been in place. This was also the case for some supportive housing facilities used in our crime-impact analysis. As far as we can ascertain, ours represents the first empirical test of the efficacy of such impaction standards.

Notes

1. Geocoding was done using MapMarker software from MapInfo Corporation.
2. ZIP+4 codes are roughly equivalent to a city block. The centroid of a ZIP+4 would be the geographical center of a block.
3. To ensure that we are only dealing with "typical" homes conveyed in arm's-length transactions, we eliminated the top and bottom 2 percent of sales according to sales price and land area.
4. It should be kept in mind that these are rates of *reported* crimes, which are not necessarily all crimes that occurred. The variation of crime rates across different parts of the city and across different crime categories may be partially due to variations in reporting rates.
5. The two dotted tracts were left out of the map range because their extremely small population resulted in extraordinarily high crime rates.
6. The BCHO data also contained information on 131 Section 8 Moderate Rehabilitation properties. Because this program was not the subject of our analysis, we excluded these sites from our models. Furthermore, to avoid confusing the price impacts of the two programs, we excluded

from our models all sales in Baltimore County that were within 2,000 feet of a Section 8 Moderate Rehabilitation site.

7. Unique locations mean distinct street addresses, not apartment or unit numbers. Tenants living in different apartments at a multifamily property were counted as living at a single site.

8. Of the 72 Section 8 sites, 56 had only one subsidized tenant at the address, 14 sites had two, and one each had three and four tenants. Similarly, the vast majority of the 92 dispersed sites consisted of single-family units.

6

The Impacts of Dispersed Public Housing in Denver

This chapter presents our findings related to property-value and crime impacts of the Denver Housing Authority's (DHA's) dispersed public housing program. Our statistical impact models provide both estimates of the average impact of all dispersed housing sites and nuances for the type of neighborhood and concentration of dispersed housing sites. We use information obtained from key informant interviews and homeowner focus group participants to contextualize our assessment of the impacts.

Overall, we found that the dispersed public housing program as implemented by the DHA had a *positive* impact on house prices in Denver neighborhoods, on average. In general, the area within 500 feet of a dispersed housing site experienced an upward trend in house prices relative to the prices of similar homes not near dispersed housing. This reversed a relative decline in house prices that existed in these areas prior to the presence of the DHA housing site. As one moved further away from the dispersed housing site, however, the positive effects became attenuated.

Though the *average* impact of dispersed housing was to increase house prices, not all neighborhoods in Denver experienced the same positive effects, and the effects depended on the concentration of dispersed housing. When we stratified our statistical models to measure the differences in impacts for different types of neighborhoods and tested for interaction effects with the concentration of sites, we found clear threshold effects. Dispersed housing sites located in all types of Denver neighborhoods (but less so in low-value ones) had a positive effect on house prices within 1,001–2,000 feet, but only if they did not exceed four or five in number. In higher-valued neighborhoods, by contrast, positive impacts also occurred within 1,000 feet, but only if one dispersed site was present.

We attributed positive effects to the effective rehabilitation and management practices of the DHA, and potential negative effects to the overconcentration of low-income renter households. Although we were unable to ascertain the definitive cause of negative impacts on home sales prices, we ruled out crime as a possibility. We could find no quantitative or qualitative evidence that dispersed housing increased crime rates nearby, regardless of concentration or neighborhood context. We emphasize, however, that all these results apply only to a set of small-scale facilities.

Quantitative Estimates of Property-Value Impacts of Dispersed Public Housing

We start by examining the results of our basic house price impact model for Denver, which measures the average impact of dispersed public housing projects across the entire city.[1] Figure 6.1 summarizes the regression results in graphical form for selected models and distance rings. The figure shows the relative percentage differences in prices over time in single-family home sales prices in proximity to DHA dispersed housing sites, compared with prices for similar dwellings elsewhere in the same census tracts but not within 2,000 feet of any dispersed (or other public housing) units.

In figure 6.1, the vertical axes indicate the percentage differences in house prices over the baseline. The horizontal axes indicate time, starting with the beginning of our Denver home price data, the first quarter of 1987. The first dotted line indicates a representative

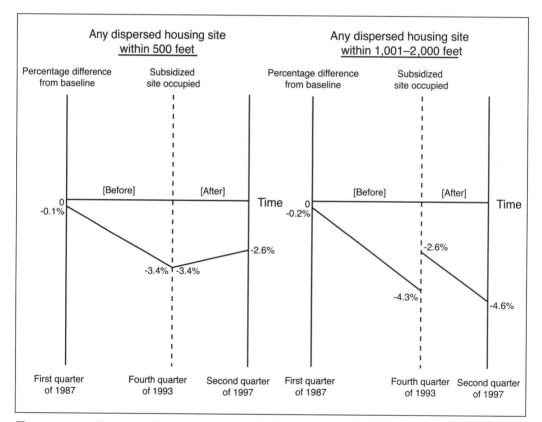

Figure 6.1.   Estimated price trends within 2,000 feet of any dispersed housing site(s), Denver County (relative to baseline areas of same tracts not within 2,000 feet)

Note: There were no statistically significant impacts of dispersed housing observed in the range of 500–1,000 feet. Baseline prices control for seasonal and countywide quarterly trends, plus housing stock characteristics.

Source: Authors' calculations.

starting date chosen as the point of first occupancy of the typical dispersed housing site. Therefore, the section of the graph to the left of the dotted line is the price trend *before* the dispersed housing site was occupied, and the section to the right of the dotted line is the price trend *after* the site was occupied.[2]

Sales Price Trends before Dispersed Sites Are Occupied

The results of our analysis show that in Denver there was a systematic tendency for dispersed housing sites to be acquired in declining, lower-priced pockets in census tracts. The negative and statistically significant coefficients on the time-trend variables indicate that areas within 2,000 feet of sites acquired for dispersed housing developments evinced price trends in the late 1980s and early 1990s that were falling relative to other areas within their same census tracts. These declines can also be seen in the downward-sloping trend lines in the left-hand sides of the price trend graphs in figure 6.1. These declines were roughly constant across all three distance rings. During the period 1987–93, home sales prices within 2,000 feet of future dispersed sites fell about 3 to 4 percent relative to comparable homes located in other areas within the same census tracts.

Our key informant interviews and subsequent discussions with DHA operational staff provided confirmation and further explanation of this empirical finding. First, the DHA typically acquired vacant, boarded-up properties for their dispersed units. Insofar as these units had been generating negative externalities for the surrounding neighborhood for oftentimes considerable periods prior to DHA acquisition, the 2,000-foot circular neighborhoods defined by proximity to these units would tend to have lower values.

Second, there were two sources of potential self-selection bias in the DHA's purchasing strategy. Because the DHA was required to do a variety of time-consuming property inspections prior to purchase, buildings in "hotter" housing submarkets would often be purchased by private interests before the DHA could acquire them. Moreover, the DHA itself was likely to search more intensively for buildings for purchase in areas where "they could get the most building for the money," and thereby stretch their scarce programmatic resources as far as possible.

Property-Value Impacts for Denver Neighborhoods as a Group

On average across Denver, the regressions showed clear and convincing evidence of positive property price impacts associated with nearby DHA dispersed housing. As is shown in the first panel of figure 6.1, after a dispersed housing site was occupied, sales prices within 500 feet reversed their previous relative downward trend evinced before occupancy. Fourteen quarters after occupancy, prices at this distance were only 2.6 percent less than the baseline; immediately preceding occupancy, they were 3.4 percent less. Had pre-occupancy trends continued, the area's sales prices would have been estimated to be 5.1 percent less than the baseline. Thus in the course of only three years after the opening of a

DHA dispersed development, housing values improved, on average, 2.5 percentage points (i.e., 5.1 minus 2.6) in the immediate neighborhood within 500 feet.

Within 1,001–2,000 feet, proximity to a dispersed site apparently provided an initial additional upward boost of 1.7 percentage points to house prices relative to other areas (figure 6.1, second panel).[3] This one-time increase did not result in a change in the previous downward relative price trend, however; and fewer than four years after the occupancy of the dispersed housing site, prices were back down to their pre-occupancy levels. Though the wider neighborhood's price trend was not "turned around" as it was in the case of closer proximity, the DHA dispersed units apparently provided some nontrivial benefits to property values over a broader area.

The price-enhancing impacts observed for the Denver dispersed housing program can most likely be attributed to the structure of the program itself. Under the program, the DHA acquired vacant, often deteriorated properties and on average invested $21,432 per unit for rehabilitation.[4] The improvement of the physical appearance of these properties and the return of vacant buildings to occupancy might have served to stem the decline of the areas where they were located. As these activities were carried out, the declining price trends within a small area of the neighborhood (i.e., within 500 feet of the site) were apparently reversed.

Meanwhile, at larger distances from the site (i.e., 1,001–2,000 feet), we observed a fixed positive price impact. Unfortunately, this upward shift in home values was eventually overcome by the continuing downward trend in prices. It would therefore appear that, while the housing market perceived a short-term boost in the desirability of an area from the act of rehabilitating units, such activity was insufficient to reverse the preexisting overall negative trends in a larger neighborhood.

Property-Value Impacts for Different Types of Neighborhoods

Our basic impact model was replicated for different clusters of census tracts in Denver. We stratified census tracts according to the racial and ethnic composition,[5] median 1990 home values, and real changes in median home values from 1990 to 1996. Stratification by terciles of median 1990 home values proved to yield the most interesting results. Only some of the overall positive results attributed to proximity to DHA dispersed housing occurred in the same fashion across all types of neighborhoods in Denver regardless of their spatial concentration. Positive impacts occurred consistently, however, at the farthest distances—1,001 to 2,000 feet—in neighborhoods with low, moderate, and high property values as long as dispersed housing sites remained below threshold concentrations.

In addition, we experimented with a variant of our basic regression, which allowed both the level and the trend of home prices post-occupancy to vary with the number of DHA dispersed sites that may have been developed later near our original set of analysis sites.[6] Due to the siting restrictions imposed on the DHA, however (see chapter 2), the variation in concentration was extremely limited in our sample. Nevertheless, we were able to observe clear threshold effects associated with concentrations observed in our sample. Moreover, there appear to have been distinct differences in sensitivity to concentrations of dispersed housing in different neighborhood contexts.

In the higher-value neighborhoods, long-run positive impacts were observed at all ranges within 2,000 feet, as long as the number of dispersed sites remained below the threshold appropriate for the particular range. The impact of one dispersed site within 500 feet was strongly positive, such that, over the long run, prices were boosted by about 7 percent annually. At ranges of 501–1,000 and 1,001–2,000 feet, the increments were lower by a factor of 6 and 12, respectively. However, if even *two* dispersed units were present within 1,000 feet (which occurred in our higher-value sample), the impact turned strongly negative, with roughly the same magnitude of impact noted above, but in the opposite direction. The corresponding threshold value in the range of 1,001–2000 feet range was five sites.[7]

The least positive impacts occurred in lower-valued neighborhoods at all distances from the dispersed sites. There were no statistically significant impacts or threshold effects observed within 1,000 feet of a site. At the range of 1,001–2,000 feet, there were statistically significant positive impacts in both the short and long term, but they were comparatively small in magnitude. With one dispersed site in this range, long-run sales price trends would be boosted in low-value areas only about half as much as in higher-value neighborhoods.

Moreover, the results suggest a lower threshold concentration of dispersed sites within 1,001–2,000 feet—four sites instead of the five in higher-value areas—that triggers a negative impact on home price trends in lower-value neighborhoods. These findings suggest that the market may be picking up on some structural weaknesses in an already vulnerable part of the housing market. Lower-value neighborhoods in Denver are characterized by higher poverty rates, rates of out-of-wedlock births, crime rates, and concentrations of black and Hispanic households.[8]

Thus, these neighborhoods may be exhibiting the effects of concentrated disadvantage. More DHA dispersed public housing in such a vulnerable market context apparently provides little lasting neighborhood benefit even if prices are boosted in the short run as housing is rehabilitated, perhaps because it further contributes to poverty concentration.

Before leaving the discussion of quantitative home price impact measures, an important caveat is in order. The results given above were generated by a set of small-scale public housing facilities developed by rehabilitating existing units. The vast majority of our dispersed housing analysis sample consisted of single-family homes. Indeed, no site in the entire DHA dispersed program exceeds 20 units. Thus, although we can analyze impacts of various spatial concentrations of small-scale facilities, the DHA sample does not permit robust investigations of the impact of facility scale. We do, however, report the results of such an investigation in the context of discussing supportive housing in chapter 7.

Key Insights of the Focus Groups Regarding Impacts

Awareness of Dispersed Housing Sites

The statistical results given above underscore that the real estate market in Denver is receiving consistent and accurate information regarding the location of dispersed housing units and that house pricing systematically reflects this information. Indeed, since the enactment of the intergovernmental agreement between the City Council and the DHA in late 1989 that stipulates public hearings with regard to the purchase of dispersed units, both the market and homeowners are made aware of the purchase of units in their neighborhoods. Further, according to our key informants, the DHA works directly with real estate agents to identify and purchase potential dispersed units. This would suggest that the market is responding directly to the rehabilitation and management of these units by the DHA.

It is interesting, then, that none of our focus group participants specifically mentioned the dispersed public housing units in their neighborhoods. This suggests that the DHA has been successful, through its maintenance and tenant screening efforts, in blending its dispersed projects into the larger community.[9] Our focus groups did, however, consistently emphasize elements of neighborhood quality that are relevant to subsidized housing policymakers: the physical condition of the neighborhood, the presence of vacant and abandoned buildings or rental properties, social cohesion, and crime and public safety. The DHA seems to have been able to successfully address many of these issues in the dispersed housing program. The fact that it operates small-scale, reasonably scattered facilities also undoubtedly contributes to their low profile.

One of the primary concerns raised during the 1989 controversy regarding dispersed housing was the potential for physical degradation of the neighborhood and how that would negatively affect property values. Focus group participants underscored the importance of this issue. Participants were very interested in the upkeep not only of residential units, but also of yards, streets, commercial establishments, and other features of the neighborhood infrastructure. The consensus among participants was that poor upkeep contributed to the decline in property values in a neighborhood: "There's trash everywhere. People aren't cleaning up their front yards. It gives kids the impression that people don't care," according to a respondent living in the Berkeley neighborhood.

The DHA has tried to address fears of neighborhood degradation by maintaining a strict maintenance and inspection schedule for all of its dispersed properties. Housing managers have worked to enhance their speed in responding to complaints, including those made by the neighbors of dispersed public housing tenants. DHA staff told us that their properties are often some of the best maintained on the block, and our own on-site inspections of selected properties confirmed this. These proactive and comprehensive maintenance policies have undoubtedly helped the DHA achieve greater acceptance of its dispersed developments in neighborhoods.

Related to resident worries about the physical upkeep of the neighborhood was their apprehension about abandoned or vacant properties. Focus group participants expressed concern about having homes left vacant for extended periods of time, especially multiple vacant units on a single block. The presence of many vacant units was thought to harm property values severely. It is therefore significant that a key element of the DHA dispersed housing program is the acquisition and rehabilitation of abandoned or foreclosed properties. The act of returning these housing units to active occupancy may signal a beneficial change to the community, as indeed our statistical estimates quantified.

Homeowners also expressed concerns regarding the high number of rental units in their neighborhoods and the potential problems that might result from having a large renter population. One respondent from the Platte Park neighborhood stated: "I think it makes a huge difference about how many rental houses there are. That was a major problem here—there were so many rentals. There was no stability here." The general consensus was that neighborhood life, particularly a sense of community and commitment to the neighborhood, was enhanced by the presence of homeowners.

Although participants acknowledged that some fraction of the housing in the neighborhood needs to be set aside for rental use, they were very concerned that, past a certain threshold, the number of rental units in the area would adversely affect property values. These comments provide one explanation for the threshold effects we observed. Unfortunately, we were unable to probe this issue further because dispersed housing was not mentioned by focus groups in areas (Berkeley, Colfax) where its concentration exceeded thresholds we estimated statistically.

The presence of large numbers of rental properties was seen to weaken social cohesion in a neighborhood, which was another issue raised by the focus group participants. Homeowners in all six groups indicated that the most important factor affecting their quality of life was having good neighbors and feeling some sense of connection with others in the neighborhood. *Who you lived with* in the neighborhood was equally, if not more, important than *where you lived*.

The focus group discussions underscored how important it was for participants to feel a sense of community with neighbors. This sense of community was described in terms of knowing one another, looking out for one another, interacting with each other, and protecting one another. However, being neighborly did not necessarily mean being totally immersed in the lives of one's neighbors. Rather, it reflected a commitment to others as well as to the neighborhood. Although our participant homeowners did not identify dispersed housing developments as being the source of neighborhood problems, we must point out that they were very aware of larger, conventional public housing developments and Section 8–occupied units in their neighborhoods. For example, residents in both of the Berkeley focus groups mentioned disparagingly the conventional public housing projects in their neighborhoods.

Participants in all six of the focus groups discussed at length their concerns about the maintenance and management of rental properties in their neighborhoods, particularly those owned by "Section 8 landlords." Their knowledge of these landlords was not based on mere speculation. Some homeowners in our groups claimed that they identified "problem" landlords by calling the city property assessor's office directly. Although our focus group respondents did not directly mention dispersed housing, homeowners still approached the DHA to check whether the "problem" property was owned by the DHA. According to our key DHA informants, most of the inquiries they received proved to be for privately owned units.

On the basis of this discussion, it is important to emphasize that the positive property-value impacts observed here cannot necessarily be generalized to public housing dispersal programs run by other housing authorities without the safeguards of the Denver program. It is the particular characteristics of the DHA's program—the acquisition and rehabilitation of run-down, small-scale, widely scattered properties; the effective ongoing maintenance practices; and the strict screening and monitoring of tenants—that arguably contribute to the beneficial, or at least nonharmful, effects that we have found. One might expect that comparable programs operating in other cities would have similar impacts, but this question can only be answered by further research.

Reactions of Homeowners in a Booming Housing Market

To further explain the responses of the Denver focus groups and their failure to implicate dispersed housing as a negative factor in their communities, it is necessary to place their comments within the context of a city and county that has experienced tremendous growth in property values during the past few years. The housing market in Denver has been booming after a decade-long drought. Participants from all of the focus groups indicated that the value of their homes had increased sharply, with most indicating a twofold to threefold increase from their original purchase price.

Although some participants expressed concern about the effect of higher prices and accompanying rapid population growth on their neighborhoods, most homeowners were quite happy with the increases they noted in the value of their property. Several focus group participants felt that these price increases were good for their neighborhoods, particularly in terms of improving physical conditions. A respondent from East Colfax explained: "Yes. As property values rise, it makes people in the neighborhood a bit more caring because of the value of their homes." Other homeowners echoed the opinion that in a climate of rising property values, neighbors were more likely to look after their properties. They noted that homes were being fixed up and that a number of properties were converting from rental use to homeownership.

The reactions of homeowners to assisted housing programs need to be viewed in this environment of rising house prices. Though it is true that our focus group participants did not hesitate to speak negatively about other forms of subsidized housing, and that the policies described above no doubt help shield the DHA's dispersed housing program from such criticism, one must also recognize that homeowners are less likely to notice small price differentials in a booming housing market. As long as house prices are rising, a typical homeowner may not be as concerned about the possible price impacts of subsidized housing.

This reaction might change, however, in an environment where house prices are declining or stagnating. The perceptions of homeowners could become more attuned to anything that might explain why property values are not increasing. Even a well-designed program like the DHA's could come under scrutiny and attack in such a situation, as happened in Denver in 1989 during an era of housing price stagnation. As we shall see in the case of Baltimore County in chapter 8, the comments and concerns of homeowners become quite different when house prices are not appreciating rapidly.

Mechanisms of Property-Value Impacts of Dispersed Housing

The property-value-impact results given above introduce a theme reinforced by findings reported in upcoming chapters: (1) Positive impacts can become negative ones when threshold concentrations of assisted housing are exceeded; and (2) sometimes no net impacts can be observed close to the assisted housing site, only farther away. We systematically explore these superficially baffling findings in chapter 9, after the totality of results has been presented. Suffice it to note here as way of introduction that we introduce the concept of "countervailing externalities" as a means of explanation.

Both of these conclusions suggest that the market differentially evaluates two distinct elements of dispersed housing. One element, the rehabilitation of the dwelling acquired, is viewed positively; the other, occupancy by a low-income, renter household, is viewed negatively (though we cannot be sure precisely why from our study). Apparently, the positive is evaluated as a linear function of the number of sites, whereas the negative is evaluated as a nonlinear function, such that the latter predominates past the threshold.

Homeowners clearly perceive a threshold of renters past which the neighborhood suffers, but we cannot be sure what role this plays in the observed threshold effects associated with overconcentrations of dispersed housing, as opposed to other characteristics of the units or their occupants. If one posits that the magnitude and spatial extent of these countervailing externalities are highly contingent on neighborhood context, then the finding of nonlocalized impacts can be explained as well.

An Evaluation of Impaction Standards for Dispersed Housing

Our property-value-impact model's parameters allow us to reflect on the limitations on dispersed housing by the 1989 intergovernmental agreement. Recall from chapter 2 that one standard was a limitation of dispersed units to census tracts having poverty rates lower than 20 percent in 1990. Given our finding of attenuated positive and lower-concentration threshold impacts in lower-value Denver neighborhoods, and the correlation between property values and poverty rates, we view this limitation as reasonable. Another standard was that individual sites had to be separated by a minimum of 950 feet. Given our finding that, at least in higher-value neighborhoods, negative impacts ensued if the number of dispersed sites exceeded one within 1,000 feet, this was a remarkably prescient standard indeed.

Finally, there was a standard that limited the number of sites to eight and/or the number of dispersed housing units to 1 percent of the housing stock per census tract. Given that we found thresholds of negative impacts at four or five sites in the range of 1,000–2,000 feet in all Denver neighborhoods, and that the typical census tract in Denver is a square mile, one can imagine configurations in which the standard could be met but our estimated threshold exceeded. For example, take a square-mile census tract and divide it into nine equal squares, with a dispersed housing site located in eight of the nine sectors; each could be separated from all others by at least 950 feet. But homes located in the very center of this tract could have all eight dispersed housing sites within the range of 1,000–2,000 feet. This suggests that the impaction standards might well be fine-tuned to better ensure a somewhat smaller number of sites beyond 950 feet than currently permitted.

Quantitative and Qualitative Analyses of Crime Impacts of Dispersed Housing

We estimated our basic crime-impact statistical model described in chapter 4, and explored variants that permitted the concentration of sites and units in the vicinity to affect crime rates. We also explored various neighborhood strata analogous to the property-value-impact analysis. We found that neighborhoods in which dispersed housing was developed generally had a higher level of reported crimes in most categories compared with other neighborhoods, prior to the introduction of dispersal housing, consistent with our finding of lower property-value trends there.

In none of these trials, however, did we uncover any evidence that the introduction of dispersed housing boosted any sorts of reported crime rates in the vicinity, regardless of neighborhood context. This is not surprising, of course, given our previous finding that dispersed housing did not generally create any negative property-value impacts. We again caution that this finding must be placed in context: a scattered-site public housing program operating small-scale facilities in rehabilitated dwellings widely scattered across the city.

Our focus groups provided indirect evidence that, indeed, DHA dispersed housing was not causing a neighborhood crime problem, rather than our quantitative finding being produced by a statistical anomaly. None of the focus group participants associated crime with the presence of subsidized or unsubsidized renters and, as noted above, none mentioned the dispersed housing program in any context.

This was not because homeowners in Denver were indifferent to issues of public safety. On the contrary, focus group participants expressed a concern closely related to neighborhood stability and cohesion: the perceived threat of increased criminal activity. In particular, participants were concerned about safety on the streets and in the schools: "It used to be when you saw kids you could ask them why they weren't in school. In this day and age you can't do that because they might have a gun or knife or will track you down" (Berkeley respondent). Other ongoing issues of concern in the neighborhoods included youth crime (mainly vandalism and petty thefts, graffiti, unsupervised children, and truancy), gang violence, and drugs.

The DHA's tenant screening procedures and occupancy policies have tried to diminish these concerns with regard to the dispersed housing program. Prospective tenants of dispersed housing are rigorously screened by the DHA and must continue to exhibit good behavior throughout their tenure to maintain residency. These prospective tenants must have an acceptable rent payment history and no record of criminal activity. They are also expected to exhibit a high degree of motivation toward self-sufficiency and community involvement. These tenants also are expected to cooperate with the DHA in maintaining the interior and exterior of the property and must be able to pay for snow removal and lawn care. DHA staff informed us that they will not hesitate to remove a tenant who cannot maintain the required standards.

It thus appears to us that it is no accident that neither our statistical model nor nearby homeowners could ascertain any crime impacts from dispersed housing in Denver. Enlightened management in a variety of dimensions clearly has paid off in promoting measurable neighborhood benefits, avoiding neighborhood harm, and rendering the assisted housing program virtually invisible to neighbors.

Conclusion

The presence of DHA dispersed public housing units generally enhanced the value of nearby single-family homes across Denver as a whole. It provided the least salutary consequences in lower-valued neighborhoods and adversely affected property values only in circumstances when its concentrations exceeded thresholds. Fortunately, this did not occur frequently; hence, our finding of overall positive impacts.

These findings of neighborhood-contingent property value impacts and concentration threshold effects foreshadow forthcoming chapters. Moreover, we could identify no impacts of dispersed housing on neighborhood crime rates, in any neighborhood context. Recall, however, that these impacts were observed for a set of small-scale, widely scattered developments, mainly single-family dwellings.

The data from the homeowner focus groups were consistent with these conclusions. The failure of any of these groups to identify dispersed housing sites as a problem suggests that the DHA overall avoided overconcentrations of dispersed housing, maintained their dispersed units well, and worked to blend both the small-scale facilities and their occupants into the neighborhood. Rigorous tenant screening by the DHA for the dispersed housing program also likely contributed to the lack of complaints by participants regarding DHA tenants in dispersed units.

It is interesting that positive impacts of DHA dispersed units also were not noted in our focus groups, implying that although the DHA itself and the sites it operates maintained a relatively low profile in the perceptions of owners, the market clearly valued the renovation and occupancy of previously vacant units through the dispersed housing program. This lack of visibility of the dispersed housing program in Denver stands in marked contrast to supportive housing programs in Denver and, especially, to the Section 8 program in Baltimore County—and, we believe, is a prime contributor to its observed successes.

We further found that poorly managed rental apartments, especially those housing assisted tenants (beyond the dispersed housing program) were often identified as a problem by our Denver focus group participants. This theme of concern over poorly managed rental property and its stereotypical association with assisted housing resonates with what we report in the next chapters regarding supportive housing in Denver and Section 8 households in Baltimore County.

Notes

1. Overall, the aggregate model for Denver performed extremely well, with adjusted R^2s of .81. Not surprisingly given the exceptional sample sizes, virtually all of the [*Struct*], [*Tract*], and [*Quarter*] control variables evinced coefficients that were significantly different from zero. All the coefficients of the [*Struct*] characteristics of homes proved to have the expected signs.

2. In these graphs, we only show the effect of regression coefficients significant at the 95 percent confidence level.

3. Though coefficients of both post-occupancy shift and trend variables were positive in the range of 501–1,000 feet, neither was statistically significant.

4. This figure was provided via a written communication with the DHA on July 7, 1998, and is based on rehabilitation costs on dispersed housing acquired after 1988.

5. White tracts were defined as those containing fewer than 5 percent black and 5 percent Hispanic residents. Black and Hispanic tracts were those that were substantially integrated (20–49 percent) as well as those that had a majority of black or Hispanic people.

6. Because all of the DHA dispersed developments were of small scale, there were virtually no differences between models testing impacts of numbers of sites vs. numbers of units.

7. Note that the observed sample maximum was nine sites in this range in these neighborhoods.

8. Data on these neighborhoods were obtained from the Neighborhood Facts database found at the Piton Foundation Web site (http://www.piton.org).

9. By design, none of the focus group participants in Denver was informed that HUD was a sponsor of this study. This withholding of information did not prevent participants from mentioning other HUD-subsidized housing programs, however, such as Section 8.

7

The Impacts of Supportive Housing in Denver

In chapter 6, we reported how the Denver housing market responded to the Denver Housing Authority's (DHA's) acquisition and rehabilitation of single-family, duplex, and small multifamily structures and their subsequent conversion to occupancy by low-income families. This chapter presents analogous findings related to property-value and crime impacts of the supportive housing programs in Denver. Some of the types of structures rehabilitated are similar in both dispersed and supportive housing programs, whereas some in the supportive program are of much larger scale; the sponsors and operators and the clientele clearly are different. As in chapter 6, the house price and crime-impact models allow us to obtain both overall measures of the average impact of all supportive housing analysis sites in Denver and stratified measures of how impacts vary across areas or subsets of analysis sites. We then apply information obtained from the homeowner focus group participants to add context to our statistical assessment of the impacts and probe potential causal mechanisms.

Overall, we found that for the set of 11 small-scale supportive housing facilities scrutinized, the property-value impact analysis was associated with a *positive* impact on single-family house prices in the surrounding neighborhood. In general after the opening of the facility, the area within 1,001 to 2,000 feet of a supportive housing analysis site experienced both an increase in general level and an upward trend in house prices relative to the prices of similar homes not near such facilities. This reversed a *relative decline* in house prices (compared with elsewhere in the census tract) that existed in these areas prior to the presence of the supportive housing site.

This positive relationship between this set of supportive housing facilities and house prices in the range of 1,001–2,000 feet was manifested for all sorts of neighborhoods, though less so in ones with lower property values. Lower-value neighborhoods also evinced more mixed effects at closer proximity, whereas other neighborhoods sometimes showed negative price impacts at 500-foot proximity. However, because sets of our supportive sites tended to fall within a common category for multiple neighborhood stratification criteria, we stress that we cannot unambiguously distinguish here between results that were generated by a certain type of neighborhood or by a set of supportive housing sites that differed systematically in their clientele or operators.

Regarding crime impacts during the 1990–97 period for the set of 14 facilities analyzed, rates of all types of reported offenses initially were higher in areas where supportive housing was developed than in other areas in Denver not near such facilities. We found no statistically significant changes overall in the rates of reported property, criminal mischief, and disorderly conduct crimes before and after a supportive facility opened, at any distance. We did, however, identify a modestly statistically significant, direct relationship between the rates of violent and total crime reports and 500-foot proximity to a supportive site after it opened.

Further stratified analyses revealed that these relationships emanated solely from the larger supportive housing facilities, not those conventionally thought to house the least desirable clientele. The issue of facility scale and impact thus comes to the fore. The bulk of the statistical and focus group evidence suggests, however, that it was not the residents of these large facilities who were perpetrators of crime. Rather, large facilities attracted more crime because they provided a mass of prospective victims and/or eroded the collective efficacy of the neighborhood.

Quantitative Estimates of Property-Value Impacts of Supportive Housing

We start by examining the results of our basic property-value-impact model, which was designed to measure the average impact of the sample of 11 supportive housing analysis sites across the entire city.[1] As before, we summarized the regression results in graphical form.[2] Because there were no statistically significant impacts of supportive housing observed at distances closer than 1,000 feet, figure 7.1 depicts price trends only within the 1,001–2,000 foot range.

Figure 7.1 shows the relative percentage differences in prices over time in single-family home sales prices in proximity to supportive housing sites, compared with baseline prices for similar dwellings elsewhere in the same census tracts but not within 2,000 feet of any supportive housing sites. The figure's vertical axis indicates the percentage differences in house prices over the baseline. The horizontal axis indicates time, starting with the beginning of our study period, the first quarter of 1987. The dotted line indicates a representative starting date chosen as the point of first occupancy of the archetypal supportive facility. Therefore, the section of the graph to the left of the dotted line is the estimated relative price pattern *before* the supportive housing site was occupied, and the section to the right of the dotted line is the price pattern *after* the site was occupied.

Sales Price Patterns before Supportive Housing Sites Are in Operation

In Denver, there was a systematic tendency for our sample of supportive housing sites developed during the early 1990s to be located in relatively lower-valued or declining pockets within census tracts. Home prices within 500 feet of areas that were to be acquired for

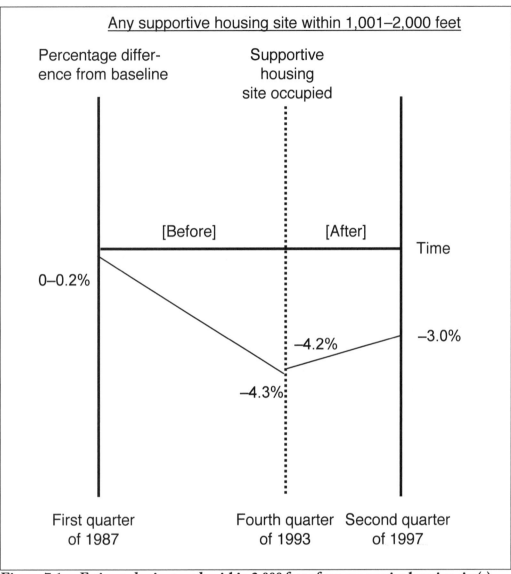

Figure 7.1. Estimated price trends within 2,000 feet of any supportive housing site(s), Denver (relative to baseline areas of same tracts not within 2,000 feet)

Note: There were no statistically significant impacts of supportive housing observed at distances closer than 1,000 feet. Baseline prices control for seasonal and countywide quarterly trends, plus housing stock characteristics.

Source: Authors' calculations.

supportive facilities were 8 percent lower, on average, than prices of comparable homes elsewhere in the census tract. The corresponding estimates for the distance rings of 501–1,000 feet and 1,001–2,000 feet were, respectively, roughly 5 and 2 percent.

Interviews with Denver key informants provided two potential (but not mutually exclusive) explanations for this finding. First, providers of supportive housing often acquired vacant, sometimes deteriorated property for their facilities. Insofar as these properties had been generating negative externalities for the surrounding neighborhood for oftentimes considerable periods prior to their acquisition, the neighborhoods near these properties tended to have lower values.

Second, as was noted in chapter 4, the purchasing strategies of supportive housing developers were a source of potential self-selection bias. Because these developers were likely to search more intensively for buildings to purchase in areas where "they could get the most building for the money," thereby stretching their scarce programmatic resources as far as possible, supportive housing facilities would tend to be located in less expensive niches within census tracts. Developers also would search in such areas because they expected less opposition there (Pendall 1999).

Property-Value Impacts for Denver Neighborhoods as a Group

The regressions using all home sales near the 11 study sites[3] showed statistically significant evidence of *positive property price impacts* associated with the opening of this particular set of supportive housing facilities as a group, at least at some distance. During the late 1980s to mid–1990s for some distance ranges, we observed overall increases in property value levels and trends as a result of proximity to this group of supportive housing sites under investigation, with greater numbers of proximate supportive housing beds magnifying the apparent beneficial impacts.

We reiterate that these results were produced by a sample of small-scale special care facilities; no correctional facilities or homeless shelters could be analyzed in the property impacts analysis. Nevertheless, because a wide range of special care programs is represented (see table 5.10), no conclusions should be drawn about the impacts of particular program types.

The impacts of proximity to one or more supportive housing sites are shown in the post-opening segment of figure 7.1. After a supportive housing facility was occupied, sales prices within 1,001–2,000 feet reversed their previous relative downward trend evinced before occupancy. Fourteen quarters after occupancy, prices at this distance were only 3.0 percent less than the baseline within the census tract; immediately preceding occupancy, they were 4.3 percent less. Had the pre-occupancy trend persisted, by the second quarter of 1997 the properties within this distance ring would have been 6.5 percent below baseline. Thus, on average across all 11 supportive sites opening during our 1989–95 study period, sales prices 3.5 years after opening were about 3.5 percentage points higher within 1,001–2,000 feet of a supportive facility than they would have been in the facility's absence.

Unlike the case of dispersed public housing in Denver, here we could discern no threshold effects. On the contrary, there was no indication in the sample as a whole that the above-mentioned positive impacts were attenuated when there were either more sites or more units in this range of 1,001–2,000 feet. Any interpretation of concentration effects for this sample must be treated with extreme caution, however, because (1) there was little variation in the number of proximate sites, and (2) the distribution of observations by number of units was highly bimodal and generated by only a few sites; see table 5.10.

Why were there no price impacts at closer ranges? What is curious about the results given above is that statistically significant impacts for the overall sample were observed only 1,001–2,000 feet from the supportive housing sites, not closer. We believe that these results are consistent with the hypothesis of "countervailing externalities." We hypothesize that supportive housing sites may (depending on neighborhood context, structure, facility scale, clientele, and management) generate several distinct types of externalities, some positive and others negative, some extending relatively short distances and others considerably farther. At certain distances where both positive and negative externalities are operating they can, in effect, cancel each other out, yielding no net effects on observed sales prices at that range. But at other distances, only one sort of externality may predominate.

Interviews with our key informants and reviews of the literature suggest that several potentially countervailing externalities may be at play when it comes to supportive housing, each with its own associated range of impact:

- Increased parking and traffic congestion: a negative externality, usually confined close to the site.
- Resident behavior (e.g., noise, littering) on-site: a negative externality, usually confined close to the site.
- Resident behavior (e.g., panhandling, crime) off-site: a negative externality, which may extend far from the site.
- Rehabilitation or construction of the facility: a positive externality signaling investment in the area, a spark to investor confidence, and possibly the removal of a blighting prior use of the property, which may extend far from the site.
- Upkeep of the property: This could be a positive or negative externality, depending on its intensity and in comparison with others on the block face, usually confined within sight of the facility.

Here, our statistical observations are consistent with the notion that positive externalities associated with improving the property before the supportive facility opens and/or comparatively superior maintenance of the facility during operation predominate at farther distances. By contrast, at closer proximity, positive and negative externalities are countervailing to the point where either no net impact is produced or a slightly negative impact emerges (as in the higher-value neighborhoods). These results foreshadow those of our Section 8 property-value-impact model reported in chapter 8. This notion of countervailing externalities is an important finding, which we discuss at greater length in chapter 9.

Property-Value Impacts for Different Types of Neighborhoods and Supportive Housing Sites

We replicated each of the three specifications of our property-value-impact models for different clusters of census tracts in Denver. We stratified census tracts according to the racial and ethnic composition,[4] median 1990 home values, and real changes in median home values from 1990 to 1996. As before, the stratification by median home value proved most robust. Note, however, that due to small sample sizes this geographic stratification simultaneously produced oftentimes-idiosyncratic sets of supportive housing programs and operators, which fell within similar clusters of neighborhoods categorized by multiple criteria. Thus here, unlike the analyses of DHA dispersed housing and Section 8, we could not unambiguously examine the consistency of the same assisted housing program in different neighborhood contexts.

The overall positive price effects attributed to proximity of 1,001–2,000 feet to supportive housing beds in the overall model occurred consistently across neighborhood values, but not in equal magnitudes. The relationship in the lowest tercile of values[5] was weaker, such that over time property values were boosted by smaller amounts than in higher-value neighborhoods. After 2.5 years, values are estimated to have been about 5 percent higher within 1,001–2,000 feet of a supportive housing facility, across all ranges of neighborhood values. After five years, however, housing prices in the lower-value stratum had inflated in this range by 3 percentage points less.

By contrast, within 500 feet of a facility there were no consistent impacts in lower-value neighborhoods, but some negative property value impacts in other ones. The estimated magnitude of impact was considerable: a 3 percent annual reduction in value. Neither the scale of facilities nor the range of clientele differed substantially in the lower-and higher-value neighborhoods; see table 5.10.

However, we caution again that, given such small samples, we could not be sure that we identified a contextual difference or consequences of one or more idiosyncratic sites in the stratum. Our further explorations revealed that the negative impacts were produced only at two small-scale sites: Hilltop (developmentally disabled clientele) and Speer (chronically mentally ill clientele). The latter site was noticeably deficient in upkeep from other properties on the block face, according to our windshield survey.

The lower-value neighborhoods evinced an interesting pattern suggesting mixed impacts from supportive housing in the range of 501–1,000 feet. In the short run, the development of a supportive housing facility provided a small boost to home prices but reduced the trend in prices thereafter more than otherwise would have occurred. In the case of a typical eight-bed facility, the initial fillip was about 1 percent, but this would have completely eroded by 2.5 years. By the end of 5 years, property values were a bit more than 1 percent lower than in comparable areas with no proximate supportive housing. There also was an interaction effect here, with greater numbers of supportive housing units (beds) in the vicinity leading to a more rapid falloff in prices after the initial boost. This suggests negative concentration effects consistent with those reported in other chapters.

Thus, the totality of statistical evidence regarding the variability of property-value impacts of supportive housing across various sorts of Denver neighborhoods is mixed, and simple conclusions are not possible. We stress, however, that context and concentration effects can be observed much less clearly, given the small sample of supportive housing facilities we were able to analyze.

Key Qualitative Insights of Focus Groups Regarding Property-Value Impacts

Awareness of Supportive Housing Sites

Since the enactment of the Denver Large Residential Care Use Ordinance in 1993, which stipulated that developers of supportive housing must notify affected neighborhood associations and that all licensed supportive sites must be listed publicly, presumably both the market and homeowners have ample opportunity to gain information on the location and characteristics of supportive housing facilities. It is thus understandable that the statistical results suggest that the real estate market in Denver is receiving consistent and accurate information regarding the location of supportive housing sites and that house pricing systematically reflects this information. The fact that the effect seems to vary across sites and tracts may merely indicate that no generalizations about impact can be made without the particulars of the site (e.g., its operator and clientele) and its surrounding neighborhood context, as opposed to inaccurate market information.

It is fascinating, then, that four out of our nine homeowner focus groups did not specifically mention the (one or more) supportive housing facilities we knew to be operating within 2,000 feet of the participants' homes. In other groups, unsolicited complaints were made about some supportive housing facilities, but other sites in the vicinity were either not mentioned or participants volunteered that these other sites were "not a problem." This suggests that many (but not all) operators of supportive housing facilities have been successful, through their maintenance, tenant screening, and management efforts, in blending their facilities into the larger community. Generalizations about "supportive housing" impacts are thus risky.

Comments about Supportive Housing Sites

Our focus groups consistently emphasized elements of neighborhood quality of life that are relevant to supportive housing developers and policymakers alike: the physical condition of the neighborhood, the presence of numerous or poorly kept rental properties, social cohesion, increased traffic, and public safety. In turn, when operators of supportive facilities seem able to address many of these issues effectively, the supportive housing facility becomes virtually invisible to nearby homeowners as a major determinant of their neighborhood quality of life.

This interpretation is consistent with the DHA dispersed housing effects presented in chapter 6, and with scholarly literature that has found that people's often negative expectations about what supportive housing will bring to the neighborhood are typically not substantiated after the fact (Cook 1997). Denver homeowners participating in our focus groups attest to this:

> At the time it [the home for Cerebral Palsy children] went in, we were very concerned about therapists coming and going, but there's been no problems. The house is right across the street from us. It's been there for eight years. We never noticed any increased traffic. (Respondent, Hilltop)

> They're low impact—there isn't a spotlight on them existing on the block. (Respondent, Speer)

> They had to vote on a half-way house—Hazel Court—it is a home for women with schizophrenia. We don't have any trouble with them. I live right in back of the house. (Respondent, Harvey Park)

> I think that one of the things that people worry about is that this is okay with exactly what they [the developer of supportive housing] said, but when are they going to shove something in that's not acceptable? They didn't shove anything else in and that worked. Yet, I'd hate to see if they brought something else in—like if they would bring criminals in, [or] a halfway house. (Respondent, Hilltop)

Participants repeatedly volunteered, however, that nearby supportive housing facilities negatively influenced the quality of neighborhood life through one or more of the dimensions, but particularly in terms of impacts on property values and safety:

> But if I were to show my house, I might not choose to tell them [prospective buyers] that [supportive housing] is what is there. (Respondent, Hilltop)

> I don't have anything against halfway houses but I don't think they should be across the street from an elementary school. (Respondent, Speer)

> When the registered pedophiles moved in—convicted felons—we weren't told. This is my neighborhood and I want them out. (Respondent, Harvey Park)

Moreover, respondents from several neighborhoods indicated that although they understood the need for supportive housing, they were concerned that some neighborhoods disproportionately shouldered the burden of providing these accommodations. This concern is illustrated by the following comments:

> I guess that another thing that our [Park Hill] Neighborhood Association is always concerned about is that they have taken unfair advantage of our part of the city. They have put all of the group homes here and not just mental health but also criminal offenders and they are not well supervised. The concept is good but they've put them all in the same neighborhoods and they don't spread them out. Park Hill has become the beneficiary—a kind of dumping grounds in a lot of ways because of the attitude of more popular, more wealthy neighborhoods that said, "We don't want those kind of people living here."

They are dumping these people on our neighborhoods where we have lived for years and years. None of us makes tons of money, but for example, how many halfway houses are in Cherry Creek [a wealthy Denver area]? How many are there in Washington Park? (Respondents, South Park Hill)

Quantitative Estimates of Crime Impacts of Supportive Housing

Public safety was uniformly viewed by our focus groups as a key component of the quality of life in a neighborhood. Given these attitudes, results of the statistical models of supportive housing crime impacts take on added saliency. We start by examining the results of our model designed to measure the *average* impact across the entire city of our analysis sample of 14 supportive housing facilities, which were not close to any other facility before they opened and commenced operations between 1992 and 1995. Recall from chapter 5 that this sample only modestly overlapped with that employed for the property value analysis, so one should not attempt to compare results across crime and property-value impact analyses.

Crime Trends before Supportive Housing Sites Are in Operation

There was a systematic tendency for our analysis sample of supportive housing sites to be developed in areas already evincing comparatively higher crimes than other neighborhoods. The levels of reports of property crimes, violent crimes, criminal mischief, and total crime within 501–1,000 feet of the areas where these facilities were placed were 42 to 48 percent higher, on average, than those in other areas—though crime rates within 500 feet of our analysis sites were no different. In the case of disorderly conduct, the differences were even more dramatic: in the range of 501–1,000 feet of our analysis sites they were twice as high, and in the range of 1,001–2,000 feet they were 60 to 75 percent higher than in other areas.

These results strongly confirm the hypothesis given in chapter 4 that there are strong forces leading to the self-selection of sites into areas evincing higher crime initially. The implication is that simple, cross-sectional regressions relating locations of supportive housing sites and neighborhood crime rates will likely overstate the causal impact of the former because they fail to control for the self-selection bias, unless they employ the pre/post specification used here.

Moreover, there were clear spatial patterns in several rates of reported crimes. The coefficient of our spatial lag variable was strongly positive and statistically significant ($p <$ .01) for violent crime and criminal mischief, and less so for disorderly conduct and property crime ($p <$ .10). This shows that there is a strong correlation between these crime rates in nearby (up to 15,000 feet) neighborhoods, a finding that has been observed before (Griffith 1987; Anselin 1992; Bailey and Gatrell 1995; Morenoff, Sampson, and

Raudenbush 2001). It also indicates that cross-sectional regression studies of crime that do not control for such spatial autocorrelation may face serious econometric problems.

Crime Impacts for Denver Neighborhoods as a Group

The regressions measuring the average effect of the 14 crime analysis sites as a whole showed no evidence of any impacts within any distance of an operating supportive housing facility for all types of reported crimes, when using the statistical significance levels conventionally employed. We did, however, identify a modestly statistically significant ($p < .10$) direct relationship between trends in the rates of violent and total crime reports and 500-foot proximity to a supportive housing site. The parameter estimates were large enough to warrant further exploration.

Crime Impacts for Different Types of Neighborhoods and Supportive Housing Sites

As before, we stratified our sample into several subsets of neighborhoods, but none proved revealing. In particular, it did not appear that the crime impacts of supportive housing in the lower-value and higher-value neighborhoods differed systematically; neither evinced the aforementioned patterns for total and violent crime reports.

The variation in the nature of the facilities in our analysis sample permitted some additional sorts of stratification; see table 5.11. The first involved examining crime impacts from the supportive housing what we presumed might represent the most threatening clientele: the community correctional facility, the substance abuse rehabilitation facility, and two facilities for the chronically mentally ill. To our surprise, they did not manifest any apparent effects on violent crime, or any other type of crime.

The second test involved examining large-scale facilities. Recall that, unlike our property impacts analysis, here our sample involved several large facilities housing various types of clientele (cf. tables 5.10 and 5.11). Five facilities contained 53 beds or more, with a maximum of 164 beds. It was this stratum that clearly was associated with the negative crime impacts in a statistically significant fashion. Magnitudes were impressive as well. Indeed, they suggest that total crime report rates near these large supportive housing facilities increased by about 30 percent of the sample mean each year after opening; the comparable figure for violent crime report rates was 40 percent.

These findings provide important implications for the standards limiting the scale of supportive housing facilities. Recall from chapter 2 that Denver's Large Residential Facilities Ordinance of 1993 established limits on Special Care Facilities of 40 beds and Community Corrections Facilities of 60 beds (40 in some contexts). However, all the facilities in our analysis stratum vastly exceeded these limits because they were approved before the ordinance went into effect. This timing appears unfortunate, indeed, because these larger facilities were associated with significant upsurges of crime nearby.

The Mechanisms of Crime Impacts

Though there is no extant theory about how supportive housing might influence crime, it is reasonable to posit both direct and indirect links. The direct link is conventionally articulated; residents of supportive housing facilities are more prone toward criminal activity than would be occupants of the structure were it developed "generically." The plausibility of this direct link depends upon the facility's clientele. The residents of a hospice or elderly care center, for example, may pose little risk of committing crimes.

However, if the residents of the supportive housing facility in question are chronically mentally ill, recovering alcoholics or drug addicts, and/or criminal offenders, these traits indeed may be predictive of a higher future propensity toward some types of criminal behaviors, even if nothing more severe than disorderly conduct. Given that the routine activity spaces of these residents may be locally constrained due to limited income and the nature of their special needs, this alleged criminality would then be manifested in the immediate environs.

One indirect link between supportive housing and neighborhood crime may transpire through its effects on collective efficacy. The collective efficacy of the neighborhood—its capacity to enforce norms of civil, lawful behavior through informal social controls—has been cited as a key vehicle for deterring crime (Sampson, Raudenbush, and Earls 1997). Residents of supportive housing, especially if they are disabled in some fashion, may be more difficult compared with a generic resident for the community to enlist as an instrument of collective efficacy. Heumann's (1996) study of mixing mentally ill and recovering substance abusers amid elderly residents of an apartment complex gives an illustration of the eroding collective efficacy hypothesis.

Another indirect link may occur because the clientele of the supportive housing facility is particularly prone to victimization. Developmentally disabled or frail elderly residents in particular may prove to be attractive targets for criminals, or a group home for troubled teenagers may be targeted by a violent gang because it houses members of a rival group. This indirect mechanism suggests that, though crime rates may rise in the vicinity of supportive housing, the victims will primarily be residents of the facility, not its neighbors.

Of course, there may be a spurious relationship between crime reports and offenses. Neighbors of supportive facilities may be more likely to call the police than other households who witness the same behaviors, perhaps because their sensitivity to crime or the general level of anxiety is heightened.

We emphasize that our statistical method cannot definitively identify mechanisms—but it is suggestive, for three reasons. First, our pre/post model makes it very likely that some aspect of the presence of a large supportive housing site in the area is contributing to this effect, not spurious events. The finding provides additional support that the coefficients for the post-opening crime trend variables grew progressively smaller in magnitude and statistical significance when one moved farther away from the site. This is consistent with the existence of highly localized negative externalities created in the vicinity of large supportive housing facilities.

Second, one would hypothesize that if the supportive housing residents themselves were perpetrating crimes, the set of facilities housing the most threatening clientele would have evinced the greatest impacts. However, even with the contrary finding we cannot reject this possibility completely, for it may be that all sorts of clientele become more difficult to supervise and manage behaviorally in larger facilities.

Third, if it were the case that neighbors of larger facilities merely grew more prone to report crimes or purported crimes, then we would not expect such a large impact on violent crime. Arguably, violent crime has the least reporting error.

We believe that the evidence is most consistent with the hypothesis that larger supportive housing facilities attract criminals, for either of two reasons: lower collective efficacy or more potential victims. Neighbors may sense that they cannot possibly exercise effective informal social controls over public spaces around such a massive facility, so their vital sense of collective efficacy is eroded (Sampson, Raudenbush, and Earls 1997; Morenoff, Sampson, and Raudenbush 2001). Moreover, criminals may be attracted to the site because they see a large mass of relatively defenseless potential victims or low collective efficacy in the area. To explore the causal connections further, we employed data derived from a series of focus group discussions with homeowners residing in close proximity to supportive housing.

Key Qualitative Insights of Focus Groups Regarding Crime Impacts

Analysis of our focus group data leaves no doubt about the importance homeowners place on safety and the *potential* impact on crime that supportive housing may have. However, the link between threats to public safety and supportive housing was not generally made. Although homeowners in five of the nine groups were aware of the supportive facilities located in their neighborhoods, a number of homeowners were adamant in their acceptance of both the facilities and their residents. Several focus groups attested to this acceptance, most clearly represented by the comment of a homeowner in a high-income white neighborhood:

> At the time it [the home for Cerebral Palsy children] went in, we were very concerned . . . but there've been no problems. The house is right across the street from us. It's been there for eight years.

There were only three instances where feared or perceived criminal behavior of any sort was linked directly to supportive housing, and there was no pattern linking these comments to larger facilities. One comment made by a homeowner from a near-downtown, predominantly renter-occupied neighborhood with many supportive housing facilities was revealing:

The city doesn't show much respect for the schools. They put a halfway home for criminals right across the street from the Catholic elementary school. I don't have anything against halfway homes but I don't think that they should be across the street from an elementary school.

Another homeowner in an upper-income, racially diverse neighborhood asserted that a fear of violent behavior emanating from supportive facilities was justified, given what occurred in an adjacent neighborhood:

[They] had a home for criminal-rehab type of people. That is what I feel does not belong in a neighborhood. I feel that [facility] should never be allowed, and by virtue of the fact that there was one [in the neighborhood], a young lady was killed.

This quotation raises an intriguing issue. If (1) public safety is salient to homeowners, (2) they know instances when public safety is less than satisfactory, and (3) most of them know about the existence of a supportive facility nearby, why did they *not* make more of the link between crime and supportive housing, given our strong statistical results? We consider three non–mutually exclusive potential explanations.

First, in a regime of declining overall crime rates, as was the case in Denver, deleterious crime impacts associated with a supportive housing facility may have less salience for neighbors. Participants in all but one of the focus groups agreed that crime had fallen in their neighborhood "over the past few years." It may be the case that, in such a context, neighbors are less worried that crime did not fall as fast as it likely would have in the absence of proximate supportive housing. Second, in many of the neighborhoods that were examined there are likely other, more visible geographic loci of criminal activity besides supportive housing facilities about which to express concerns. For example, poorly managed rental properties were sometimes blamed in our groups for eroding public safety. In the words of a participant living in a working class, heavily Hispanic neighborhood:

There are some rental properties that are not controlled, and too many people move in— there were sometimes five families living there, with lots of partying and drug dealers.

Ironically, other forms of subsidized housing were also mentioned as a source of crime. Several participants from a working-class, predominantly black area cited a "Section 8 home" as the center of gang activity, noise, and "fast street life" in their neighborhood. A participant in an upper-income, racially diverse area echoed this theme: "There's been crack houses set up in some of these Section 8 houses."

A main thoroughfare with multiple entertainment venues was seen as an "importer" of crime into the area, as revealed by several comments from homeowners living in an upper-income, racially diverse area:

When I came here my friends asked if I was afraid—even now, they say, "You're just two blocks away from Colfax Avenue."

I don't like what happens with people coming off Colfax and pulling up in front of my house.

It's not traffic, it's prostitution. There's a motel down the street that has given us a lot of problems. I called the police the other night.

There was some unfortunate [crack cocaine] traffic associated with the bars and abandoned bars. . . .

In addition to the above-mentioned problems, homeowners residing in three of the neighborhoods near large supportive housing facilities identified absentee landlords, high densities, substance abuse, gangs, unsupervised teens, transients, and the influx of non-English-speaking immigrants as contributing to crime and safety concerns in their neighborhoods—not supportive housing. These homeowners' comments suggest that a potential causal link between supportive housing and crime may be obscured if there are other visible candidates or significant changes occurring within the neighborhood to which residents attribute patterns of crime.

Third, there may be no *actual* relationship between supportive housing facilities and proximate crime rates—especially in the case of small facilities—and this is why our respondents rarely made the link. When operators of supportive facilities are able to address neighborhood quality-of-life issues effectively, the supportive housing facility apparently becomes virtually "invisible" to nearby homeowners. Indeed, in four of our nine groups the issue of supportive housing never arose, even though we knew all participants lived within 1,400 feet of such a facility. Of interest, three of these groups were located in areas housing only one small facility, but one was close to a facility housing more than 100 residents.

We believe that these comments by homeowners (or, more precisely, their absence) are inconsistent with the hypothesis that supportive housing residents are major sources of crime. Unfortunately, the focus groups did not definitively disentangle whether it was a mass of potential victims or an erosion of collective efficacy that more likely generated our observed statistical patterns. There was, however, a suggestion that homeowners in neighborhoods near large facilities perceived their own inability to maintain social control. In one neighborhood that experienced gang activity, teens hanging out, and a considerable influx of immigrants, residents expressed the following concerns regarding neighborhood social control:

Sometimes we don't have control over what happens in the neighborhood. You go with the flow or you leave.

What we need to do is be better informed about how we can be effective. Need someone to do it but there's a sense of frustration.

We feel a little helpless.

Unfortunately, we are left to speculate about the degree to which the large supportive housing facility may have contributed to this apparent lack of collective efficacy. To our knowledge, we are the first to hypothesize a link between large-scale supportive housing facilities and crime through victimization and collective efficacy; more research is clearly warranted.

Conclusion

Our findings suggest that the fears commonly expressed by residents faced with the prospect of a supportive housing facility being developed nearby may be unfounded, at least in the case of scattered, small-scale facilities. Although our archival reconnaissance, key informant interviews, and focus groups identified cases where particular supportive housing facilities are reputedly causing problems for a neighborhood, these cases clearly are not the typical pattern in Denver. Overall, we found no statistical evidence in the sites we examined that the development of small-scale supportive housing generally reduced property values or increased rates of crime reports nearby.

On the contrary, widely separated, small-scale supportive housing as observed in Denver can generate a positive fillip to property values. We believe that this results when a developer succeeds in rehabilitating a dilapidated property and subsequently maintains and manages it well.[6] It is less clear, however, if these generalizations are robust in all sorts of neighborhood contexts. Because sets of our supportive sites tended to fall within a common category for multiple neighborhood stratification criteria, we cannot unambiguously distinguish between property-value impacts that are generated by a certain type of neighborhood or by a subset of supportive housing sites that differ systematically in their clientele or operators.

We found a pattern of significantly greater reporting rates of violent crimes and total crimes within 500 feet of large (53 beds or more) supportive housing sites after they open. Ironically, none of these sites would have been approved had Denver's Large Residential Care Use Ordinance been enacted a few years earlier.

We believe that the weight of the evidence suggests, however, that it is *not* the residents of these large supportive housing facilities who are perpetrating these crimes, despite conventional wisdom to the contrary. There is little doubt that supportive housing residents and crime remain linked in the minds of some Denver homeowners. When our focus groups expressed concerns about supportive housing, it was typically within the context of specific types of reputedly dangerous clientele, yet we could find no evidence that facilities housing criminal offenders, recovering substance abusers, or the mentally ill increased crime nearby.

Several focus groups, which we knew to live near such clientele, voiced no concerns. Indeed, the topic never arose in most of our discussions. Other groups were fervent about "nice" supportive housing near them where residents "gave no problems to anyone." Our focus group participants more often voiced vociferous complaints that poorly maintained and managed rental housing, unsavory commercial establishments, gang activity, substance abuse, unsupervised teens, and transients were the prime sources of crime, not supportive housing.

We think it more likely, therefore, that the apparent crime impact occurs because large facilities either provide a pool of potential victims or make it difficult for the neighborhood to maintain collective efficacy. Though this likely causation cannot be stated conclusively, homeowners near such facilities offered unambiguous commentary about their lack of social control in the area.

Notes

1. Overall, the model performed extremely well. The adjusted R^2 was 0.82. Not surprisingly given the exceptional sample sizes, virtually all of the [*Struct*], [*Tract*], and [*Quarter*] control variables evinced coefficients that were statistically significant. All the coefficients of the [*Struct*] characteristics of homes proved to have the expected signs.

2. In graphs, we show only the effect of regression coefficients significant at the 95 percent confidence level (two-tailed test).

3. All regressions also used all sales that were not within 2,000 feet of any supportive site.

4. White tracts were defined as those containing less than 5 percent black and 5 percent Hispanic populations. Black and Hispanic tracts were those that were substantially integrated (20–49 percent black or Hispanic) as well as those that were majority black or Hispanic.

5. We had six of our analysis sites in this lowest tercile: Berkeley, Clayton, and the Montbello sites; see table 5.10.

6. This finding is consistent with those of previous studies; see Hogan 1996, chap. 7.

8

The Impacts of Section 8 in Baltimore County

Scattered-site public housing programs and supportive housing programs, such as those in Denver analyzed in the last two chapters, are distinguished by the fact that there is a particular *building* in the neighborhood that is earmarked for exclusive use by assisted tenants and is operated by a public or nonprofit agency. In contrast, the Section 8 certificate and voucher program provides assistance to tenants who typically live in privately operated apartment buildings that have a socioeconomic mix of residents. In principle, assisted housing provided under the tenant-based Section 8 program therefore should be less visible to the neighborhood than that provided under the site-based approach.

As we shall see in this chapter, our findings related to the property-value impacts of Section 8 households in Baltimore County suggest that this is not the case in some neighborhood contexts.[1] We first provide a graphical portrayal of the results of our property-value-impact statistical models. We then analyze whether these aggregate patterns persist over various neighborhood types and concentrations of Section 8 households. Finally, we provide a richer view of these quantitative findings by juxtaposing them against results of our four Baltimore County homeowner focus groups.

Overall, the results for Baltimore County Section 8 housing echo a theme established earlier in the cases of Denver dispersed public housing or supportive housing: Impacts depend on context and concentration. Across the entire sample, there was an average *upward impact* on prices associated with the occupancy of Section 8 households within 500 feet of a single-family home sale. The impact changed to a relative *decline* in post-occupancy house prices, however, if there were more than six Section 8 sites or eight units within 500 feet of the same house. Smaller negative impacts were observed at distances up to 2,000 feet from the sale, generally in proportion to the number of nearby Section 8 units.

As was the case in Denver, Section 8 households did not have the same impacts on all types of neighborhoods in Baltimore County. Positive price effects occurred only in neighborhoods with higher house values, but they turned to negative effects here if the concentration of Section 8 sites or households exceeded three within 500 feet of the home sale. Negative price impacts were the norm in neighborhoods with lower-value homes, even those with only one Section 8 unit within 2,000 feet. Our focus groups suggest that homeowners' perceptions that their area is "vulnerable" are associated with these strong negative impacts.

Quantitative Estimates of Property-Value Impacts of Section 8

We start by examining regression results for all our analysis sites across Baltimore County.[2] The net effects of the model coefficients are easier to see when portrayed graphically. Figure 8.1 shows the estimated home sales price trends within 1,000 feet of any Section 8 site in Baltimore County for the study period, based on the estimated (statistically significant) coefficients of our basic model (as was shown in chapter 4).[3] Figure 8.2 portrays results from a variant of this model that allows both the level and trend of post-occupancy impact to vary with the number of Section 8 sites. The trends are plotted before and after occupancy of an archetypical Section 8 site, computed at the median of the occupancy dates—the fourth quarter of 1993—shown by the dotted vertical lines in figures 8.1 and 8.2.

Sales Price Trends before Section 8 Sites Are Occupied by Assisted Households

As figures 8.1 and 8.2 make clear, the neighborhoods into which Baltimore County Section 8 households moved tended to be valued somewhat lower than other neighborhoods within the same census tract. By the fourth quarter 1993, just prior to occupancy by a representative Section 8 household, prices for areas within 500 feet of the future site were 4.1 to 6.6 percent lower (depending on the specification; see figures 8.1 and 8.2). There were no statistically significant indicators that areas beyond 500 feet from an eventual Section 8 site were priced any differently from other locations in the tract.

These results indicate that there was a tendency for Section 8 households to locate in weaker market niches of Baltimore County, independent of any subsequent impacts of such choices on the neighborhoods thereafter. From this information we are unable, however, to distinguish among several plausible hypotheses: (1) Landlords in declining market niches are more likely to participate in Section 8 or more actively recruit Section 8 households; (2) Section 8 voucher (not certificate) holders seek to stretch their subsidy by occupying less expensive sections of neighborhoods; (3) selective information and kin and friendship networks lead Section 8 households to cluster in the less expensive niches within neighborhoods; and (4) clusters of rental housing depress single-family house prices. Regardless, this systematic selection effect provides further support for our claims in chapter 4 that a statistical method like our pre/post model is required to make unambiguous conclusions about the causal impacts of Section 8.

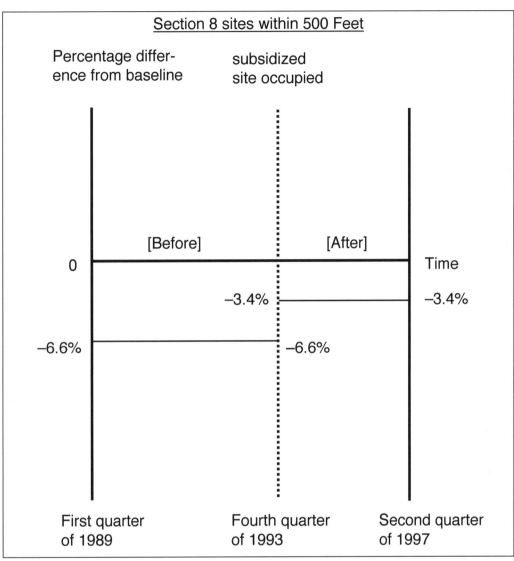

Figure 8.1. Estimated price trends within 500 feet of any Section 8 site, Baltimore County (relative to baseline areas of same tracts not within 2,000 feet)

Note: Baseline prices control for seasonal and countywide quarterly trends, plus housing stock characteristics.

Source: Authors' calculations.

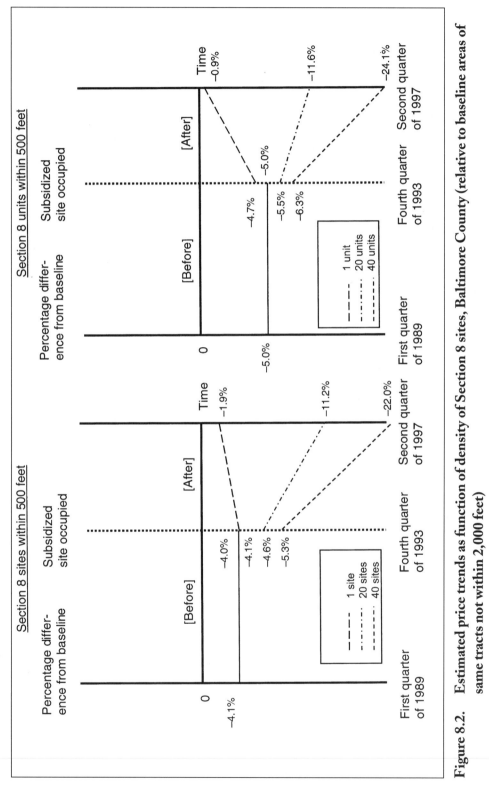

Figure 8.2. Estimated price trends as function of density of Section 8 sites, Baltimore County (relative to baseline areas of same tracts not within 2,000 feet)

Note: Baseline prices control for seasonal and countywide quarterly trends, plus housing stock characteristics.
Source: Authors' calculations

Property-Value Impacts for Baltimore County Neighborhoods as a Group

Our statistical estimates showed that, within 500 feet, there was a distinct *upward shift* in local area single-family home price patterns associated with the occupancy of a site by one or more Section 8 households. Figure 8.1 indicates that the price level within 500 feet of the occupied site was 3.4 percentage points higher compared with the level of prices in that area prior to occupancy (i.e., only 3.4 percent below the baseline after occupancy instead of 6.6 percent below). Even though the neighborhoods within 500 feet of Section 8 sites still were valued somewhat lower than elsewhere in the tract, the apparent impact of the Section 8 occupancy itself appears positive and significant, both statistically and substantively. No such positive impact was observed beyond 500 feet.

These positive effects must be qualified in important ways by considering the impacts of the *number* of Section 8 sites and occupied units nearby, not merely whether any were present or not. There proved to be a strong interaction between the post-occupancy trend in prices and the number of occupied Section 8 sites in the given distance range. As the first panel of figure 8.2 demonstrates, the greater the number of occupied Section 8 sites within 500 feet of a sale, the greater the initial shift downward in values and the greater the rate of decline thereafter. There appears to be the possibility of net *positive* price trend, however, as long as the number of sites was limited. Specifically, if the number of Section 8 sites within 500 feet remained below 6, there was a positive post-occupancy price trend.

With larger numbers of nearby sites, such as those well below the observed sample maximum of 39, the net impact on price proved substantively *negative*, both immediately following occupancy and thereafter. Figure 8.2 shows that when, for example, 20 Section 8 sites began operating within 500 feet of a home, the immediate impact was to reduce its price by half a percentage point (4.6 percent below the baseline instead of only 4.1 percent below before occupancy). Moreover, this negative impact grew over time, such that by 14 quarters after occupancy its price was 7.1 percent lower (11.2 percent vs. only 4.1 percent below the baseline) than if no Section 8 sites were nearby. These results point to a clear threshold effect: A few Section 8 sites can be good for a neighborhood, but too many can harm property values.

Similar insights are gained from consideration of the results for Section 8 unit counts, portrayed in the second panel of figure 8.2. The results for Baltimore County as a whole indicate that 500-foot proximity to a greater number of occupied Section 8 *units* (as opposed to distinct addresses) was associated with *higher* sales prices, as long as the number of units did not exceed 8. As with the first panel of this figure, the result is encouraging, inasmuch as the vast majority of observations met this criterion. Conversely, the parameters suggest that when a sale occurred within 500 feet of more than 8 units (and noting that the observed sample maximum number of Section 8 units in this range was 67), substantial price decrements were observed, especially as more time elapsed between the sale and first occupancy of the units.

Taken together, the results for the area described by a 500-foot radius from the site provide clear implications about impacts from various scales of Section 8 occupancy at a single address. At one extreme, if the area had only one Section 8 household, the estimated initial impact in the quarter after occupancy was virtually nil. Subsequently, a positive impact transpired, rising to roughly 2 to 4 percentage points after 14 quarters since the first occupancy. If the area continued to have only one address at which Section 8 tenants resided, the net impact on prices was positive until the building's occupancy reached eight Section 8 tenants, whereupon there was no estimated impact, either immediately after occupancy or thereafter.

The parameters clearly show that the net positive impacts are enhanced if more Section 8 tenants occupy a single site, as opposed to the same number of tenants scattered across an equal number of sites. As was noted above, if more than five distinct Section 8—occupied sites are present within 500 feet of a sale, there was a net negative impact on property values, both initially after occupancy and accelerating thereafter. Thus, as in the case of supportive housing in Denver, not only concentration of Section 8 tenants within a geographic area but also the *scale* at which they occupy a given building matters for neighborhood impacts.

Unlike at closer distances, no threshold effect appeared for the 501–2,000 feet range. Instead, even one Section 8 site or unit had a negative impact on home sales values in this range, reducing values there from 2 to 4 percentage points after 14 quarters. Variation in the number of Section 8 sites or units had relatively muted effects compared with those in the 500-foot range. In comparison with the results for 500 feet, these findings raise a challenging question. Why might small numbers of sites or units yield a positive price impact on properties within 500 feet while simultaneously yielding a negative impact at farther distances? This apparent conundrum disappears when we disaggregate the results by neighborhood type and find that positive and negative impacts transpire in different kinds of neighborhoods, as is explained next.

Property-Value Impacts for Different Types of Neighborhoods

We replicated our econometric specifications for different clusters of census tracts in Baltimore County, which were stratified according to racial composition,[4] median 1990 owner-occupied home values, and real changes in median values from 1990 to 1996. As in the case of Denver, the most dramatic and consistent results emerge when neighborhoods are differentiated by median home values.

These stratified regressions show that the results reported above for the aggregate, countywide portrait above require important qualification. Positive price impacts from close proximity to a small number of Section 8 sites did not occur in all sorts of Baltimore County neighborhoods, but appeared to be an exclusive feature of census tracts that ranked in the highest third of 1990 median values.[5] Moreover, the magnitude of the implied impacts was great: an extra 1-percentage-point increase in value each succeeding year after one Section 8 site or unit was occupied within 500 feet. In these areas, dramatic Section 8 threshold effects emerged, however. Our models suggest that the positive impacts quickly became attenuated the more units were occupied within 500 feet, such that the impact became nil at three units, whether located in one building or divided among three sites. With any more than this threshold, the impact on proximate home values became negative in these higher-value areas. This, in fact, rarely occurred in our sample, because the maximum number of Section 8 sites and units within 500 feet in the higher-value stratum was only four.

Negative price impacts—statistically significant impacts occurring at all distances up to 2,000 feet—appear mainly confined to neighborhoods in the lowest-median-value tercile.[6] Here the magnitude of negative impact grew with each Section 8 site or unit in the range, with no threshold. Within 500 feet, there was a 0.4-percentage-point drop; and from 501–2,000 feet, there was a 0.1-percentage-point drop in value level per occupied Section 8 site or unit.

In conjunction, these results mean that positive and negative price impacts were not being manifested in the same neighborhoods, as the countywide aggregate results might erroneously lead us to believe. Rather, the positive impacts generated by the small concentrations of Section 8 in higher-value neighborhoods were apparently outweighing the negative impacts in lower-value neighborhoods within the 500-foot range. At longer distances, only the negative impacts in lower-value neighborhoods were manifest.

What is less clear from these results is whether racial composition per se or its correlation with median property values is the driving force. As our focus group results made clear, the answer relates much more to median values. Predominantly white but lower-valued neighborhoods clearly can feel vulnerable to changes they perceive as being wrought by Section 8.

We were able to explore econometrically another intriguing racial dimension of these stratified results. Because we had information on the race of the first Section 8 household to occupy each of our analysis sites, we were able to estimate our models for all four combinations of race of first Section 8 occupant and racial composition of the neighborhood. There were virtually no substantive differences among the four race-of-Section 8-household/neighborhood cells, regardless of distance. Not only were the same coefficient sign and statistical significance patterns evinced, but also the magnitude of the price effects did not differ appreciably across the combinations.

These results lead us to conclude that it is not some racially identifiable aspect of the Section 8 program in Baltimore County that produced the strong, consistent property-value impacts we observed. Below, we hypothesize about the likely mechanism of impact.

Key Qualitative Insights of the Focus Groups Regarding Impacts

Awareness of Section 8 Sites

The results examined above make it clear that the real estate market is gaining consistent information about the location of Section 8 households in Baltimore County and is pricing proximity to these locations in a systematic fashion. In other words, Section 8 is not as "stealthy" a program as some might believe or wish. As was the case with Denver's dispersed or supportive housing, we cannot tell directly from our statistical study whether it is Section 8 per se that is signaling the market or some more visible *correlates* of Section 8, such as exterior building conditions or behavioral problems with tenants. Our focus group findings suggest that homeowners know about Section 8 but have erroneous impressions about where it is present in Baltimore County. Nevertheless, they can identify "problem rental properties," and there apparently is sufficient connection between such properties and Section 8 occupancy to produce the observed neighborhood impacts. In other words, the market does not price Section 8 housing as such, but rather some conditions associated with it. This finding has important policy implications, which will be discussed in chapter 9.

Especially in Dundalk, but at other sites as well, homeowners were highly attuned to the issue of Section 8, volunteering their concerns about the program by name without any encouragement from the group facilitator.[7] Several homeowners were so concerned about Section 8 occupancy that they told us they have personally questioned new tenants and landlords about whether their apartments were subsidized. Another participant found out about Section 8 sites from a friend who was a real estate broker. These homeowners apparently gathered quite accurate information, given that several locations they could identify during the focus group as "Section 8–occupied" were indeed so, according to our database.

Nonetheless, even the Dundalk focus group incorrectly identified some addresses as Section 8–occupied and overlooked others that in fact were so occupied. This failure to identify Section 8–occupied units accurately was typical in the other focus groups. Indeed, the Rodgers Forge group confidently (if erroneously) asserted the absence of all such sites near their homes. Thus, although some Section 8 sites clearly were known to nearby homeowners, and apparently to some local real estate agents, this direct evidence appears to be generally inaccurate and spotty, especially where few Section 8 sites were present.

Additional qualitative evidence suggests that homeowners' failure to identify proximate Section 8 apartments was directly related to the state of repair and the behavior of tenants in these units. Significantly, one of the sites that the Dundalk group failed to identify was the apartment at the center of the neighborhood from which we drew focus group participants. Our exterior inspection of this unit revealed that it was indistinguishable from all the other rowhouses in the area. In Millbrook, focus group participants commented favorably about the civic-minded behaviors of Russian immigrants who lived in a large, well-maintained garden apartment complex across the street from them, without any reference to the fact that this complex had the largest spatial concentration of Section 8 tenants in our sample and that many of these immigrants received housing subsidies.

We believe, therefore, that it is not Section 8 occupancy in and of itself, but rather the correlation (albeit imperfect) between Section 8 and "bad properties" that the market is observing (and pricing). This finding is crucial, for it implies that if policymakers succeed in developing and operating well-functioning subsidized housing it will likely be invisible to neighboring homeowners and to the market.

It is quite clear that "problem properties" were visible to homeowners and of great significance to their quality of life and the perceived value of their properties on the market. All focus groups were acutely aware of rental properties that were poorly managed and maintained, and whose occupants engaged in visibly uncivil or disreputable behaviors, such as loud partying, selling drugs, or "having a lot of men hanging around." Moreover— as our key informants, the Patterson Park experience, and a national survey of public housing authorities (HUD 2001) all would have led us to predict—our focus group participants generally perceived problematic rental properties as "Section 8 apartments." Several comments by focus group participants illustrate this point:

> [There is a] Section 8 person on my street who is a headache for everyone . . . government pays the rent and this person doesn't care [about neighbors or neighborhood]. (Respondent, Twelve Trees)

> Families will be moved in [through subsidized housing programs] . . . [who] will be on welfare and will not be good neighbors. (Respondent, Rodgers Forge)

> Our tax dollars are being used for MTO [Moving to Opportunity] programs and undesirables are moving [in]. (Respondent, Rodgers Forge)

Our statistical results imply that there must be some validity to this perception in Baltimore County, for otherwise there would be no statistically significant negative relationships between sales prices and proximity to Section 8 units, at least when the number of units passes a critical amount. Our focus groups indicated that homeowners (and, presumably, prospective buyers) were extremely sensitive to rental properties with visibly problematic maintenance or tenants. They perceived (often incorrectly) that most "problem properties" housed subsidized tenants, but they apparently were not cognizant of Section 8 sites that did not exhibit these problems. They thus seemed unaware of Section 8 when it occurred in a less-vulnerable neighborhood and the occupied property created no problems. Unfortunately, in Baltimore County there apparently was a strong statistical association between Section 8 sites and problem properties, at least in the more vulnerable neighborhoods, as we explore further below.

Section 8 Impacts in More Vulnerable Neighborhoods

There were consistently negative property value impacts at all distances up to 2,000 feet from a Section 8 site in low-valued neighborhoods. Our focus groups in Twelve Trees, Millbrook, and especially Dundalk revealed much about the nature of the perceived vulnerability of such neighborhoods.

Most of the concerns suggesting neighborhood vulnerability were remarkably similar across these three sites, despite the fact that they differed dramatically in their racial composition. We interpret this as evidence that weak market values signaling a threat to the quality of neighborhood life are the key ingredient of "vulnerability" as applicable here, not racial composition.

A split in views between generations was evident, however. Older residents recalled times in the neighborhood before "central air conditioning kept everyone indoors" and when "women were home to visit during the day" that connections among neighbors seemed stronger and ties to the community ran deeper. In general, longtime residents believed that people with different values were coming into their neighborhood. These different values they attributed partly to society at large ("the rise of the 'me' decade") and partly to "a different class of people." Younger focus group participants with a less experience in their neighborhoods shared the second concern. Indeed, all age groups were concerned about an influx of owners and tenants who did not take care of their homes, attracted or committed crimes, and did not care about their neighbors.

All groups in vulnerable neighborhoods mentioned concerns about the encroachment of "the city" as bringing an increase in crime and deterioration to their neighborhoods.[8] "The city is coming closer and that is scary," said one homeowner in Dundalk. Respondents pinpointed these in-movers in particular as having different values and standards than the current residents hoped for in their neighborhood. In this regard, our focus group participants echoed themes that have arisen across the nation in the context of Section 8 (HUD 2001).

Sources of racial anxiety varied among the three neighborhoods, however. Millbrook participants were explicitly concerned about racial and cultural shifts in their community. This area had once been historically occupied by white residents but was now racially and ethnically diverse. Focus group participants, all of whom were white, supported integrated living. As one homeowner put it: "[Who lives here?] Russians, whites, blacks, Orientals . . . there is a nice mixture." They were concerned, however, about the growing concentration of racial minorities in their neighborhood. They believed that their community could no longer attract new white buyers, which depressed resale prices and encouraged a "rougher" type of new resident. More units were becoming available as longtime residents were moving who did not want to live in a neighborhood with a growing number of minorities, they noted with regret: "I lost neighbors when they [referring to minorities] moved in."

Respondents from Twelve Trees, a predominantly black-occupied community, also were very concerned about changes that they thought were contributing to physical deterioration and to a decrease in the quality of life in the neighborhood. Resident change was described as both a change in resident values and a change in the overall racial composition of the community. This group of black respondents described many of the newer (mainly black) residents as a "different culture within our culture" and feared this new resident had adverse effects on neighborhood life. Moreover, longtime residents moved to the neighborhood when the residents were predominantly white and chose the area because they desired an integrated community. They were concerned that as the racial composition shifted toward black predominance, the benefits of integrated living would be lost and property values would decrease.

It is important to note that all focus groups in the three vulnerable neighborhoods perceived that adverse influences on their neighborhood were not merely the product of broad social forces or inexorable metropolitan trends. Rather, they explicitly and consistently portrayed the real estate brokerage industry or assisted housing policies as major contributing factors to their neighborhoods' vulnerability. For example, residents of Millbrook and Twelve Trees thought that real estate and rental agents were steering minorities to their community:

> Realtors will do anything for a sale . . . they don't care if a person can keep up the house or not . . . bringing borderline buyers. (Respondent, Millbrook)

> A lot of Realtors will steer black people to Randallstown [the broader community of which Twelve Trees is a part]. (Respondent, Twelve Trees)

Dundalk and Twelve Trees groups spoke pointedly about subsidized housing as a destructive force now operating in their communities. One Dundalk homeowner put it quite clearly: "Everyone seems to say there are Section 8 houses throughout the neighborhood. People don't want to live near Section 8."

The anxiety about rental housing in general and assisted housing in particular brings together concerns about physical conditions, safety, and resident characteristics. One Dundalk participant went so far as to volunteer that what makes for a good neighborhood is having few Section 8 households. Though some participants talked about "good renters" or about how "not everyone on Section 8 does bad," rental and assisted housing was strongly perceived as associated with declining physical standards of dwellings, increased crime, and bad neighbors. In this sort of skittish neighborhood context, it is understandable that the market apparently views substantial numbers of additional Section 8 households as forces of decline.

One Dundalk respondent, however, saw Section 8 as the last resort of owners in already declining neighborhoods: "If people can't sell their home, they turn it over to the government and get Section 8." His views correspond with our statistical result that, indeed, there often is a prior condition of relative or absolute neighborhood decline in values prior to Section 8 occupancy.

Section 8 Impacts in Less Vulnerable Neighborhoods

In Rodgers Forge, focus group participants generally expressed more confidence in the future of their neighborhood and the lack of current deleterious forces, compared with other groups. Indeed, whereas the other three groups in vulnerable, lower-valued neighborhoods typically listed a dozen or more problems eroding their neighborhood's livability, those in Rodgers Forge only mentioned that some owners were building fences that violated the covenants and that there was a bit more vandalism. The group viewed their property values as remaining strong, thereby implicitly supporting and endorsing their neighborhood standards and covenants. Indeed, it was this very strength of property values, buttressed by the force of housing covenants, that led the group to believe that they were less vulnerable to the "wrong sort of people moving in," as they put it.

This high degree of confidence did not mean, however, that there was any less distaste for the prospect of assisted housing in the vicinity. Rodgers Forge respondents were united in strong opposition to assisted housing coming to their neighborhood but said (erroneously) that such housing was not currently in their neighborhood and, as such, was not a problem for them.[9] Participants believed strongly that assisted housing brought physical decay and vandalism. "When subsidized housing comes, it's bad," said one homeowner.

In a context of less neighborhood vulnerability, the Rodgers Forge focus group indicated that, despite opposition in principle to subsidized housing, there was less likelihood (1) that the relatively isolated Section 8 household would be noticed and (2) that any negative market consequences would follow. On the contrary, our econometric results clearly showed that in such higher-valued neighborhoods as Rodgers Forge the effect on sales prices within 500 feet was consistently positive if the number of Section 8 units did not exceed three.

We speculate that this positive effect may be due to the physical improvements to the dwelling that are made at the time of initial Section 8 occupancy, although unfortunately we have no direct evidence on this point from the focus group. We could go even further, and speculate that it is precisely because the Section 8 unit in question apparently was renovated and well maintained and because there were no serious behavioral issues with the Section 8 household(s) that the respondents did not think of it as a subsidized site, given the stereotypes they held about such sites.

Reactions of Homeowners in a Stagnant Housing Market

In contrast to the environment in Denver, house prices throughout most of Baltimore County increased only modestly or even declined in the 1990s. The comments made by our homeowner focus groups and their concerns about assisted housing need to be evaluated in this context. Three of the four focus group locations, Dundalk, Millbrook, and Rodgers Forge, experienced virtually no price appreciation from 1990 to 1996. We believe that such an environment can heighten homeowner sensitivity to potential threats to property values and can lead them to look for scapegoats on which to focus their frustration.

Although, overall, our focus group participants in areas with low price appreciation liked their neighborhoods and planned to stay in them, all groups were concerned about the current value of their homes and prospects for future appreciation. This concern was not only financial, but was also because property-value decline was seen as an indicator of eroding quality of neighborhood life. Across the focus groups in Baltimore County, participants attributed property-value decline to similar factors: (1) physical upkeep, (2) safety, and (3) resident values. Issues related to the physical condition of homes and yards were at the forefront for many participants, with widespread scorn for people who did not keep up their properties, particularly owners of rental units. Echoing a theme in Denver, for many focus group participants an increase in *any* amount of rental housing was seen as a harbinger of neighborhood decline, whether occupied by Section 8 tenants or not.

Groups in the neighborhoods with low price appreciation were especially anxious about neighborhood changes in terms of both physical conditions and resident characteristics and thought that these shifts would soon be manifested in slowing or declining values. Their comments projected dual themes—both high regard for neighborhood living and anxiety about the future of their valued environment and asset:

> This is a quiet, family neighborhood and we want to keep it that way. (Respondent, Millbrook)

> There are a lot of "For Sale" signs . . . that is very disturbing. (Respondent, Twelve Trees)

> When I see a house go up for sale, I get worried. (Respondent, Dundalk)

The 1994 controversy over the MTO program occurred in the middle of the stagnating housing market being experienced by most of Baltimore County. In Dundalk, one of the centers of the MTO protests, average property values had increased less than 1 percent from 1990 to 1996. Even though most areas in Dundalk were ineligible to receive MTO households because they exceeded 10 percent poverty rates in 1990, and despite the fact that no MTO households ever moved there,[10] homeowners were highly sensitized to any potential threats to property values and to the quality of life in their neighborhoods.

Four years after the controversy over MTO erupted, our focus groups indicated that many homeowners in Dundalk and elsewhere in Baltimore County continue to be alarmed by the prospect of more assisted housing entering their communities. We view such a reaction as a product of ongoing homeowner concerns regarding a wide array of changes and problems in these areas, not simply Section 8. But even if Section 8 had not been, in reality, a major contributor to these problems, it would have been difficult to develop a more welcoming environment for such a program given the unfavorable conditions in the larger housing market. If the building maintenance and tenant behavior issues had been addressed, however, it might have been possible to make assisted housing more palatable to existing homeowners. We consider this issue at greater length in the next chapter.

Mechanisms of Property-Value Impacts of Section 8

Our statistical models and focus group results for Baltimore County hold five interesting implications about the sources of impact of nearby Section 8 sites. We stress that these implications are suggestive and not definitive, and are limited to the context of Baltimore County. Further research and replication are needed to validate these claims more generally and for other areas.

First and foremost, inasmuch as there were a variety of statistically significant relationships between single-family home prices and proximity to Section 8 sites, (1) neighbors and the market as a whole were aware (with some systematic degree of accuracy) of the presence of Section 8 units in Baltimore County; and (2) one or more attributes associated with those units were quickly capitalized into property values. That the market consistently priced proximity to these units implies that the Section 8 program was visible, not necessarily because households were identified as "Section 8," but rather because there were some identifiable characteristics of Section 8 households or landlords with which they were associated.

Second, inasmuch as small numbers of occupied Section 8 units or sites within 500 feet improved the price trends subsequent to occupancy, there was support for the notion that Section 8 landlords in Baltimore County used the enhanced rental revenues gained from Section 8 to reinvest in their properties (and perhaps manage them better) more than if Section 8 had not been available, at least in higher-value neighborhoods. An additional factor might have been at play: Prospective Section 8 landlords failing to meet HUD Housing Quality Standards required for Section 8 program participation might have been required to rehabilitate their building.[11]

Third, neighborhood context mattered. The positive externality effect at close proximity to Section 8 occurred solely in higher-value census tracts, whereas negative externality effects were observed in lower-value, more vulnerable tracts. There must have been systematic, cross-neighborhood differences in one or more of the following: (1) how effective the Housing Quality Standards inspections were in triggering renovations; (2) how well Section 8 landlords maintained and managed their properties; (3) how Section 8 households behaved; (4) how likely neighbors and the market were to identify the Section 8 site, and (5) how the market evaluated the other four attributes.

Fourth, at all distances studied in low-value neighborhoods, the larger the number of Section 8 sites or units that were occupied at the time of sale, the greater the negative impact on proximate home prices. We thus found support for (nonmutually exclusive) hypotheses that (1) uncivil behaviors of the Section 8 households; (2) poor property maintenance or management by certain types of Section 8 landlords (such as those owning properties almost exclusively housing Section 8 tenants); and/or (3) class prejudices of segments of the home-buying market (which might not have been behaviorally validated by actual Section 8 sites) caused the adverse effect on property values. Inasmuch as the Baltimore County Section 8 program participants were racially diverse and we could discern no differences in impacts when white or black Section 8 households moved into either predominantly white or black-occupied neighborhoods, we could not attribute the observed effects to racial prejudices.

Fifth, the strong negative threshold effect evinced for larger concentrations of Section 8 sites within a 500-foot radius in a higher-valued area echoed the findings for Denver's dispersed public housing program. This empirical threshold may have been correlated with a "threshold of visibility." As our Rodgers Forge focus group manifested, a few Section 8 sites were not identified as such, if they were well maintained and well managed. However, if a small area exceeded the threshold, "Section 8" apparently came to be perceived as a neighborhood problem, whereupon the market reduced its property valuations accordingly.

Conclusion

Households receiving rental subsidies through the Section 8 program in Baltimore County were not located randomly across space, but rather concentrated disproportionately in the lower-value niches of local housing markets. Although we cannot identify precisely the reason for this strong selection bias, we believe that a combination of factors related to both landlord and tenant behaviors were responsible.

Despite this neighborhood selection bias, we discerned in Baltimore County a clear causal effect when Section 8 households moved into an area. The property value impacts appeared highly contingent, however, on context, concentration, and scale. The magnitude and even direction of impact depended upon the intensity at which Section 8 households moved into an area, the neighborhood market context and, to a lesser degree, the scale at which they clustered within a single building. Negative impacts extending up to 2,000 feet from any number of Section 8 sites or units were manifested in lower-valued neighborhoods, areas in which we found homeowners worried about the vulnerability of their neighborhood's quality of life. In higher-value, less vulnerable neighborhood contexts, low concentrations of Section 8 households had a positive impact on the immediate environs, although there was a low threshold value beyond which additional numbers of Section 8 households resulted in lower property values among surrounding single-family homes. A given number of Section 8–subsidized tenants produced modestly smaller consequences for a neighborhood if they occupied a single building as opposed to a larger number of sites.

Homeowners in the vicinity of Section 8 households were not reticent to express their opposition to the program because they perceived it as a threat to the stability of their neighborhoods, regardless of context. These homeowners were aware of some (but not all) the Section 8 households in their midst, but most of them "learned" of this fact by the observation of poorly maintained rental properties that often evinced uncivil behavior by their occupants. Section 8 was almost synonymous with badly managed rental properties, so anytime such a property appeared, homeowners assumed that "it must be due to Section 8." However, well-managed properties occupied by Section 8–supported households were typically "invisible" to neighboring homeowners. In concert, these findings about context, concentration, and rental management point in clear directions of programmatic reform, to which we now turn.

Notes

1. We remind the readers that we were unable to replicate our crime-impact analysis here because locations of crime reports were not made available to us.

2. Overall, the aggregated models for Baltimore County performed extremely well. The adjusted R^2s were .81 in the regressions and did not vary significantly across model specifications. Not surprisingly given the exceptional sample sizes, virtually all of the [Struct], [Tract], and [Quarter] control variables evinced coefficients that were significantly different from zero. All the coefficients of the [Struct] characteristics of homes proved to have the expected signs.

3. In figure 8.1, only coefficients statistically significant at the 95 percent confidence level are portrayed.

4. We included substantially integrated (20–49 percent black) tracts with majority-black tracts due to paucity of the latter.

5. We note that all these areas also have fewer than 5 percent black residents, though predominantly white-occupied neighborhoods are found across the value spectrum.

6. We also note that all Baltimore County neighborhoods that are 20 percent or more black-occupied fall into this category, although a much larger number of predominantly white-occupied ones do as well.

7. All homeowners in the Baltimore County focus groups were informed that HUD was the sponsor of this study. They were not told that the study involved specific programs, however, only that we wished to obtain information about the views of homeowners on the quality of life in neighborhoods.

8. Three of the four neighborhoods represented (Dundalk, Millbrook, and Rodgers Forge) were relatively close to the city limit of Baltimore, including one community where a neighborhood boundary was the city line. See map 4.5.

9. Though all of our focus group sites contained some Section 8 households, only one such household was living within the vicinity of Rodgers Forge as of late 1997.

10 Lucas 1997, map 5A.

11. This point was suggested to us at a briefing with Baltimore County housing officials. They also suggested that housing quality inspectors also took note of housing code violators in the vicinity of Section 8 buildings, and reported such to the appropriate county department for enforcement. If this enforcement were to generate rehabilitation activities from other property owners near the Section 8 building, the positive externality effect of course would be magnified.

9

Conclusions and Policy Implications: Toward a Neighborhood-Friendly Strategy for Deconcentrating Assisted Housing

Programs to deconcentrate assisted housing constitute a major policy thrust both nationally and in many local areas. Advocates of deconcentration cite evidence suggesting that such programs, regardless of whether the subsidies are attached to sites or to tenants, have more positive consequences for participants than residence in traditional, large-scale facilities located in neighborhoods of concentrated poverty. However, the question of whether one agrees that this evidence is persuasive or not misses the key policy point. The benefits for assisted households must be compared with the costs for prospective neighbors before one can assess the wisdom of the policy (Galster, 2002, 2003; Johnson, Ladd, and Ludwig 2002).

In this book, we have analyzed this key issue of neighborhood impacts through a multimethod, quantitative and qualitative reconnaissance into three case studies where fears about the neighborhood impacts of deconcentrated assisted housing programs led to major political controversies and subsequent program modifications. In Denver, we investigated the dispersed public housing program and a set of supportive housing programs. In Baltimore County, we investigated the Section 8 certificate/voucher program.

We begin this final chapter by highlighting our main findings, which focus on the themes of context, concentration, and scale. In sum, deconcentrated assisted housing:

1. had positive or insignificant effects on the environs in higher-value, less vulnerable neighborhoods unless it exceeded thresholds of spatial concentration or facility scale;
2. evinced more modest prospects for positive impacts in lower-value, more vulnerable neighborhoods, with the strength of frequently negative

impacts being directly related to the concentration of sites and scale of the facilities.

What are the implications from these findings about how assisted housing deconcentration policy should be reformed? We propose a comprehensive strategy, which is described below. We repeat our caveat that these conclusions are necessarily limited by the specific programs and areas we studied and that more research should be done to confirm our findings in different settings.

Two basic assumptions underlie our approach to the issue of policy reform. First, we believe that it is desirable to expand the opportunities for low-income and special-needs households to live in low-poverty neighborhoods where their quality of life and future opportunities may be enhanced.[1] Second, we believe that deconcentration policy must take seriously the potential impacts on recipient neighborhoods, and be tailored to maximize its potentially positive impacts while minimizing its potentially negative ones. Our policy recommendations are designed to advance both dimensions: expanding opportunities for assisted households while being "neighborhood friendly."

What Have We Learned?

The Geopolitical Context of Controversy over Deconcentrating Assisted Housing

Superficially, it might appear that the two sites we investigated could not be more different. Baltimore County was more affluent, with much higher homeownership rates. It had a much smaller minority population, and the predominant and fastest-growing minority group was blacks, whereas in Denver it was Hispanics. None of these differences are surprising, inasmuch as Baltimore County is a largely suburban area outside of the City of Baltimore, whereas Denver is a jurisdiction comprising both a central city and a county with suburb-like communities.

What is perhaps more surprising is that the two areas show several similarities in their demographic and market trends. In the five-year period prior to their major political controversies over assisted housing, both metropolitan areas' housing markets saw declines in the real values of most homes. Both had increasing median household ages, percentages of female-headed households, and absolute numbers and relative percentages of minorities, whereas their white populations declined absolutely and relatively. Both witnessed increasing economic polarization among blacks, Hispanics, and whites. Finally, in both contexts the predominant participant in the deconcentrated assisted housing program was the most impoverished, fastest-growing racial or ethnic group in the area. Thus, despite their differences, the geopolitical context in both situations demonstrated some crucial similarities that rendered Baltimore County and Denver vulnerable to local political demagoguery centered on efforts to deconcentrate assisted housing.

The motive of electoral victory spurred some local politicians to whip up opposition to the deconcentrated assisted housing program in "threatened" neighborhoods by playing on fears of property value declines, unsavory tenantry and associated social problems, and the unfairness of assistance to the "undeserving poor." The deconcentrated assisted housing policy thus became the convenient vehicle for political opportunism. In all three cases, there were allegations of housing provider insensitivity to local concerns, and a subsequent lack of preparation in dealing with a surprisingly vehement public reaction. Ironically, in each case, essentially similar programs had been operating without significant public attention for many years prior to the controversies, but subsequently their operations were significantly changed as a result of the controversies.

We do not infer from this that neighbors' worries over assisted housing were groundless or that the policy response represented an overreaction, however. On the contrary, our study shows that concerns about the concentration of sites, the scale of the facilities, and the behavior of assisted housing managers and their clientele are eminently justified in certain circumstances. Indeed, the ensuing policy responses proved sensible.

The Nature of Assisted Housing's Neighborhood Impacts: Context, Concentration, and Scale

These political controversies appear especially intriguing in light of our primary statistical findings, which are summarized in table 9.1. The general pattern during the late 1980s through the mid-1990s was that a dispersed public housing site in Denver, a supportive housing site in Denver, or a Section 8 household in Baltimore County did *not* lower single-family home prices or raise crime rates in their neighborhoods, contrary to conventional wisdom. In many cases, such proximity even resulted in *higher* home prices.

This is not to say that some of the concerns voiced during the political controversies were groundless; on the contrary. The magnitude and direction of impacts were clearly contingent on the neighborhood context and the spatial concentration and facility scale of the assisted housing. There was a widespread pattern of threshold effects, whereby home price impacts became negative when more than a critical mass of assisted housing sites or units were located in a neighborhood. This danger of "reconcentration" was most acute in lower-value neighborhoods, especially where homeowners perceived a vulnerability to their quality of life. Indeed, in some circumstances in Baltimore County, we observed that *any* additional Section 8 households would have harmful impacts on property values. But even in the most favorable neighborhood contexts, we estimated that fewer than literally a handful of assisted housing sites or units could be concentrated within 2,000 feet before negative impacts ensued; see table 9.1. In the case of supportive housing, facility scale, more than clientele, appeared to be the critical variable in predicting whether any crime impacts would be forthcoming.

Our focus group discussions provided a rich texture for these statistical patterns. In focus group sites representing "vulnerable" neighborhoods, homeowners expressed deep anxieties over demographic, tenure, and physical changes taking place in their communities. Rental properties in general, especially if they were poorly maintained and had disruptive

Table 9.1

Summary of Statistical Estimates of Neighborhood Impacts:
The Importance of Context, Concentration, and Scale

		Type of Assisted Housing	
Neighborhood Context	*Dispersed Public Housing (Denver)*	*Supportive Housing (Denver)*	*Section 8 Subsidies (Baltimore County)*
Higher-value, less vulnerable	*Property values:* positive impacts within 2,000 feet if and only if below threshold; negative impact if $N>1$ within 1,000 feet, $N > 5$ within 1–2,000 feet	*Property values:* positive impacts 1–2,000 feet; negative impacts within 500 feet; impacts unrelated to N	*Property values:* positive impacts within 500 feet if and only if below threshold; negative impacts if $N > 3$ within 500 feet (maximum N observed = 4)
	Crime: 0 impact, all concentrations (but only small facilities tested)	*Crime:* 0 impact, small facilities at any distance; negative impact, large facilities within 500 feet	*Crime:* no data available
Lower-value, more vulnerable	*Property values:* positive small impacts 1–2,000 feet if and only if below threshold; negative impacts if $N > 4$ within 1–2,000 feet	*Property values:* positive small impacts 1–2,000 feet; mixed impacts 501–1,000; 0 impacts within 500 feet	*Property values:* negative impact, all distances; size of impact grows with N, no threshold; impacts slightly mitigated if same number of tenants in fewer N
	Crime: 0 impact, all concentrations (but only small facilities tested)	*Crime:* 0 impact, small facilities at any distance; negative impact, large facilities within 500 feet	*Crime:* no data available

Note: N = number of assisted housing sites operating within specified distance

tenants, were seen as key contributors to decline. Several groups in both cities spoke pointedly about Section 8 subsidized housing as a destructive force in their communities because it was stereotyped as involving "problem rental properties." Yet focus group participants in all neighborhoods typically were unaware of the presence of small-scale Section 8 sites nearby that were physically indistinguishable from other homes in the neighborhood. The same was true for dispersed public housing and most cases of supportive housing.

In sum, our focus groups consistently emphasized elements of neighborhood quality of life that are relevant to those who design and operate deconcentrated assisted housing programs: the physical condition of the neighborhood, the presence of numerous or poorly kept rental properties, social cohesion, increased traffic, and public safety. In turn, when operators of assisted housing programs seem able to address many of these issues effectively, the assisted site becomes virtually invisible to nearby homeowners as a major determinant of their neighborhood quality of life. This revelation provides powerful policy guidance, as we shall discuss below.

The Origins of Assisted Housing's Neighborhood Impacts: Countervailing Externalities

Our quantitative and qualitative findings yield important insights regarding the origins of deconcentrated assisted housing's neighborhood impacts. Although these findings are specific to the situations and programs we studied in Denver and Baltimore County, we believe that they are suggestive for many programs elsewhere.

The findings summarized in table 9.1 can best be explained by positing *countervailing externalities*. That is, assisted housing sites may have both positive and negative spillover effects on their environs that, depending on their relative magnitudes and spatial extents, may partially or completely offset each other. Countervailing externalities can explain the two consistent patterns of property-value impacts we observed: (1) Positive impacts can become negative ones when threshold concentrations of assisted housing are exceeded, and (2) sometimes no net impacts can be observed close to the assisted housing site, only farther away. If the positive were evaluated as a linear function of the number of sites but the negative as a nonlinear function, it is easy to see how the latter could predominate past some threshold. Moreover, if one posits that the magnitude and spatial extent of these countervailing externalities were highly contingent on neighborhood context, then the finding of nonlocalized impacts can be explained as well, as we will amplify below.

We believe that start-of-program building renovations and good property management after initial occupancy are the principal sources of any positive externalities here. However, it is possible there are at least three, non-mutually exclusive sources of negative externalities: (1) poor property maintenance or management by certain types of landlords; (2) uncivil or illegal behaviors of the assisted households; and/or (3) class prejudices of large segments of the home-buying market (which may not be behaviorally validated by actual assisted housing sites).

The totality of the evidence we have uncovered suggests that these positive and negative countervailing externalities differ in their strength across space according to two parameters: concentration of sites and neighborhood context. We illustrate this point with the aid of figures 9.1 through 9.4, which portray countervailing positive and negative externality functions, along with the net property-value impact of both curves, drawn to be consistent with our empirical findings in less vulnerable and more vulnerable neighborhoods, respectively.[2]

These four figures show situations in which the assisted housing in question is provided by rehabilitating an existing, undermaintained structure, instead of using Section 8 to place a needy tenant in an existing, well-maintained apartment. They illustrate the two qualities of these externality functions that are necessary to produce the range of net property-value impacts we observe: (1) At low concentrations of sites, the positive externalities extend further than the negative ones; and (2) past threshold concentrations, the positive externalities rise near the sites but extend no further than originally, but the negative externalities both rise and increase their spatial extent.

Figure 9.1 shows the situation in a higher-value, less vulnerable neighborhood context.

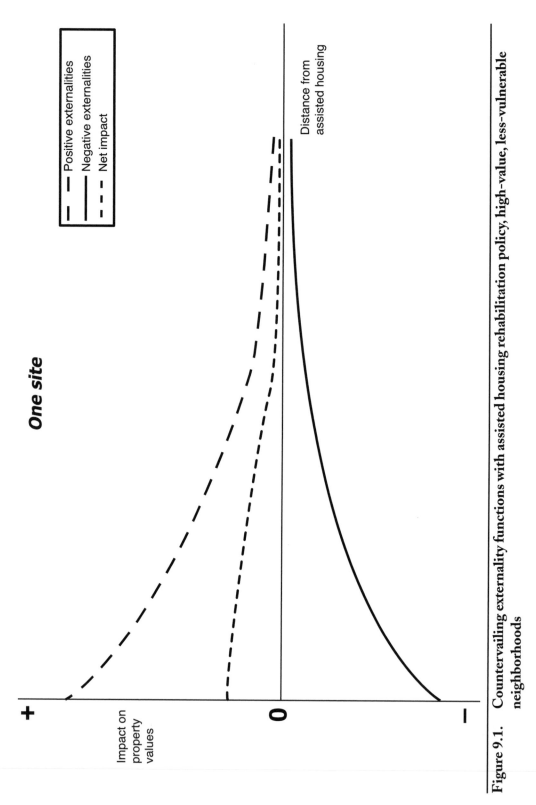

Figure 9.1. Countervailing externality functions with assisted housing rehabilitation policy, high-value, less-vulnerable neighborhoods

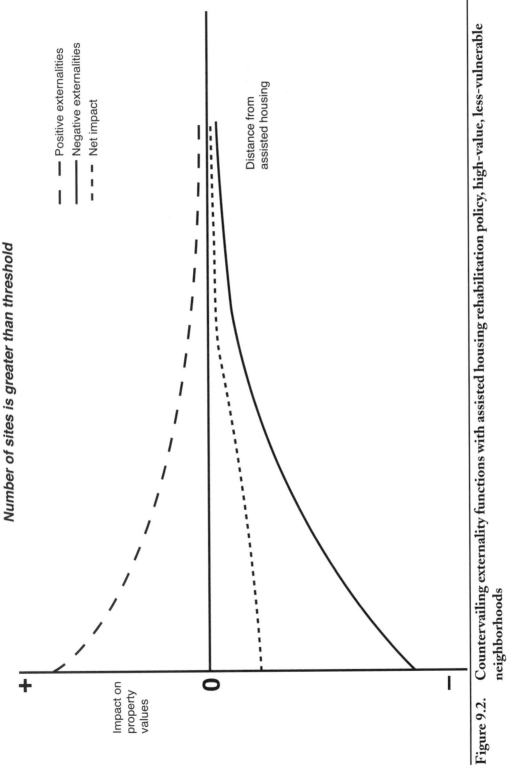

Figure 9.2. **Countervailing externality functions with assisted housing rehabilitation policy, high-value, less-vulnerable neighborhoods**

181

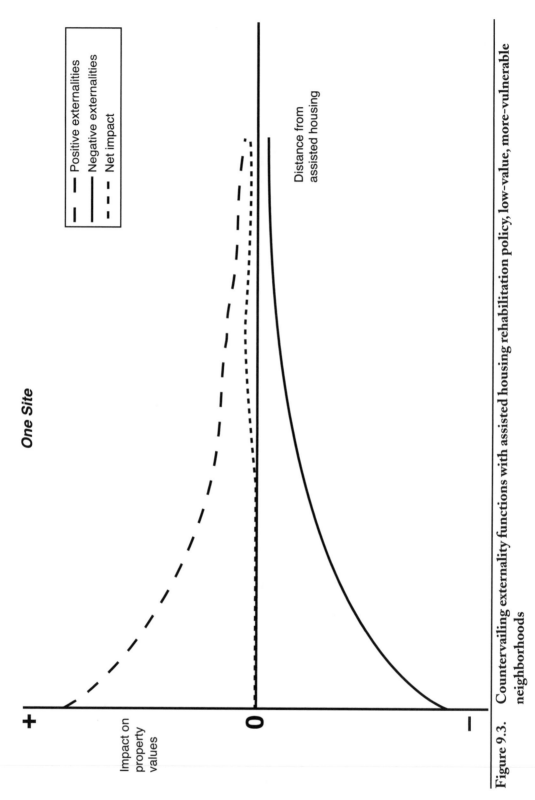

Figure 9.3. Countervailing externality functions with assisted housing rehabilitation policy, low-value, more-vulnerable neighborhoods

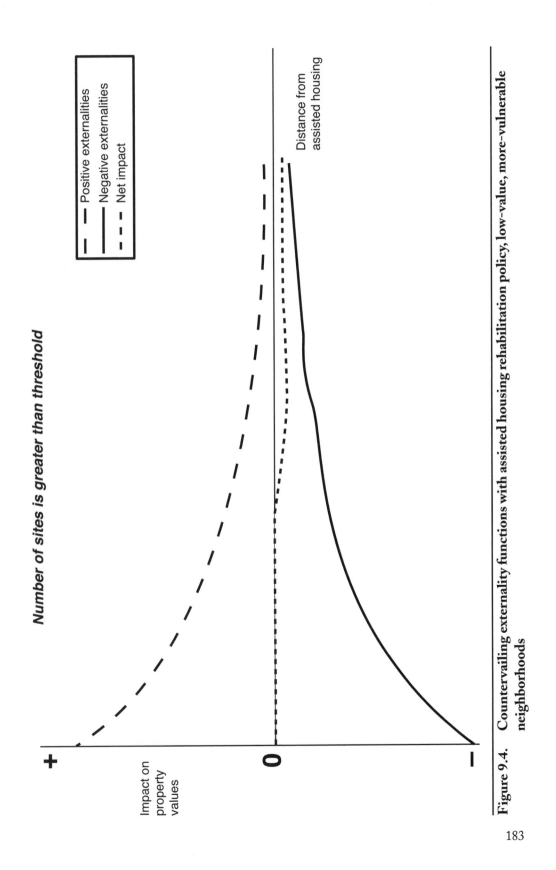

Figure 9.4. Countervailing externality functions with assisted housing rehabilitation policy, low-value, more-vulnerable neighborhoods

Here, when one assisted site is developed, the positive externalities associated with reha-bilitation are substantial and extend at least 2,000 feet. By contrast, negative externalities are modest, with limited extension into the neighborhood. The net effect is a positive fil-lip to property values at all ranges within 2,000 feet of the site, precisely what we observed for low concentrations of dispersed housing in higher-value Denver neighborhoods.

Past the threshold concentration, however, we posit that the rehabilitation of addi-tional dwellings for assisted housing is subject to severe diminishing returns. Thus, figure 9.2 portrays a smaller increase in the positive externality function relative to the single-site case. Negative externalities, conversely, are relatively greater both near the sites and, even more important, at farther distances. These latter effects apparently can swamp the former at all distances within 2,000 feet, generating net negative impacts on property val-ues, as we witnessed for dispersed housing concentrations exceeding thresholds in higher-value Denver neighborhoods.

Context matters as well, as we show in figures 9.3 and 9.4. In lower-value, more vul-nerable neighborhoods, the results are consistent with the hypothesis that the marginal positive property value impact generated by the first assisted housing rehabilitation is less than in higher-value areas (figure 9.3). When coupled with countervailing negative exter-nalities within close range of the site, the net impact may well be nil. But as positive ex-ternalities declined less rapidly at further distances, a positive net impact nevertheless could be observed there. This we observed in the cases of dispersed and supportive housing in lower-value neighborhoods.

The data suggest that diminishing returns from dwelling rehabilitation do not set in as quickly (though their marginal effect may still be smaller than in higher-value areas). Hence, we portray a relative upward shift in the positive externality function in figure 9.3, though once again its spatial extent is not altered significantly. Past threshold concentra-tions, however, negative externalities decrease less rapidly, as shown in figure 9.4. Within close proximity to the sites, the countervailing externalities may cancel out; only at farther distances will the negative impact predominate. This pattern was consistent with dispersed housing exceeding thresholds in lower-value Denver neighborhoods.

The same analysis can easily be extended to the case of assisted housing provided through Section 8. In general, the positive externality effect will be weaker, inasmuch as Section 8 typically does not involve major rehabilitation of the structure in question. When it involves some nontrivial renovations, however, as apparently was the case in higher-value neighborhoods in Baltimore County, a positive impact within close range of the site can be observed. In more vulnerable neighborhoods or when no renovations occur, however, there is no offset to the negative externality function. In these cases, we find what tran-spired in the lower-value areas of Baltimore County: negative property value impacts near the Section 8 site, which grew in magnitude and spatial extent the larger the concentra-tion of sites.

The Selection of Assisted Housing into Weaker Neighborhood Niches: Implications for Research and Politics

A crucial, if incidental, finding of our statistical analyses was that, in both Denver and Baltimore County, deconcentrated assisted housing sites of all varieties studied systematically tended to be located in the lower-value, (often) slower-appreciating, sectors within any given census tract. These patterns can be traced to the behaviors of assisted tenants, Section 8 landlords, supportive housing developers, and the local housing authorities themselves, although we cannot disentangle the relative contributions of these causes here. Perhaps of more import, however, are two implications of this finding.

First, from a research perspective, it implies that statistical models of neighborhood impacts must be specified carefully to avoid erroneous conclusions. For example, if one merely does a cross-sectional comparison of home prices near assisted housing sites with those less proximate, one will tend to observe lower prices in the areas near the sites. But this clearly cannot be attributed necessarily to an independent impact from the assisted sites, given the initial conditions before the sites were developed. As another example, if one merely compares levels of home prices before and after occupancy of a nearby assisted site, there will be a bias toward observing a lower post-occupancy level because of a preexisting trend of depreciation in the area, not because of assisted housing. In the absence of carefully specified empirical tests such as those reported here, any claims related to neighborhood impacts will be founded on suspect causality.

The second implication relates to politics and the public support that can be mustered for a deconcentrated assisted housing program. Assisted housing currently has a tendency to be located in lower-value neighborhoods with property values of lower appreciation, precisely where local residents and the market as a whole are most likely to be anxious about the area's future. Moreover, local residents and the market are unlikely to make the subtle distinctions in causality that our statistical analyses permitted here. From their perspective, assisted housing will be seen as highly correlated with incipient neighborhood decline, and this probably is sufficient for them to attribute causation to the former. Of course, both our Denver and Baltimore County analyses showed that this attribution may be correct if the census tract in question is in a vulnerable market situation and the spatial concentration of assisted households or scale of assisted facilities becomes excessive.

Finally, consider our focus group finding that many residents in neighborhoods containing assisted housing have a habitual tendency to equate "bad landlords of bad properties housing bad tenants" with such programs. Although clearly not generalizable, this conventional wisdom erodes support for such initiatives and provides another, apparently "factual" justification for recipient neighborhood NIMBY-ism. In any event, the empirical and perceptual conditions surrounding the geography of deconcentrated assisted housing appear to prime ongoing public opposition to such housing by recipient neighborhoods, needing only the spark of political opportunism to set off an explosion.

It follows that the cornerstone for building a political constituency for deconcentrated assisted housing and defusing potential local opposition must be an attack on the stereo-types surrounding such housing. We believe that this attack requires changing both the *objective* conditions associated with deconcentrated assisted housing and the public's *per-ceptions* of these conditions. This will necessitate comprehensive revisions in deconcentrated assisted housing program design and operations, including siting and type of assisted hous-ing, selection and monitoring of tenants and landlords, homeownership initiatives, and pub-lic education and relations. Moreover, it will require a realignment of deconcentration housing policy within the larger realm of local housing policies, perhaps requiring new institutional delivery systems. We believe that the results will produce a neighborhood-friendly strategy that is both more socially optimal (better balancing opportunities for as-sisted households and legitimate concerns of their neighbors) and less politically vulnerable.

A Neighborhood-Friendly Strategy for Deconcentrating Assisted Housing

Policies for deconcentrating assisted housing have been established nationally and in many locales. Whether sufficiently justified by careful research or not, this direction represents the status quo. We believe that there are many reasons to support this direction in prin-ciple, though not always in the way it has been practiced. Throughout this book, we have taken seriously the concerns often voiced by neighbors when confronted with the pros-pect of an assisted housing facility or household located nearby. We have not presumed that all sorts of neighborhood protests against assisted housing are ill-informed, based on prejudice, or illegal. Rather, we have sought to better understand (through qualitative re-search methods) the nature and sources of the opposition and measure (through quantita-tive research methods) the degree to which opposition seems warranted in terms of negative neighborhood impacts, and in what contexts.

Although our findings suggest that commonly expressed fears about assisted hous-ing typically are exaggerated, important contextual caveats remain. Our key informant in-terviews, statistical analyses, and focus groups all identified circumstances in which deconcentrated assisted housing has apparently caused real problems for the neighborhood. In other cases, however, deconcentrated assisted housing clearly benefited neighborhood property values. Therefore, it behooves policymakers to learn from both of these situations in order to create more successful, socially beneficial, and politically acceptable programs.

Our results from multiple methods and study sites reinforce common themes for policy reform. Policymakers, developers, and operators of deconcentrated assisted housing must pay close attention to

- siting and concentration,
- development type and scale,
- monitoring of tenants and operators,
- management of buildings, and
- collaboration with neighborhoods and public education.

Nearby homeowners and the market clearly can distinguish between low concentrations of small-scale assisted housing that are well designed, well maintained, and well managed and those that are not. Public opposition to development of additional assisted housing likely is fueled by a few lurid vignettes regarding the latter, which reinforce conventional stereotypes (HUD 2001). The former sort of "good" assisted housing, conversely, apparently can become cognitively invisible to homeowners as a potential concern or factor contributing to neighborhood change.

Thus, our policy recommendations are designed holistically to confound negative public stereotypes about deconcentrated assisted housing programs by striving for universally well-conceived and well-operated programs. Our recommendations imply added responsibilities for all parties involved in deconcentrated assisted housing: program designers and administrators, facility developers and managers, assisted households, and neighbors alike. Correspondingly, they hold promise to create programs that confer more benefits on all these parties.

Again, we caution that the results presented in this book do not necessarily apply to all types of deconcentrated assisted housing programs in other locales. Nevertheless, we think it valuable to discuss what our findings imply for policy were they to prove generally applicable. In this spirit, we offer the following six recommendations for those who design, implement, and administer deconcentrated assisted housing policies. We recognize that not all of these recommendations may be desirable or practical in all situations. National and local policymakers will have to decide which policy reforms would yield the most benefit for specific programs and communities. Nevertheless, we feel strongly that a multifaceted approach incorporating several of these recommendations will much more likely be successful.

Siting to Ensure Sufficient Deconcentration

We have found that too many Section 8 households or dispersed public housing sites clustered in a small area, especially within vulnerable neighborhoods, result in negative impacts on home sales prices. Conversely, widely scattered, small-scale facilities or assisted households have no impacts (or even positive impacts if building rehabilitation is involved) and are virtually invisible to their neighbors. If harmful concentration is to be avoided, policymakers must encourage, or perhaps even mandate, particular spatially related choices on the part of local public housing authorities (PHAs), private developers, municipalities, Section 8 landlords, and assisted households themselves. A laissez-faire approach may merely continue the current perverse selection process, whereby assisted housing gravitates toward the very neighborhoods where its presence can do the most damage.

The four components of our recommendation aim to increase the opportunities for low-income and special-needs households to live in low-poverty neighborhoods providing enhanced opportunities *over the long term*. Three of our recommended components are specifically targeted at expanding the number of assisted housing sites in such neighborhoods, about which potential occupants are aware, and that all can access regardless of race, gender, familial status, or source of income. The fourth, and probably most controversial, component is to require that assisted housing and tenants locate in higher-value, less-vulnerable housing submarkets that have not already been significantly impacted by assisted housing programs or poverty in general. Though limiting the choices of some assisted households in the short-term, this component serves to expand the desirable neighborhood choices of assisted households as a group in the long term, because it avoids the reconcentration of poverty and associated neighborhood deterioration.

Incentives to Spatially Diversify Assisted Housing Opportunities

We suggest that a variety of pilot programs might be initiated and funded by the U.S. Department of Housing and Urban Development (HUD) or by state and local governments that would provide substantial, behavior-modifying financial incentives for relevant parties to create opportunities for assisted housing where they are now sorely underrepresented. Local PHAs should have stronger incentives to recruit landlords for Section 8 programs in less vulnerable neighborhoods than in vulnerable ones, and be rewarded for helping their Section 8 household make the corresponding sorts of deconcentrating moves (Briggs 1997; Hartung and Henig 1997; Turner 1998). The reward structure should also facilitate the deconcentration of their existing public housing stock. Private developers of supportive housing should receive incentives if they produce in neighborhoods with few assisted housing facilities. Landlords of market-rate units should receive bonuses for participating in the Section 8 program for the first time. Local governments should be financially encouraged to permit the development of rental housing that either provides site-based assistance (through public housing; HOME; or Low Income Housing Tax Credit, or LIHTC, programs) or is priced at Fair Market Rent levels that would permit its participation in the Section 8 program (Pendall 2000). Such financial incentives could emanate from either federal or state governments.

We recognize that there are several decades' worth of experience with state and local efforts to expand the geographic scope of assisted and affordable housing through mandates like "fair share" or "inclusionary zoning" laws, most notably in California, Maryland, Massachusetts, and New Jersey (Downs 1973; Lake 1981; Mallach 1984; Advisory Commission on Regulatory Barriers to Affordable Housing 1991; Keating 1994). More recently, these efforts have been echoed in more than a dozen federal court-ordered remedies in local housing authority segregation cases (Popkin et al. 2000). We certainly applaud and encourage such efforts, though we question how politically feasible they may be in many contexts. By contrast, there has been little prior use of economic incentives. Our view is that a great deal of experimentation is required before we can ascertain which sort of subsidy mechanism and what degree of incentive will be required to produce the desired outcome. The following are thus merely suggestive of what we hope will be a wide variety of trials:

- "deconcentration bonuses" attached to PHA Section 8 administrative fees granted by HUD, perhaps through the new Management Assessment Program (Turner 1998);
- "enrollment bonuses" and/or "rehabilitation grants" for landlords who open up new apartments for Section 8 occupancy and commit to maintaining Section 8 occupancy for a specified future period;
- expedited zoning, permitting, and approval processes from local governments for supportive housing developers who choose deconcentrated sites;
- altered formulas for awarding federal (such as McKinney) or state (LIHTC allocations) housing development funds so that proposals for facilities in higher-value neighborhoods are favored; and
- "opportunity housing" bonuses for local governments, funneled through a formula-altered Community Development Block Grant Program or through the Internal Revenue Service, which would permit greater write-offs of local property taxes and/or mortgage interest payments on residents' federal taxes if their community met its "fair share" of assisted housing sites (Boger 1996).

Assist the Mobility of Section 8 Households

Numerous analysts have considered how to facilitate moves into low-poverty areas by holders of Section 8 vouchers and certificates (Turner and Williams 1998; Goering et al. 1999; Cunningham, Sylvester, and Turner 2000; Pendall 2000; Turner, Popkin, and Cunningham 2000; Popkin et al. 2000). We believe that many of these suggestions have merit, including

- intensive, hands-on mobility counseling and relocation assistance to the household in locating and inspecting apartments and neighborhoods;
- financial assistance for moving costs, furnishings, apartment and utility security deposits, contingent upon moving to low-poverty areas;
- simplifying the "portability" features of the vouchers or certificates that permit holders to move to different PHA jurisdictions; and
- postmove follow-ups, to provide counseling, information, and other assistance aimed at heading off move-outs by discouraged households.

Intensify Fair Housing Enforcement and Expand Protected Classes

Assisted households may be reluctant to move into deconcentrated contexts because they fear (often with justification) ostracism and discrimination, especially if they are members of a racial or ethnic minority group (Yinger 1998; Turner, Popkin, and Cunningham 2000). Developers of supportive housing, public housing, or even rental housing priced to be eligible for Section 8 may be precluded from using the program by local zoning and housing codes (National Law Center on Homelessness and Poverty 1997; Pendall 1999). Thus, efforts to remove such private and public discriminatory barriers should be intensified (Pendall 2000).

In the realm of private discrimination, we already possess at the federal and most state and local levels substantially equivalent legal prohibitions on the basis of race, ethnicity, gender, disability, and family composition. These are protected classes of relevance to virtually all participants of deconcentrated assisted housing programs. More enforcement resources, directed in a more effective manner, are certainly needed to effectively thwart discrimination in these veins, but at least the legal framework is in place (Galster 1990a).

Yet another crucial category, source of income, is not protected from private discrimination either under federal law or in virtually any state and locality. Consideration could therefore be given to amending federal, state, or local fair housing statutes to make it illegal to refuse to rent to a household because that household receives child support, public assistance, or housing assistance (e.g., Section 8). Such an amended statute has been enacted in Massachusetts and in Montgomery and Howard Counties, Maryland (Beck 1996). By implication, landlords would no longer have the option of not participating in the Section 8 program, were a prospective tenant with a voucher or certificate to request such and if there were no other legitimate reasons for denying the household's application.

In the realm of public-sector discrimination, increasing numbers of communities have been revising their zoning laws as a means of excluding low-income and special-needs households (National Law Center on Homelessness and Poverty 1997). Arresting this trend could be accomplished both by legal action and by employing financial disincentives applied by federal and state governments, as discussed above. The 1988 federal Fair Housing Amendments Act and the 1990 Americans with Disabilities Act apparently provide sufficient legal foundation for effective challenges, but continued legal pressure would likely be needed to effect greater change in this area.

Establish Impaction Standards

It would be our hope that the previous three components of our deconcentration initiative would significantly expand the geographic range of assisted housing opportunities throughout all parts of metropolitan areas. However, such actions may not be adequate, at least in the short run, to guarantee that neighborhood-harming concentrations of assisted housing or households will not appear, given the powerful forces of selection to which we have alluded above. Thus, various levels of government, as appropriate, might consider establishing "impaction standards" for either assisted households or developers that would comprehensively limit the concentration and scale of assisted housing of various types in all or certain types of neighborhoods (Briggs 1997; Hartung and Henig 1997). For instance, special attention could be given to avoiding concentrations in more vulnerable neighborhoods (Pollock and Rutkowski 1998).

On the demand side of the equation, policymakers might restrict additional Section 8 certificate recipients from occupying units in particular neighborhoods, much in the way Moving to Opportunity (MTO) now restricts the experimental group to census tracts having poverty rates of 10 percent or less. Many sorts of similar restrictions on Section 8 usage have previously been imposed in the context of settling PHA desegregation cases. The Gautreaux remedy, for example, required that the special certificates issued under the consent decree be used in neighborhoods where black residents made up less than 30 percent of the population (Goering, Stebbins, and Siewert 1995). Consent decrees in both Memphis and Cincinnati limited Section 8 assistance issued as part of the settlement to neighborhoods with black populations of less than 40 percent, and a Dallas settlement restricted Section 8 to areas with less than 10 certificates or vouchers per census tract (Goering, Stebbins, and Siewert 1995). Another option would be not to allow additional Section 8 households in neighborhoods where existing Section 8 levels exceed a certain percentage of the population.

To gain some perspective on how limiting these restrictions may be, consider the findings of Kingsley, Johnson, and Pettit (2001) regarding Section 8 household locations in 31 metropolitan areas. They found that only 2 percent, on average, of the census tracts containing any Section 8 households had 10 percent or more of their population made up of such households. Eight percent of the tracts had Section 8 households representing 5.0–9.9 percent of the population. They also found that, on average in their sample, 10 percent of all Section 8 households resided in tracts where they constituted 10 percent or more of all households; 27 percent resided in tracts where they constituted 5.0–9.9 percent of the households.

On the supply side of the equation, analogous sorts of impaction standards could be enforced to prevent individual landlords from overconcentrating Section 8 households within a single apartment complex, or to prevent additional landlords from participating in the program if the neighborhood is already sufficiently impacted. Developers of scattered-site public housing units similarly should be restricted in which neighborhoods they can develop units and how many they can develop there within certain separations. Such restrictions are similar in principle to the long-standing HUD impaction standards for privately owned, subsidized complexes or to those imposed on the Denver Housing Authority (DHA) and supportive housing developers by the Denver City Council, as described in chapter 2.

We also recommend that impaction standards be instituted for developers of LIHTC developments, given that past patterns indicate their tendency to concentrate in lower-income, predominantly minority-occupied neighborhoods (Cummings and DiPasquale 1999; Freeman and Rohe 2000). In some contexts, the deconcentration of preexisting clusters of subsidized and public housing that give rise to some vulnerable neighborhoods should be considered, for example, "de-densification" programs for conventional public housing sites, such as those funded under the HOPE VI program.[3]

Finally, our findings suggest that the scale of individual supportive housing facilities be limited. Recall that it was only the set of large supportive housing facilities in Denver—all of which exceeded by large margins the Large Special Care and Community Correctional Facility scale limitations subsequently legislated soon after their opening—that were associated with higher crime rates.

There are ample precedents for such supply-side impaction standards. The 1996 consent decree settling the public housing desegregation suit in Baltimore City required that scattered-site public housing replacing demolished units be built in areas with less than 26 percent minorities, less than 10 percent poverty rates, and less than 5 percent subsidized housing. The 1984 consent decree resolving the Cincinnati public housing suit required that more than half the new scattered-site public housing units be constructed in areas with less than 20 percent minorities and less than 15 percent subsidized housing (Varady and Preiser 1998). The FY2001 HUD appropriations bill set a maximum of 25 percent of units with project-based assistance in any apartment complexes newly developed by PHAs. The standards established in Denver were, of course, discussed in chapter 2.

We have insufficient data to recommend definitive impaction standards, the degree to which such standards should be flexibly applied at the local level, or how standards might be modified for vulnerable neighborhoods. Nevertheless, our findings suggest that the lowest terciles of median home value are a robust indicator of neighborhood vulnerability, whereas racial and ethnic composition is not. Poverty rates exceeding 20 percent might be superimposed as well for this purpose. For such vulnerable areas in our study sites, we found negative impacts when two or more Section 8 and four or more assisted sites employing dwelling rehabilitation were within 2,000 feet of each other. For higher-value, less vulnerable neighborhoods, we found negative impacts beyond one site-based and three tenant-based assisted units within 500 feet, and roughly five units of any sort within 2,000 feet. For supportive housing scale, the limit of 40 beds per facility chosen in Denver seemed an appropriate standard.

Such standards would need to be formulated taking into account the specific conditions in the community. However operationalized, impaction standards must be based on easily available, frequently updated information.[4] The resulting distributions of assisted households must be continuously monitored and standards reviewed and revised as needed. We suggest that impaction standards have a schedule for review, evaluation, and potential revision established at the same time that they are enacted.

Despite the precedents, opponents of impaction standards argue that they unfairly restrict the freedom of assisted tenants and/or developers and other providers of assisted units. There are four possible reasons, however, why such restrictions may not be as undesirable as critics contend.

First, such impaction standards should be instituted only in conjunction with the aforementioned comprehensive package of incentives for expanding the geographic spread of assisted units. Thus, the larger set of options would be expanded at the same time that a subset of options is foreclosed.

Second, impaction standards might be fairer for assisted households as a group in the long run. No assisted households seeking low-poverty neighborhoods of opportunity, including those whose choices may be constrained by the standards, are well served if they are permitted to undermine, albeit unwittingly, the very thing they seek. It is well known that households, behaving in uncoordinated, unconstrained ways will overconsume collective goods in a way that renders them unavailable to all (Schelling 1978). Such is the case with low-poverty neighborhoods; if too many assisted and other low-income households are permitted to move in, the class composition of the area will "tip" and that which all our in-movers sought will prove illusory to all. To preserve an area with a mix of poor and nonpoor households over the long run is to maintain for at least some low-income households an option that cannot otherwise be sustained.

Third, the rights of assisted tenants and housing providers should not necessarily take precedence over valid neighborhood concerns or overall social efficiency. To allow some assisted tenants to benefit modestly while potentially imposing much greater costs on other residents and property owners already in a neighborhood might not be considered desirable social policy. We have shown that excessive clustering of assisted housing in vulnerable neighborhoods can lead to severe losses in home equity for property owners there. This circumstance is not only unfair to these owners (who may be of modest incomes themselves) but is also inefficient and inequitable from an overall societal perspective.

If such neighborhoods were to become places where poverty is newly concentrated because of assisted housing weakening the private market, policy would have merely re-created the undesirable context that deconcentrated housing strategies were designed to counter in the first place. Moreover, the evidence on the relationship between neighborhood poverty rates and the propensity of individuals to engage in socially problematic behaviors tentatively suggests that there will be a net *increase* in the aggregate incidence of such behaviors if low-income households are merely shifted from high-poverty neighborhoods to moderate-poverty (15 to 30 percent), vulnerable ones (Galster and Zobel 1998; Galster, 2002, 2003).

Fourth, impaction standards are key elements for rebuilding political support for deconcentrated assisted housing policy. We believe that all sorts of assisted housing facilities, whether deconcentrated or not, are vulnerable to mounting political opposition in the United States today. If ill-directed deconcentration efforts continue to needlessly harm vulnerable neighborhoods, they risk significant retrenchment in *all* assisted housing appropriations. The MTO debacle could prove to be a foreshadowing. Impaction standards provide assurances to such neighborhoods that they will not be asked to bear an undue share of assisted housing in the region, and thus trump a potential source of political grievance.

Thus homeowners, society as a whole, and in a fundamental sense assisted households themselves and their advocates have an interest in ensuring that assisted housing policy is not a vehicle for destabilizing neighborhoods and reconstituting them as places of concentrated poverty. Impaction standards might be the last line of defense for preventing this until the other components of the deconcentration strategy succeed in expanding the geographic scope of assisted housing options.

Monitor the Concentration of Assisted Housing Sites and Households

If a formal impaction standard is adopted in a community, it will certainly be necessary to monitor the concentration of assisted housing sites and households to ensure that these standards are being met. Even where no such requirements exist, however, it may still be highly desirable to monitor concentration levels. Such information could provide useful feedback on the performance of mobility counseling, financial incentives, and other more voluntary means of encouraging the dispersion of assisted housing.

Such a monitoring system should not be prohibitively difficult to implement, at least for federally funded housing programs. Housing authorities are already required by HUD to keep automated records of the locations of households in Section 8 and other housing assistance programs that they oversee. These records include the address of each household, which can be "geocoded" using mapping software and then displayed as points on a map.[5] Through more sophisticated mapping analysis, it should be possible to automatically identify areas with higher concentrations of assisted sites.

Accessing information for supportive housing sites may be more difficult, however. Not all communities have a central registry of the locations of such sites or allow easy access to this information. In Denver, all supportive housing sites must be licensed with the city, which made it possible to obtain a list of addresses from a single source. Furthermore, in Denver these data are considered public information; they may not be elsewhere. Other communities may need to modify their record-keeping practices for supportive housing if they wish to include these programs in a monitoring system.

Encourage the Rehabilitation of Structures as Assisted Housing

Programs to deconcentrate assisted housing clearly can generate positive externalities if they are done correctly. The evidence from our property-value impact studies suggests that a key component of successful deconcentration is the transformation of a neighborhood eyesore into a well-maintained assisted housing site. We recommend a variety of incentives that might be considered to encourage this form of deconcentration strategy.

To the extent feasible, site-based deconcentrated assisted housing programs should attempt to acquire and rehabilitate vacant, poorly maintained properties. HUD might alter its expense reimbursement formulas for PHAs in ways that encourage development through rehabilitation rather than new construction. The Denver Housing Authority's approach to acquisition and rehabilitation for developing its dispersed housing represents a model in this regard. In similar fashion, localities could provide financial or administrative and procedural incentives favoring a rehabilitation strategy for supportive housing development.

Tenant-based assisted housing deconcentration programs could seek to recruit owners of deteriorated properties, especially in otherwise-strong neighborhoods, and then apply incentives for the rehabilitation of said properties prior to qualification for Section 8 lease-up. The Baltimore County experience suggests some efficacy from the initial Housing Quality Standard inspections in stimulating repairs before owners qualify for Section 8 contracts. We believe that additional financial incentives may be required, however, to encourage more major property rehabilitation as a precursor to participation in the Section 8 program. Localities might well collaborate with PHAs, nonprofit providers, and for-profit rental property owners to allocate some local housing repair monies (typically funded through HOME, Community Development Block Grants, local revenues, or housing trust funds) for this purpose.

Intensify Oversight of Deconcentrated Assisted Housing

Of course, as the efforts of the DHA, many supportive housing developers, and landlords of Section 8 tenants manifest, the ongoing conscientious supervision and maintenance of assisted properties is required if the positive effect of property acquisition and rehabilitation is to persist. Implicit in a policy to ensure good management is the need to carefully monitor *both* demanders and suppliers. Mechanisms should be implemented to screen tenants who participate in deconcentrated housing programs, to monitor tenants' behavior once they begin to participate, and to oversee the performance of those who operate the facilities where these tenants live. Only by rigorous oversight can the superior performance levels be reached that will enable public stereotypes of assisted housing to be refuted.

Screen and Monitor Tenants

Administrators of deconcentrated assisted housing programs should give consideration to screening potential tenants on the basis of past rental performance (including housekeeping, behavior, and financial responsibility). Otherwise, public stereotypes that "subsidized tenants are bad neighbors" may not be disconfirmed. Once subsidized tenants are in residence, local housing authorities and supportive housing operators should ensure that the tenants obey all the financial and behavioral conditions of the lease, and that all violations are dealt with swiftly, through counseling, disciplinary action, or, in extreme cases, eviction. For instance, DHA officials claim that vigilant screening and lease enforcement results in fewer than 5 percent of their dispersed tenants creating any problems. Stringent screening of applicants' credit records and housekeeping skills rendered one-quarter of Gautreaux Section 8 program applicants ineligible, but was cited as a key ingredient in the ultimate success of the program (Rosenbaum 2000).

It might be argued that screening and close monitoring of tenants constitutes an unwarranted invasion of privacy and affront to their dignity. This is a valid concern, but we offer two responses. First, screening and monitoring could be viewed as a necessary quid pro quo associated with the acceptance of a rare and valuable form of public assistance. Without rigorous screening and monitoring, scarce program monies may be wasted because tenants are evicted, landlords and developers may be discouraged from future participation, and political capital will be squandered (Rosenbaum and Miller 1997; Rosenbaum 2000). Second, public housing residents themselves are often quick to call for better screening and monitoring of tenants in their own complexes.[6] Once again, impositions on the individual must be compared with benefits accruing to the larger group.

Some might see this recommendation as an undesirable shift from the current emphasis on providing assistance to the "neediest." First, we do not believe that there is a high correlation between need and behaviors of the sort that would be screened. Second, should need- and behavior-based criteria come into conflict, there may be strong strategic reasons why the latter should take precedence. Given the political precariousness of assisted housing programs in general and deconcentration strategies in particular, it behooves policymakers to put the most positive face on the program that is possible. Focusing the program on the low-income families who are most ready and/or able to take advantage of deconcentrated housing (and then publicizing this fact, as we explain below) may be one way to achieve this.

We recognize that many potential participants in deconcentration efforts, such as current residents of public housing, may not pass more stringent screening standards (Popkin et al. 2000). We therefore also propose that supportive services be provided to applicants for and participants in deconcentrated assisted housing programs so that more may meet stringent screening and monitoring requirements. For example, local housing authorities might well form partnerships with local social service agencies to achieve this goal (Turner, Popkin, and Cunningham 2000). In other cases, community development corporations, faith-based groups, and other community-based organizations could offer these services to low-income individuals moving into their communities through assisted housing programs.

Monitor Dwellings and Landlords

Once subsidized tenants are in residence, local housing authorities must ensure that the property is maintained at a level equal or superior to the general upkeep of the neighborhood, to confound public stereotypes and make the unit less likely to be identified as assisted (MaRous 1996; Hogan 1996, chap. 4). Our study, like others, has shown that well-maintained, small-scale assisted housing is rendered essentially invisible to neighbors (Wahl 1993). However, our focus group participants seemed very concerned with the potentially deleterious effects of proximity to poorly maintained and managed Section 8–subsidized units.

In the case of Section 8, ensuring good maintenance generally means ongoing, frequent inspections of participating private apartments by the administering PHA, and the imposition of appropriate sanctions until remediation occurs (Turner, Popkin, and Cunningham 2000). In the case of scattered-site public housing, it means the conscientious investment of housing authority resources in building upkeep and semiannual apartment interior inspections, as has been done in Denver. In the case of supportive housing, it means periodic inspections of facilities by the local licensing agency as a condition of continued licensure.

The Housing Authority of Baltimore City has recently initiated several policies aimed at precisely these goals. These policies include stepping up maintenance checks on landlords and tenants, encouraging intensified lease violation reporting by landlords, and developing neighborhood service centers to deal with community complaints. The Baltimore County Housing Organization also now appears to be stricter in screening Section 8 tenants and in requiring Housing Quality Standard compliance of landlords than do many other jurisdictions (Varady and Walker 1998). Nevertheless, it has expressed frustration at HUD's regulatory limits on which tenant screening criteria could be applied and on sanctions for Section 8 landlords who proved weak property managers and lease enforcers. The Cincinnati Housing Authority has made one creative response to this issue by forming an association of Section 8 landlords, with the goal of enhancing their skills in property management.[7]

Develop Stepping Stones to Homeownership through Assisted Housing

As our homeowner focus groups repeatedly made clear to us, a key characteristic of a good neighborhood is a high proportion of owner occupancy. From these discussions, we gleaned that part of their aversion to rental properties comes from a fear of irresponsible managers and absentee owners, and part from a worry over tenants who damage and defile property because they "have no stake in it." We believe that the sorts of enhanced monitoring proposed above can allay many of these concerns. More may be required, however.

We recommend that another ingredient for building acceptance of deconcentrated assisted housing into a neighborhood is tying the assistance to a homeownership development process. That is, if deconcentrated assisted housing can be oriented (and then marketed) as a vehicle for helping low-income households become homeowners, public acceptance may be accentuated. We recognize that not all low-income households (especially those who reside in supportive housing facilities) can be expected (or even want) to become homeowners. Nevertheless, to the extent that those with both the motivation and feasible prospects of such can be placed in deconcentrated assisted housing, more benefits should be forthcoming.

Two sorts of initiatives provide encouraging guidance in this regard. Local housing authorities may foster homeownership both directly and indirectly. The new homeownership component of the Section 8 program, introduced as part of the Quality Housing and Work Responsibility Act of 1998 and implemented with final HUD rules in the fall of 2001, offers a direct means of tying deconcentrated Section 8 assistance to homeownership.[8]

Under this policy, PHAs are permitted to devise, within broad guidelines, plans for allowing eligible households to purchase homes, condominiums, and cooperatives and use monies from their Section 8 certificates to repay the mortgage for up to 10 years.[9] Households must meet a range of requirements for participating, including (1) meeting down-payment and Federal Housing Authority underwriting guidelines, (2) being a first-time homebuyer, (3) working more than a minimum number of hours per year and earning more than a prescribed income (if not elderly or disabled), and (4) buying a property meeting certain quality and legal standards. Homeownership certificates are portable to other jurisdictions, but the PHAs will recapture a pro-rata share of the support provided if the homebuyer sells the house before 10 years. Unfortunately, under the current structure there are no financial or other incentives to encourage PHAs to develop such Section 8 homeownership programs or employ them aggressively (National Housing Law Project 2001).

Several PHAs have operated programs to enhance the economic self-sufficiency of their residents and thereby indirectly boost their homeownership potential (Bogdon 1999). As typical parts of these programs, participants are eligible for intensified social work counseling for goal delineation, needs assessment, and training plans, homeownership assessments, free credit reports, assistance with credit repair, money management counseling, home repair classes, and matching savings accounts created from escrowed rental payments. The Charlotte Housing Authority's Gateway program, as an example, has been shown to dramatically increase participants' rates of becoming homeowners (Rohe and Stegman 1991; Rohe 1995; Rohe and Kleit 1997). Similarly, the Denver Housing Authority's Foundations for Home Ownership program has enabled dozens of residents of dispersed public housing and Section 8 projects to become homeowners during the past several years, with no reported foreclosures to date (Santiago and Galster 2001).

Burnish the Image of Deconcentrated Assisted Housing

Beyond the above-mentioned programmatic and operational changes, our findings lead us to suggest initiatives aimed at altering the *perceptions* of deconcentrated assisted housing programs held by residents in potential recipient neighborhoods and the public at large. Although changing the functional reality of assisted housing programs is a necessary condition for changing public perceptions and assuaging opposition, it may not be sufficient. We therefore recommend two sets of initiatives in this regard, related to collaboration with neighborhood groups and public education.

Collaborate with Neighborhood Groups

The recent housing policy history of Denver and Baltimore County demonstrates how a campaign of misinformation and fear-mongering can mobilize powerful forces in opposition to deconcentrated assisted housing programs. Therefore, wherever possible, local developers and operators of such housing might want to develop constructive ongoing relationships with neighborhood groups, homeowner associations, and other local opinion leaders (National Law Center on Homelessness and Poverty 1997).

The predominant goal is to build the trust of the community. The Denver case shows clearly that policymakers must build trust to allow neighborhood concerns (both when a facility is proposed and after it is in operation) to be heard and responded to sensitively and promptly. The public must trust that developers of deconcentrated assisted housing will be competent and principled, and that the local government will provide effective oversight.

As an example of affirmative response, in the years since the 1989 controversy the DHA has learned to work more openly with neighborhoods receiving dispersed public housing sites, demonstrating the DHA's understanding of the neighborhood's concerns and its commitment to avoiding "problem properties." The fact that none of our focus group participants cited the DHA as a source of their neighborhood's problems, plus the good public relations currently enjoyed by the DHA as evinced from multiple sources, should be grounds for optimism in light of the vitriol of a decade ago. By contrast, the ill repute in which the Housing Authority of Baltimore City is widely held throughout Baltimore County provides fertile ground for suspicion and fear of the Section 8 program as a vehicle for the "invasion of the city."

The desired collaborations may be spurred by local regulations requiring periodic public hearings on the operation of deconcentrated assisted housing sites, perhaps as prerequisite to continued licensing in the case of supportive housing or contract renewal in the case of Section 8. For instance, the current Denver regulations could be modified to require a public hearing on the operation of each supportive housing facility as part of the biennial renewal process. Evaluations of the facility's past two years' performance might be provided by a regulator, with permit renewals contingent on achievement of certain minimum performance standards. Several studies have documented the benefits of institutionalizing mechanisms of active community participation and interactions among all interested parties (Susskind 1990; Stamato 1990; Weisberg 1993; Hogan 1996, chap. 7).

Enhance Public Education

Enhanced public education is implied by our findings fundamentally because conventional fears about the impact of deconcentrated assisted housing programs are not, in general, justified. Indeed, when done well, assisted housing can provide positive neighborhood impacts while staying "below the radar" of proximate homeowners, as our focus groups clearly demonstrated. Our results thus support opinion poll studies of other researchers nationwide, which show that residents' actual experiences with assisted housing nearby are much more satisfactory than they had predicted (Arens 1993; Wahl 1993; Cook 1997). It also supports prior public opinion work on this issue, with Denver audiences in particular (Gould and O'Brien 1997).

A concerted, ongoing campaign to publicize assisted housing success stories could be very beneficial in convincing the public that such programs serve "deserving" households and can be developed in ways that can be good for neighborhoods (National Law Center on Homelessness and Poverty 1997). Many successful developers of supportive housing in Denver and elsewhere, for example, offer tours of their smoothly operating developments to leaders of neighborhoods in which new developments are being proposed (Takahashi 1997). The DHA blanketed the media with information on successful dispersed public housing sites, though it only did so as a reaction once the 1989 furor had erupted.

Particular attention needs to be paid in this public relations campaign to alter stereotypical images of residents in deconcentrated assisted housing (Turner, Popkin, and Cunningham 2000). It has often been observed that the public equates disruptive or illegal behaviors by tenants with receipt of housing assistance. Yet official investigations into the most highly publicized claims have found that the sources of nuisance were tenants having no connection with assisted housing (Turner, Popkin, and Cunningham 2000). Such misperceptions, and the generalized resentment against the "undeserving poor" we observed in our focus groups, might well be mollified if local housing authorities were more effective in providing poignant vignettes of assisted households (preferably, with a variety of races and ethnic groups portrayed) that had achieved economic independence through deconcentration programs.

Finally, we believe that local and federal policymakers should seriously consider renaming the set of deconcentrated housing programs. Inasmuch as "public housing" and "Section 8" currently carry a stigma, the aforementioned programmatic improvements face an uphill struggle to alter public opinion if the "new wine" is still presented in "old wineskins." A new symbolic umbrella under which the above-mentioned recommendations could flourish might yield dramatic payoffs for the political viability of a deconcentrated assisted housing program agenda. In this regard, the recent re-titling of Section 8 as "Housing Opportunity Vouchers" represents an appropriate step.

Develop Adequate Institutional Mechanisms for Policy Delivery

The preceding five planks to our plan for a more neighborhood-friendly strategy for deconcentrating assisted housing make significant demands on local institutions to develop, administer, and oversee such programs. As programs are currently structured, the bulk of the recommended development and operationalizing of impaction standards, monitoring of assisted tenants and landlords, homeownership program design and operation, and public education and outreach related to scattered-site public housing developments and the Section 8 program would fall upon local housing authorities. In the case of supportive housing programs, many of the same responsibilities would be the purview of a branch of municipal government.

Undoubtedly, some PHAs and local governments have proven that they have the requisite human, technological, and financial resources to run and oversee successful deconcentrated assisted housing programs. But others just as clearly do not, as HUD itself recognizes (HUD 2001). How, then, can our programmatic reforms be delivered in a consistently effective manner across the nation?

We believe that considerable experimentation is needed to find the best method for enhancing institutional capacity to operate neighborhood-friendly deconcentrated assisted housing programs. A recent proposal forwarded by Katz and Turner (2001) offers an illustration of one such innovative experiment. Their proposal seeks to achieve more metropolitan-wide administrative capacity for the Section 8 program, instead of the typically uneven, fragmented coverage now provided by a melange of PHAs in the region. They argue that HUD should allow interagency competition for administering a seamless Section 8 program across each metropolitan region, potentially involving bids from nonprofit organizations, state agencies, and PHAs.

Though this particular proposal has its shortcomings, we agree with two fundamental principles for expanding coordinated capacity that should be reflected in any future demonstration programs. First, there should be competitive awards of federal funds for housing program administration. Second, winning organizations should have finite-term contracts, which should be renewed only upon successful attainment of clear performance criteria.

It is clear that significant organizational capacity of the type envisioned exists outside PHAs in many metropolitan areas.[10] The court-ordered settlements in more than a dozen PHA desegregation suits mandated similar sorts of interorganizational competitions for administering deconcentration Section 8 programs (Popkin et al. 2000). Analogous capacities have been built in nonprofit mobility counseling centers through HUD's Regional Opportunity Counseling demonstration program. Though none of these precedents involve the comprehensive sorts of activities we recommend above, we think they offer far more promise as a delivery vehicle than would attempted reforms administered solely by some dysfunctional PHA or municipal government. Whatever new administrative organizational structures are envisioned, it is crucial that the various programmatic elements collaborate closely across the entire metropolitan area.

Conclusion

Spatially deconcentrating households with low incomes or special needs through assisted housing programs is proceeding apace on several programmatic fronts. Supporters and substantial research argue that these initiatives generate benefits for participants and society as a whole, inasmuch as the superior neighborhood environments produced by such programs increase the likelihood that participants eventually will be able to achieve economic self-sufficiency.

Yet efforts to open up neighborhoods to those with low incomes and special needs are often met with "not in my backyard" (NIMBY) reactions from prospective neighbors. Why NIMBY? It clearly is motivated by a complex nexus of fears about what assisted housing will mean for quality of life, safety, and property values. Assisted housing is burdened by a terrible public image—an image so bad that many homeowners we observed assume that problem properties in the neighborhood are assisted housing, whether correctly or not. Sometimes, this stereotype-based NIMBY reaction marshals sufficient political opposition to significantly alter, if not actually thwart, the content and scale of deconcentrated assisted housing programs.

By comprehensively examining the dispersed public housing program, supportive housing program, and Section 8 program in Denver and Baltimore County, we found that NIMBY reactions are not always justified. When developed, sited, and subsequently administered effectively, deconcentrated assisted housing programs do not lead to upsurges of serious crime and even can produce substantial enhancements to values of single-family homes nearby when the rehabilitation of assisted properties is involved. However, we also found that deconcentrated assisted housing programs can hurt neighborhoods when they end up excessively concentrated, especially in low-value, vulnerable market contexts; are large scale; and pay insufficient attention to maintaining proper actions by assisted tenants, managers, and property owners.

Thus, NIMBY should not be universally dismissed as a phenomenon based purely on unfounded fears and stereotypes. In some cases, it may be a legitimate public reaction to badly designed and implemented assisted housing policies. Context matters. It is our hope that this book has helped provide a basis for distinguishing between the "bad" and "good" forms of deconcentrated assisted housing policy.

The cornerstone for reestablishing a strong political constituency for deconcentrated assisted housing and defusing potential local opposition must be an attack on the public images surrounding such housing. This attack requires changing both the *objective* conditions associated with deconcentrated assisted housing and the public's *perceptions* of these conditions. This will necessitate comprehensive revisions in deconcentrated assisted housing program design and operations—including the siting, concentration, scale, and type of assisted housing; selection and monitoring of tenants and landlords; homeownership initiatives; and public education and relations. Moreover, it will require a realignment of deconcentration housing policy within the larger realm of local housing policies, perhaps requiring new institutional delivery systems.

If these recommendations were implemented, they would produce a more neighborhood-friendly strategy. The strategy would ensure that only the "good" forms of deconcentrated assisted housing were promulgated and also that the public was aware of this. We believe that the reaction of neighbors to assisted housing nearby then would more typically become "Why *not* in my backyard?"

Notes

1. This position should not be confused as advocacy for *only* deconcentration as a means of supplying assisted housing opportunities. It should also not be misinterpreted as implicit criticism of community development corporations and others who seek to develop affordable housing in the context of revitalizing poverty-stricken neighborhoods.

2. These figures are meant to illustrate the interaction between positive and negative externalities that would be consistent with the net impact results from our property value models. The

externality curves themselves are not based directly on empirical findings, however, and are only meant to represent a range of possible curves that could fit the net impact results.

3. The DHA has already undertaken significant conventional public housing deconcentration efforts, e.g., converting North Lincoln Park into a "Campus of Learners" that incorporates lower on-site densities, dispersing some tenants into nonimpacted areas, and limiting the total time spent by tenants in public housing.

4. One such source for property values, which we used for this study, is the register of home sales maintained by the local property tax assessor's office. Home Mortgage Disclosure Act data, available from the Federal Financial Institutions Examination Council, is another source for annual property values at a census tract level. The Census Bureau's American Community Survey (ACS) may also prove to be a valuable source of data, if it is fully implemented. The ACS would, once operational, provide annually updated, 5-year moving averages of demographic, economic, social, and housing indicators at the census tract level of geography.

5. Almost all personal computer mapping programs, such as ArcView, MapInfo, and Maptitude, have geocoding capability built in. Furthermore, these packages are not prohibitively expensive.

6. A sample of current and former DHA residents ($N = 60$) were asked the open-ended question, "What did you dislike most about living in public housing?" Problems with neighbors and neighborhoods were cited by 23 percent of the respondents. When asked about what the DHA could do to improve its housing, the suggestion offered second most frequently was "to conduct better tenant screening" (Santiago and Galster 2001).

7. We are indebted to David Varady for bringing this to our attention.

8. The use of Section 8 homeownership certificates was mandated in the consent decree settling the case against the Housing Authority of Baltimore City, as described in chapter 3.

9. The term can be extended to 15 years if the mortgage term is 20 years or more. There is no time limit if the household contains elderly or disabled people.

10. Whether such organizations would only administer the Section 8 program, or also might be ceded some authority over supportive housing by local governments, remains to be seen.

Appendix

Econometric, Spatial Econometric, and Data Issues

Data Quality

In estimating the values of the coefficients in each of the property-value and crime models, we took a number of steps to eliminate or minimize several data conditions that could have adversely affected our estimations. These steps are described below.

Outlier observations have the potential to exert undue influence on regression estimations and bias results. In estimating our property-value models, we wished to exclude from our database home sales that were highly idiosyncratic and did not represent arms-length transactions. In this vein, we eliminated the top and bottom 2 percent of all observations according to sales price and land area.

On the basis of trial regressions, we also dropped records yielding regression residuals greater than 2 standard deviations from the mean value of all observations. Sales were also dropped for properties that did not have a complete set of house characteristics. See Galster and others (2000, annex B; 1999, annex B) for details. Similarly, we excluded any crime reporting rate area with a 1990 population of less than 40 from the crime models because the small denominator resulted in extremely high crime rates that had a distorting effect on the model estimations.

Econometric Issues

One of the key assumptions in ordinary-least-squares regression is that the error term in the regression model has finite and constant variance. Rejection of this assumption, *heteroskedasticity*, can cause inefficiency and bias in the parameter estimates (Intriligator 1978, 156). We controlled for an unknown source of heteroskedasticity of the model error terms in our property-value regressions using the White (1980) covariance matrix to estimate all standard errors. For the crime models, we used a dummy-variable approach to control for both heteroskedasticity and autocorrelation (see below).

Autocorrelation occurs when the error terms of the regression estimations are not independent of one another, violating one of the assumptions of ordinary-least-squares regression. Autocorrelation results in estimators that are not efficient and can affect tests of statistical significance (Intriligator 1978, 159). Because our crime reporting rates were panel data (i.e., both time-series and cross-sectional), we had strong reason to suspect that both autocorrelation and heteroskedasticity would be a problem. Because the source of the problem was known to us (i.e., it was related to the fact that we were looking at a fixed set of analysis sites over a period of several years), we were able to use a least-squares dummy-variable approach (Hsiao 1986, 29–32) to correct for both conditions. We defined a series of dummy variables for each supportive housing analysis site to incorporate into our crime models.

Spatial Econometric Issues

Spatial dependence, sometimes known as *spatial autocorrelation*, is analogous to serial correlation and refers to the possibility that, in the case of the property-value model, the observed price of one home is not independent of the prices of other homes nearby in geographic space. The presence of spatial dependence would violate one of the key assumptions of the error terms in the models—their independence across observations. If left uncorrected, such spatial dependence would lead to biased parameter estimates and misleading *t*-tests for statistical significance levels of parameters.

To test for this potential problem, we employed a specification that Can and Megbolugbe (1997) found to be robust. We calculated the *spatial lag* of the dependent variable (house price or crime rate) and included it in our model as an independent variable. The spatial lag is a weighted average of all of the observations of the dependent variable within a certain distance from the reference observation. The average is weighted by the *spatial weight*, which is some function of the distance between observations. Consistent with the approach of Can and Megbolugbe, we used the inverse of the distance $(1/d)$ as the spatial weight. For the property-value model, the formula for the spatial lag is

$$\text{Spatial lag } (P_i) = \sum_j \left[(1/d_{ij}) \,/\, \sum_j 1/d_{ij} \right] P_j$$

where P_i is the sale for which we are calculating the spatial lag, d_{ij} is the distance between sales i and j, and P_i is one of the set of all sales within distance D of P_j and that occurred within the six months prior to the date of P_I. For the crime models, we substituted crime rate for P in the formula above, used the centroids of the analysis subareas as points for determining d_{ij}, and calculated the spatial lag using crime rates for subareas in the same year as the reference observation.

One of the key parameters is the selection of the cutoff distance D. The choice of D depends upon the researcher's knowledge and assumptions as to how far the supposed spatial dependence is likely to be felt, but can be tested by evaluating the effectiveness of different choices. For the property-value model, we assumed that a minimum cutoff distance of 2,000 feet would be necessary to see a spatial effect.

We calculated spatial lags at this distance, but also tested spatial lags with cutoffs of 5,000 and 10,000 feet to examine the possibility that spatial dependence may exist over a larger area. Because the crime model did not use point data, it was necessary to test larger cutoff distances than for the property model. We tried distance cutoffs of 10,000, 12,500, and 15,000 feet.

Because of the large numbers of house sales, calculating the spatial lag was computationally intensive and very time consuming for the property-value models. We therefore conducted several test cases before attempting to create spatial lags for the entire set of house sales. We calculated spatial lag variables for three census tracts and estimated one of our model specifications first without any spatial lag variable, and then trying each of the spatial lag variables in turn. The test was whether the addition of the spatial lag variable significantly improved the goodness of fit (R^2) of the model.

We calculated and tested six alternative specifications of spatial lag for each census tract. We created spatial lag variables for the sales price and for the log of sales price using cutoffs of 2,000, 5,000, and 10,000 feet. To give some idea of the computationally intensive nature of determining spatial lag, calculating six spatial lag variables for each of six census tracts took more than 32 hours on a Pentium computer.

For the property-value model, none of the spatial lag variables improved the model fit by any substantial amount. If the cost of computing the spatial lag were small, one might decide to include it in the models anyway. Given the fact that creating spatial lags for more than 100,000 sales would take a great deal of time, we decided that the negligible improvement in the model estimations was not worth the cost of such an effort. We therefore did not include the spatial lag in our property-value models.

For the crime models, however, we found that the introduction of the spatial lag variable did affect the regression results. Because the largest improvement of the estimates was produced by using the 15,000-foot cutoff, we included this variable in all of the crime regressions.

Spatial heterogeneity refers to the systematic variation in the behavior of a given process across space. Here, the issue was whether the parameters of the regression equation were invariant across space or whether they assumed different values according to the local socioeconomic, demographic, and/or physical contexts of the various neighborhoods across a metropolitan area. If such were the case, the error term would be heteroskedastic. To deal with this issue, we employed the "spatial contextual expansion with quadratic trend" specification as suggested by Can and Megbolugbe (1997). This method involved adding to the models the latitude (X) and longitude (Y) coordinates of each observation in the following variables (normalized so that zero values represent the center of the city): X, Y, XY, X^2, and Y^2. Higher numerical values of X (Y) signified increasing distance from the center of the city heading west (north). These variables typically proved statistically significant in our aggregate property-value model specifications, suggesting that our various controls for local fixed effects needed further supplementation from these spatial coordinates. We therefore included these variables in all of our property-value models.

Because the observations in the crime models did not employ point data, however, we would have had to use the centroids of the different subareas to construct the X and Y coordinates. Because these variables would have been highly correlated with the site and tract dummy variables already included in these specifications, we did not include corrections for spatial heterogeneity in the crime models.

Specification of Key Property-Value-Impact Variables

The following presents our coding scheme for the property-value-impact model variables. Define distance rings of 0–500 feet, 501–1,000 feet, and 1,001–2,000 feet. Let $A_i = \{A_1, A_2, \ldots\}$ be the set of subsidized housing sites for which we want to measure impacts. For the aggregated models, A_i is a subset of all sites that were first occupied at least two years after the earliest date in the home price sales data (i.e., 1991 for Baltimore County and 1989 for Denver) and were continuously occupied through the 3rd Qtr. 1997.

The selection of A sites is further narrowed to those that have sufficient numbers of pre and post sales observations within 2,000 feet. For the disaggregated models, A_i consists of a single site. Let $B_i = \{B_1, B_2, \ldots\}$ be the set of all remaining subsidized housing sites not in A_i.

Given a house sale X and the sets A_i and B_i, let dXA_i be the distance (ring) from A_i to X and dXB_i be the distance (ring) from B_i to X. Also define $DPre\_dXA_i$ as a pre flag for the distance from site A_i to X, $DPost\_dXA_i$ as a post flag for the distance from site A_i to X, and $DPost\_dXB_i$ as a post flag for the distance from site B_i to X. These pre and post flags are coded as follows:

> For each A_i, we code $DPre\_dXA_i = 1$ if and only if (1) X occurs pre A_i, (2) there exists no other A_i such that $dXA_i \leq 2,000$ and X occurs in a quarter when A_i is occupied (i.e., post), and (3) there exists no B_i such that $dXB_i \leq 2,000$ and X occurs in a quarter when B_i is occupied (i.e., post).

> For each A_i, we code $DPost\_dXA_i = 1$ if and only if X occurs post A_i.

> For each B_i, we code $DPost\_dXB_i = 1$ if and only if (1) X occurs in a quarter when B_i is occupied and (2) there exists some A_i such that X occurs post A_i and $dXA_i \leq 2,000$.

> We delete sale X if there exists some A_i such that X occurs pre A_i and $dXA_i \leq 2,000$ and some B_i such that X occurs in a quarter when B_i is occupied and $dXB_i \leq 2,000$.

> We delete sale X if there exists some B_i such that X occurs while B_i is occupied and $dXB_i \leq 2,000$ and there exists no A_i such that $dXA_i \leq 2,000$.

To obtain the aggregated site impact variables, we add together the dummies *DPost_dXA$_i$* and *DPost_dXB$_i$* to get *Post500*, *Post1k*, and *Post2k*, and we add together the dummies *Pre_dXA$_i$* to get *Pre500*, *Pre1k*, and *Pre2k*.

To create the impact variables for unit counts, we proceed as described above but set *DPost_* and *DPre_* equal to the number of occupied units at the site instead of to 1.

To create the trend variables, we proceed as follows:

Given a distance ring *d*:
If *Post_d* = 0, then *TRPost_d* = 0

If *Post_d* > 0, then *TRPost_d* = 1 if the sale occurred in the first quarter after the first site in the distance ring was occupied, = 2 if the sale occurred in the second quarter after the first site in the distance ring was occupied, and so on.

References

Advisory Commission on Regulatory Barriers to Affordable Housing. 1991. *Not in my backyard: removing regulatory barriers to affordable housing*. Washington, DC: U.S. Department of Housing and Urban Development.

Anselin, L. 1992. *Spacestat tutorial: a workbook for using Spacestat in the analysis of spatial data*. Santa Barbara, CA: National Center for Geographic Information Analysis.

Ards, S. 1991. The role of housing vouchers in Baltimore City, Maryland. *Review of Black Political Economy* 19, 111–23.

Arens, D. A. 1993. What do the neighbors think now? Community residences on Long Island, New York. *Community Mental Health Journal* 29: 235–39.

Bailey, K. 1990. City profile of tenants under fire. *Rocky Mountain News*, May 23, p. 7.

Bailey, T. C., and A. C. Gatrell. 1995. *Interactive spatial data analysis*. New York: Wiley.

Baltimore County. 1993. *Comprehensive Housing Affordability Strategy (CHAS)*. Baltimore: Baltimore County Department of Community Development.

Bauman, J. 1987. *Public housing, race, and renewal: urban planning in Philadelphia, 1920–1974*. Philadelphia: Temple University Press.

Bauman, J. F., N. P. Hummon, and E. K. Muller. 1991. Public-housing, isolation, and the urban underclass—Philadelphia Homes, Richard Allen 1941–1965. *Journal of Urban History* 17: 264–92.

Beck, P. 1996. Fighting Section 8 discrimination: the Fair Housing Act's new frontier. *Harvard Civil Rights–Civil Liberties Law Review* 31: 155–77.

Boeckh, J., M. Dear, and S. M. Taylor. 1980. Property values and mental-health facilities in metropolitan Toronto. *Canadian Geographer–Geographe Canadien* 24: 270–85.

Bogdon, A. S. 1999. What can we learn from previous housing-based self-sufficiency? In S. Newman, ed., *The home front: implications of welfare reform for housing policy*. Washington, DC: Urban Institute Press.

Boger, J. C. 1996. Toward ending residential segregation: a fair share proposal for the next reconstruction. In J. C. Boger and J. W. Wegner, eds., *Race, poverty, and American cities*. Chapel Hill: University of North Carolina Press.

Bovard, J. 1994a. Clinton's wrecking ball for the suburbs. *Wall Street Journal*, August 4.

———. 1994b. Suburban guerrilla. *American Spectator* (September): 26–32.

Boydell, K. M., J. N. Trainor, and A. M. Pierri. 1989. The effect of group homes for the mentally ill on residential property values. *Hospital and Community Psychiatry* 40: 957–58.

Bradburn, N. M., S. Sudman, and G. L. Gockel. 1971. *Side by side: integrated neighborhoods in America*. Chicago: Quadrangle Books.

Briggs, X. de S. 1997. Moving up versus moving out: neighborhood effects in housing mobility programs. *Housing Policy Debate* 8: 195–234.

Briggs, X. de S., J. T. Darden, and A. Aidala. 1999. In the wake of desegregation—early impacts of scattered-site public housing on neighborhoods in Yonkers, New York. *Journal of the American Planning Association* 65: 27–49.

Brill, William, and Associates. 1975. *Victimization, fear of crime, and altered behavior: a profile of the crime problem in four housing projects in Boston.* Washington, DC: U.S. Department of Housing and Urban Development.

———. 1976. *Victimization, fear of crime, and altered behavior: a profile of the crime problem in William Nicherson Jr. Gardens, Los Angeles, California.* Washington, DC: U.S. Department of Housing and Urban Development.

———. 1977a. *Victimization, fear of crime, and altered behavior: a profile of the crime problem in Murphy Homes, Baltimore, Maryland.* Washington, DC: U.S. Department of Housing and Urban Development.

———. 1977b. *Victimization, fear of crime, and altered behavior: a profile of the crime problem in Capper Dwellings, Washington, DC.* Washington, DC: U.S. Department of Housing and Urban Development.

———. 1977c. *Victimization, fear of crime, and altered behavior: a profile of the crime problem in Scott/Carver Homes, Dade County, Florida.* Washington, DC: U.S. Department of Housing and Urban Development.

Brooks-Gunn, J., G. J. Duncan, and J. L. Aber, eds. 1997. *Neighborhood poverty: context and consequences for children.* New York: Russell Sage Foundation.

Calavita, N., and K. Grimes. 1998. Inclusionary housing in California. *Journal of American Planning Association* 64, 150–69.

Can, A., and I. Megbolugbe. 1997. Spatial dependence and house price index construction. *Journal of Real Estate Finance and Economics* 14: 203–22.

Carson, L. 1994a. City unqualified for MTO. *Baltimore Sun*, September 23. p. 5B.

———. 1994b. City vows to proceed on housing. *Baltimore Sun*, September 21. p. 1B.

Cisneros, H. 1995. *Regionalism, the new geography of opportunity.* Washington, DC: U.S. Department of Housing and Urban Development.

City and County of Denver. 1989. *Replacement housing plan for the housing authority of the City and County of Denver.*

———. 1998a. *Large residential care use handbook.*

———. 1998b. *Bi-annual residential care use renewal.*

———. 1998c. *Residential care uses ordinance.*

Colwell, P. F., C. A. Dehring, and N. A. Lash. 2000. The effect of group homes on neighborhood property values. *Land Economics* 76: 615–37.

Cook, J. R. 1997. Neighbors' perceptions of group homes. *Community Mental Health Journal* 33: 287–99.

Coulibaly, M., R. L. Green, and D. M. James. 1998. *Segregation in federally subsidized low-income housing in the United States.* Westport, CT: Praeger.

Cox, K. R. 1982. Housing tenure and neighborhood activism. *Urban Affairs Review* 18: 107–29.

Cummings, J. L., and D. DiPasquale. 1999. The Low-Income Housing Tax Credit: an analysis of the first ten years. *Housing Policy Debate* 10: 251–307.

Cummings, P. M., and J. D. Landis. 1993. *Relationships between affordable housing developments and neighboring property values.* Working Paper 599. Berkeley, CA: Institute of Urban and Regional Development, University of California at Berkeley.

Cunningham, M. K., D. J. Sylvester, and M. A. Turner. 2000. Section 8 families in the Washington region: neighborhood choices and constraints. Paper presented at the Annual Meeting of the Association for Public Policy Analysis and Management, Seattle, November.

Davis, M. 1993. The Gautreaux Assisted Housing Program. In T. Kingsley and M. A. Turner, eds., *Housing markets and housing mobility.* Washington, DC: Urban Institute Press.

Dear, M. 1977. Impact of mental health facilities on property values. *Community Mental Health Journal* 13: 150–59.

————. 1992. Understanding and overcoming the NIMBY syndrome. *Journal of the American Planning Association* 58: 288–300.

Dear, M., L. Takahashi, and R. Wilton. 1996. *Factors influencing community acceptance: summary of the evidence*. Washington, DC: Campaign for New Community Resource Document Series.

Dear, M., and J. Wolch. 1987. *Landscapes of despair: from deinstitutionalization to homelessness*. Princeton, NJ: Princeton University Press.

Denver Community Redevelopment Agency. No date. *Housing resource directory: providers–services–advocates in the Denver metropolitan area*.

De Salvo, J. 1974. Neighborhood upgrading effects of middle-income housing projects in New York City. *Journal of Urban Economics* 1: 269–77.

District of Columbia Association for Retarded Citizens. 1987. *Group homes for persons with mental retardation in the District of Columbia: effects of single-family house sales and sales prices*. Washington, DC.

Downs, A. 1973. *Opening up the suburbs: an urban strategy for America*. New Haven, CT: Yale University Press.

Dunworth, T., and A. Saiger. 1993. *Drugs and crime in public housing: a three-city analysis*. Santa Monica, CA: RAND Corporation.

Earls, M., and G. Nelson. 1988. The relationship between long-term psychiatric clients' psychological well-being and their perceptions of housing and social support. *American Journal of Community Psychology* 16: 279–93.

Edkins, I. 1996. *The controversy over Moving to Opportunity for fair housing*. Master's thesis, George Washington University, Washington, DC.

Ellen, I. G., and M. Turner. 1997. Does neighborhood matter? Assessing recent evidence. *Housing Policy Debate* 8: 833–66.

Epp, G. 1996. Emerging strategies for revitalizing public housing communities. *Housing Policy Debate* 7: 563–88.

Evans, J. 1996. In Baltimore, leaving behind a city's crime. *Washington Post*, p. E1.

Farber, S. 1986. Market-segmentation and the effects on group homes for the handicapped on residential property-values. *Urban Studies* 23: 519–25.

Farley, J. E. 1982. Has public-housing gotten a bum rap—the incidence of crime in St. Louis public-housing developments. *Environment and Behavior* 14: 443–77.

Fischer, P. 1999. *Section 8 and the public housing revolution: Where will the families go?* Chicago: Woods Fund of Chicago.

Freeman, L., and W. Rohe. 2000. Subsidized housing and neighborhood racial transition: an empirical investigation. *Housing Policy Debate* 11: 67–89.

Freudenberg, W. R., and S. K. Pastor. 1992. NIMBYs and LULUs: stalking the syndrome. *Journal of Social Issues* 48: 39–61.

Fuchs, E., and W. McAllister. 1996. *The continuum of care: a report of the new federal policy to address homelessness*. Washington, DC: U.S. Department of Housing and Urban Development.

Gabriel, S. A., and J. R. Wolch. 1984. Spillover effects of human-service facilities in a racially segmented housing market. *Journal of Urban Economics* 16: 339–50.

Galster, G. C. 1990a. Federal fair housing policy: the great misapprehension. In D. DiPasquale and L. C. Keyes, eds., *Building foundations: housing and federal policy*. Philadelphia: University of Pennsylvania Press.

————. 1990b. White flight from racially integrated neighborhoods in the 1970s—the Cleveland experience. *Urban Studies* 27: 385–99.

————. 2002. An economic efficiency analysis of deconcentrating poverty populations. *Journal of Housing Economics* 11, 4: 303–29.

————. 2003. The effects of MTO on sending and receiving neighborhoods. In J. Goering, T.

Richardson, and J. Feins, eds., *Choosing a better life? A social experiment in leaving poverty behind*. Washington, DC: Urban Institute Press, 365–82.

Galster, G. C., and S. P. Killen. 1995. The geography of metropolitan opportunity—a reconnaissance and conceptual-framework. *Housing Policy Debate* 6: 7–43.

Galster, G. C., K. Pettit, P. Tatian, A. M. Santiago, and S. Newman. 2000. *The impacts of supportive housing on neighborhoods and neighbors: final report*. Washington, DC: U.S. Department of Housing and Urban Development.

Galster, G. C., A. M. Santiago, R. Smith, and P. A. Tatian. 1999. *Assessing property value impacts of dispersed housing subsidy programs: final report*. Washington, DC: U.S. Department of Housing and Urban Development.

Galster, G. C., P. Tatian, and R. Smith. 1999. The impact of neighbors who use Section 8 certificates on property values. *Housing Policy Debate* 10: 879–917.

Galster, G. C., and Y. Williams. 1994. Dwellings for the severely mentally disabled and neighborhood property-values—the details matter. *Land Economics* 70: 466–77.

Galster, G. C., and A. Zobel. 1998. Will dispersed housing programmes reduce social problems in the U.S.? *Housing Studies* 13: 605–22.

Gephart, M. A. 1997. Neighborhoods and communities as contexts for development. In J. Brooks-Gunn, G. J. Duncan, and J. L. Aber, eds., *Neighborhood poverty: context and consequences for children*. New York: Russell Sage Foundation.

Gillies, F. 1972. Housing inaction scored. *Denver Post*, November 16, pp. 35, 42.

Ginther, D., R. Haveman, and B. Wolfe. 2000. Neighborhood attributes as determinants of children's outcomes: How robust are the relationships? *Journal of Human Resources* 35: 603–42.

Goering, J. M., ed. 1986. *Housing desegregation and federal policy*. Chapel Hill: University of North Carolina Press.

Goering, J., T. Richardson, and J. Feins, eds. 2003. *Choosing a better life? A social experiment in leaving poverty behind*. Washington, DC: Urban Institute Press.

Goering, J. M., and M. Coulibably. 1989. Investigating public-housing segregation—conceptual and methodological issues. *Urban Affairs Review* 25: 265–97.

Goering, J. M., H. Stebbins, and M. Siewert. 1995. *Promoting housing choice in HUD's rental assistance programs*. Report to Congress. Washington, DC: Office of Policy Development and Research, U.S. Department of Housing and Urban Development.

Goering, J. M., J. Kraft, J. Feins, D. McInnis, M. J. Holin, and H. Elhassan. 1999. *Moving to opportunity for Fair Housing Demonstration Program*. Washington, DC: Office of Policy Development and Research, U.S. Department of Housing and Urban Development.

Goetz, E. G., H. K. Lam, and A. Heitlinger. 1996. *There goes the neighborhood? The impact of subsidized multi-family housing on urban neighborhoods*. Minneapolis: Center for Urban and Regional Affairs, University of Minnesota.

Goldstein, I., and W. Yancy. 1986. Public housing projects, blacks and public policy. In J. Goering, ed., *Housing desegregation and federal policy*. Chapel Hill: University of North Carolina Press.

Gould, M., and T. O'Brien. 1997. *Neighborhood attitudes about the placement of services and housing for groups protected by the federal Fair Housing Act: final report of a year-long study involving focus groups and a survey of neighborhood residents*. Denver: Center for Human Investment Policy, University of Colorado—Denver.

Graham, L., and R. Logan. 1990. Social class and tactics: neighborhood opposition to group homes. *Sociological Quarterly* 31: 513–29.

Gray, R., and S. Tursky. 1986. Location and racial/ethnic occupancy patterns for HUD-subsidized family housing in ten metropolitan areas. In J. M. Goering, ed., *Housing desegregation and federal policy*. Chapel Hill: University of North Carolina Press.

Grieson, R. E., and J. R. White. 1989. The existence and capitalization of neighborhood externalities—a reassessment. *Journal of Urban Economics* 25: 68–76.

Griffith, D. 1987. *Spatial autocorrelation: a primer.* Washington, DC: American Association of Geographers.

Guhathakurta, S., and A. H. Mushkatel. 2000. Does locational choice matter? A comparison of different subsidized housing programs in Phoenix, Arizona. *Urban Affairs Review* 35: 520–40.

Guy, D. C., J. L. Hysom, and S. R. Ruth. 1985. The effect of subsidized housing on values of adjacent housing. *Journal of the American Real Estate & Urban Economics Association* 13: 378–87.

HABC (Housing Authority of Baltimore City). 1993. MTO demonstration program application.

Hall, G., G. Nelson, and H. Fowler. 1987. Housing for the chronically mentally ill disabled: part I—conceptual framework and social context. *Canadian Journal of Community Mental Health* 6: 65–78.

Hargreaves, B., J. Callanan, and G. Maskell. 1998. Does community housing reduce neighborhood property values? Paper presented at the American Real Estate and Urban Economics Association (AREUEA) Annual Meeting, Chicago, January 3.

Harkness, J., S. Newman, G. Galster, and J. D. Reschovsky. 1997. Life-cycle costs of housing for the mentally ill. *Journal of Housing Economics* 12: 561–77.

Harrell, A., and C. Gouvis. 1994. *Predicting neighborhood risk of crime.* Washington, DC: Urban Institute Press.

Hartung, J. M., and J. R. Henig. 1997. Housing vouchers and certificates as a vehicle for deconcentrating the poor: evidence from the Washington, D.C., metropolitan area. *Urban Affairs Review* 32: 403–19.

Hayes, T. J., and C. B. Tatham. 1989. *Focus group interviews: a reader.* Chicago: American Marketing Association.

Hendren, J. 1996. Judge approves plan to relocate 2,000 black families to white suburbs. Associated Press, June 26.

Henig, J. R. 1994. To know them is to…? Proximity to shelters and support for the homeless. *Social Science Quarterly* 75: 741–54.

Hersl, J. 1994. Move to opportunity? Please explain. *Dundalk Eagle*, May 12.

Heumann, L. 1996. Assisted living in public housing? A case study mixing frail elderly and younger persons with chronic mental illness and substance abuse histories. *Housing Policy Debate* 7: 447–72.

Hirsch, A. R. 1983. *Making the second ghetto: race and housing in Chicago, 1940–1960.* New York: Cambridge University Press.

Hogan, J. 1996. *Scattered-site housing: characteristics and consequences.* Washington, DC: Office of Policy Development and Research, U.S. Department of Housing and Urban Development.

Holzman, H. R. 1996. Criminological research on public housing: toward a better understanding of people, places, and spaces. *Crime & Delinquency* 42: 361–78.

Holzman, H. R., R. A. Hyatt, and J. Dempster. 2001. Patterns of aggravated assault in public housing. *Violence Against Women* 7: 662–84.

Hsiao, C. 1986. *Analysis of panel data.* New York: Cambridge University Press.

HUD (U.S. Department of Housing and Urban Development). 1995. *Supportive housing application: moving toward a continuum of care.* Document HUD–40076. Washington, DC.

———. 1996. *Expanding housing choices for HUD-assisted families.* Washington, DC: Office of Policy Development and Research, U.S. Department of Housing and Urban Development.

———. 1999. *Moving to Opportunity for Fair Housing demonstration program.* Washington, DC: Office of Policy Development and Research, U.S. Department of Housing and Urban Development.

————. 2000. *Section 8 tenant-based housing assistance: a look back after 30 years* (PDF). Available at http://www.huduser.org/publications/pubasst/look.html (accessed January 16, 2002).

————. 2001. *Tools and strategies for improving community relations in the housing choice voucher program*. Washington, DC: Office of Policy Development and Research, U.S. Department of Housing and Urban Development. Available at http://www.huduser.org/publications/pubasst/hcvpguide.html (accessed December 2001).

Husock, H. 1994. Voucher plan for housing: a Trojan horse. *Wall Street Journal,* December 12, p. A14.

Iglhaut, D. M. 1988. *The impact of group homes on residential property values.* Upper Marlboro, MD: Research and Public Facilities Planning Division, Prince George's County.

Intriligator, M. D. 1978. *Econometric models, techniques, and applications.* Englewood Cliffs, NJ: Prentice-Hall.

Johnson, M. P., H. F. Ladd, and J. Ludwig. 2002. The benefits and costs of residential-mobility programs for the poor. *Housing Studies* 17: 125–38.

Johnston, D. 1969. Low-income housing plan ready to go. *Denver Post,* November 20, p. 37.

Katz, B., and M. A. Turner. 2001. Who should run the housing voucher program? A reform proposal. *Housing Policy Debate* 12: 239–62.

Katz, L. F., J. R. Kling, and J. B. Liebman. 2001. Moving to opportunity in Boston: early results of a randomized mobility experiment. *Quarterly Journal of Economics* 116: 607–54.

Kaufman, S., and J. L. Smith. 1997. Implementing change in locally unwanted land use: the case of GSX. *Journal of Planning Education and Research* 16: 188–200.

Kaufman, S., and J. L. Smith. 1999. Framing and reframing in land use change conflicts. *Journal of Architectural and Planning Research* 16: 164–80.

Keating, W. D. 1994. *The suburban racial dilemma: housing and neighborhoods.* Philadelphia: Temple University Press.

Kingsley, G. T., J. Johnson, and K. Pettit. 2001. *HOPE VI and Section 8: spatial patterns in relocation.* Washington, DC: Urban Institute.

Kotlowitz, A. 1991. *There are no children here: the story of two boys growing up in the other America.* New York: Doubleday.

Krueger, R. A. 1994. *Focus groups: a practical guide for applied research.* Thousand Oaks, CA: Sage Publications.

Lake, R. W. 1981. *The new suburbanites: race and housing.* New Brunswick, NJ: Center for Urban Policy Research, Rutgers University.

Lake, R. W. 1993. Rethinking NIMBY. *Journal of the American Planning Association* 59: 87–93.

Lauber, D. 1986. *Impacts on the surrounding neighborhood of group homes for persons with disabilities.* Springfield, IL: Report to the Governor's Planning Council on Developmental Disabilities.

Leavitt, J., and A. Loukaitou-Sider. 1995. A decent home and a suitable environment—dilemmas of public-housing residents in Los Angeles. *Journal of Architectural and Planning Research* 12: 221–39.

Lee, C.-M., D. Culhane, and S. Wachter. 1999. The differential impacts of federally assisted housing programs on nearby property values: a Philadelphia case study. *Housing Policy Debate* 10: 75–93.

Leventhal, T., and J. Brooks-Gunn. 2000. The neighborhoods they lived in: the effect of neighborhood residence on child and adolescent outcomes. *Psychological Bulletin* 126, 309–37.

Lindauer, M., P. Tung, and F. O'Donnell. 1980. *The effect of community residences for the mentally retarded on real estate in the neighborhoods in which they are located.* Brockport: State University of New York at Brockport.

Lindsay, S. 1998. Denver ordered to provide housing for mentally ill. *Rocky Mountain News,* May 29, pp. 4,7.

Lucas, W. 1997. *Baltimore County's eastern sector: rental housing market study*. Boston: Economic Market Analysis Division, Massachusetts State Office, U.S. Department of Housing and Urban Development.

Ludwig, J., and S. Stolzberg. 1995. HUD's Moving to Opportunity demonstration: uncertain benefits, unlikely costs, unfortunate politics. *Georgetown Public Policy Review* 1: 25–37.

Ludwig, J., G. J. Duncan, and J. C. Pinkston. 2000. *Neighborhood effects on economic self-sufficiency: evidence from a randomized housing-mobility experiment*. Working Paper 159. Northwestern University—University of Chicago Joint Center for Poverty Research. Available at http://www.jcpr.org/wp/WPprofile.cfm?ID=165 (accessed June 25, 2001).

Ludwig, J., G. J. Duncan, and P. Hirschfield. 2001. Urban poverty and juvenile crime: evidence from a randomized housing-mobility experiment. *Quarterly Journal of Economics* 116: 655–79.

Ludwig, J., H. F. Ladd, and G. J. Duncan. 2001. Urban poverty and educational outcomes. In W. G. Gale and J. Rothenberg-Pack, eds., *Brookings-Wharton papers on urban affairs: 2001*. Washington, DC: Brookings Institution Press.

Lyons, R. F., and S. Loveridge. 1993. *An hedonic estimation of the effect of federally subsidized housing on nearby residential property values*. Staff Paper P93–6. Saint Paul: Department of Agriculture and Applied Economics, University of Minnesota.

McDougall, H. A. 1993. *Black Baltimore: a new theory of community*. Philadelphia: Temple University Press.

Mallach, A. 1984. *Inclusionary housing programs: policies and practices*. New Brunswick, NJ: Center for Urban Policy Research, Rutgers University.

Mariano, A. 1994. Hill panel halts plan to move poor families. *Washington Post*, September 3, p. E1.

MaRous, M. S. 1996. Low-income housing in our backyards: what happens to residential property values? *Appraisal Journal* 64: 27–33.

Martinez, M. 1988. *The effects of supportive and affordable housing on property values: a survey of research*. Sacramento: Department of Housing and Community Development, State of California.

Massey, D. S., and N. A. Denton. 1993. *American apartheid: segregation and the making of the underclass*. Cambridge, MA: Harvard University Press.

Massey, D. S., A. B. Gross, and M. L. Eggers. 1991. Segregation, the concentration of poverty, and the life chances of individuals. *Social Science Quarterly* 20: 397–420.

Massey, D. S., and S. M. Kanaiaupuni. 1993. Public housing and the concentration of poverty. *Social Science Quarterly* 74: 109–22.

Matulef, M. 1988. The effects of subsidized housing on property values. *Journal of Housing* 45 (November/December): 286–87.

Mechanic, D., and D. A. Rochefort. 1990. Deinstitutionalization: an appraisal of reform. *American Review of Sociology* 16: 301–27.

Mental Health Law Project. 1988. *The effects of group homes on neighboring property: an annotated bibliography*. Washington, DC.

Mercurio, J. 1995. HUD offers limit on suburban shift: Baltimore poor would be moved out. *Washington Times*, December 14. www.washtimes.com/archives.htm

Metraux, S., D. P. Culhane, and T. Hadley. 2000. The impact of supportive housing on services use for homeless persons with mental illness in New York City. Paper presented at the Annual Meeting of the Association for Public Policy Analysis and Management, Seattle, November.

Montgomery, L. 1994. U.S. plan to spread out poor creates a storm. *Detroit Free Press*, July 14. http://www.freep.com/newslibrary

Morenoff, J. D., R. J. Sampson, and S. W. Raudenbush. 2001. Neighborhood inequality, collective efficacy, and spatial dynamics of urban violence. *Criminology* 39: 517–59.

National Housing Law Project. 2001. *National Housing Law Project: Section 8 housing.* Available at http://www.nhlp.org/html/sec8/homeowenrshiprule.htm (accessed September 6, 2001).

National Law Center on Homelessness and Poverty. 1997. *Access delayed, access denied: local opposition to housing and services for homeless people across the United States.* Washington, DC.

Nenno, M. 1997. Changes and challenges in affordable housing and urban development. In W. van Vliet, ed., *Affordable housing and urban redevelopment in the United States.* Thousand Oaks, CA: Sage Publications.

Newman, O. 1972. *Defensible space: crime prevention through urban design.* New York: Macmillan.

Newman, S. J. 1992. *The severely mentally ill homeless: housing needs and housing policy.* Occasional Paper 12. Baltimore: Institute for Policy Studies, Johns Hopkins University.

Newman, S. J., Reschovsky, J. D., Kaneda, K. and Hendrick, A. M. 1994. The effects of independent living on persons with chronic mental illness—an assessment of the Section 8 certificate program. *Quarterly Journal of Economics* 72, 171–198.

Nichols, P., and C. McCoy. 1997. Section 8: a racist rallying cry? *Philadelphia Inquirer,* November 16, pp. B1, B7–8.

Nourse, H. 1963. The effect of public housing on property values in St. Louis. *Land Economics* 39: 433–41.

Otto, M. 2000. Public housing strategy riles Baltimore neighbors. *Washington Post,* November 9, p. 1.

Pankratz, H. 1998. Denver "failed" its mentally ill. *Denver Post,* May 29. p. B–01.

Paul, R. S. 1989. Open letter to Denver realtors. *Denver Realtor News,* January 11, p. 12.

Pendall, R. 1999. Opposition to housing: NIMBY and beyond. *Urban Affairs Review* 31: 112–36.

———. 2000. Why voucher and certificate users live in distressed neighborhoods. *Housing Policy Debate* 11: 881–910.

Peterson, G., and K. Williams. 1995. *Housing mobility: What has it accomplished and where is its promise?* Washington, DC: Urban Institute Press.

Polikoff, A. 1994. *Housing policy and urban poverty.* Washington, DC: Center for Housing Policy.

Pollock, M., and E. Rutkowski. 1998. *The urban transition zone: a place worth a fight.* Baltimore: Patterson Park Community Development Corporation.

Popkin, S. J., L. F. Buron, D. K. Levy, and M. K. Cunningham. 2000. The Gautreaux legacy: What might mixed-income and dispersal strategies mean for the poorest public housing tenants? *Housing Policy Debate* 11: 911–42.

Puryear, V. 1989. The effects of scattered-site public housing on residential property values. Master's thesis, University of North Carolina at Charlotte.

Quercia, R., and G. Galster. 2000. Threshold effects and neighborhood change. *Journal of Planning Education and Research* 20: 146–62.

Rabiega, W. A., T. W. Lin, and L. M. Robinson. 1984. The property value impacts of public-housing projects in low- and moderate-density residential neighborhoods. *Land Economics* 60: 174–79.

Rainwater, L. 1970. *Behind ghetto walls: black families in a federal slum.* Chicago: Aldine.

Ridgway, P., and C. A. Rapp. 1998. *The active ingredients of effective supported housing: a research synthesis.* Lawrence: University of Kansas School of Social Welfare.

Rocha, E., and M. J. Dear. 1989. *Gaining acceptance for community-based service facilities: an annotated bibliography.* Working Paper 25, Los Angeles Homeless Project. Los Angeles: Department of Geography, University of Southern California.

Rohe, W. M. 1995. Assisting residents of public housing achieve self-sufficiency—an evaluation of Charlotte's Gateway Families Program. *Journal of Architectural and Planning Research* 12: 259–77.

Rohe, W. M., and R. G. Kleit. 1997. From dependency to self-sufficiency: an appraisal of the Gateway Transitional Families Program. *Housing Policy Debate* 8:75–08.

Rohe, W. M., and M. A. Stegman. 1991. Coordinating housing and social services: the new imperative. *Carolina Planning* 17: 46–50.

———. 1994. The impact of home ownership on the social and political involvement of low-income people. *Urban Affairs Review* 30: 152–72.

Roncek, D. W., R. Bell, and J. M. A. Francik. 1981. Housing projects and crime—testing a proximity hypothesis. *Social Problems* 29: 151–66.

Rosenbaum, J. E. 1995. Changing the geography of opportunity by expanding residential choice—lessons from the Gautreaux Program. *Housing Policy Debate* 6: 231–69.

———. 2000. Relocation works. *Boston Review.* Available at http://bostonreview.mit.edu/BR25.3/rosenbaum.html (accessed January 16, 2002).

Rosenbaum, J. E., and S. Miller. 1997. Certificates and warranties: keys to effective residential integration programs. *Seton Hall Law Review* 27: 1426–49.

Rubinowitz, L. S., and J. E. Rosenbaum. 2000. *Crossing the class and color lines: from public housing to white suburbia.* Chicago: University of Chicago Press.

Rusk, D. 1995. *Baltimore unbound: a strategy for regional renewal.* Baltimore: Johns Hopkins University Press.

Ryne, C. S., and A. Coyne. 1985. Effects of group homes on neighborhood property-values. *Mental Retardation* 23: 241–45.

Sampson, R. J., S. W. Raudenbush, and F. Earls. 1997. Neighborhoods and violent crime: a multilevel study of collective efficacy. *Science* 277: 918–24.

Santiago, A. M. 1996. Trends in black and Latino segregation in the post—fair housing era: implications for housing policy. *La Raza Law Journal* 9: 131–53.

Santiago, A. M., and G. C. Galster. 2001. *Dispersing the second ghetto: the effects of deconcentrating public housing residents in Denver.* New York: Ford Foundation.

Schafer, R. 1972. The effect of BMIR housing on property values. *Land Economics* 48: 282–86.

Schelling, T. C. 1978. *Micromotives and macrobehavior.* New York: Norton.

Schill, M. 1992. Deconcentrating the inner city poor. *Chicago-Kent Law Review* 67, 795–853.

Schill, M. H., and S. M. Wachter, 1995. The spatial bias of federal housing law and policy: concentrated poverty in urban America. *University of Pennsylvania Law Review* 143: 1285–1342.

Segal, S. P., C. Silverman, and J. Baumohl. 1989. Seeking person–environment fit in community care placement. *Journal of Social Issues* 45: 49–64.

Seltzer, M. M. 1984. Correlates of community opposition to community residences for mentally-retarded persons. *American Journal of Mental Deficiency* 89: 1–8.

Shern, D. L., C. J. Felton, R. L. Hough, A. F. Leham, S. M. Goldfinger, E. Valencia, D. Dennis, R. Straw, and P. A. Wood. 1997. Housing outcomes for homeless adults with mental illness: results from the second-round McKinney Program. *Psychiatric Services* 48: 239–41.

Simpson, G. E., and J. M. Yinger. 1972. *Racial and cultural minorities: an analysis of prejudice and discrimination.* New York: Harper & Row.

Stamato, L. 1990. Planning and politics: a winning strategy. *Negotiation Journal* 6: 109–111.

Stewart, D., and P. N. Shamdasani. 1990. *Focus groups: theory and practice.* Newbury Park, CA: Sage Publications.

Sugrue, T. J. 1996. *The origins of the urban crisis: race and inequality in postwar Detroit.* Princeton, NJ: Princeton University Press.

Susskind, L. 1990. A negotiation credo for controversial siting disputes. *Negotiation Journal* 6: 309–14.

Takahashi, L. M. 1997. Information and attitudes toward mental health care facilities: implications for addressing the NIMBY syndrome. *Journal of Planning Education and Research* 17: 119–30.

Takahashi, L. M., and M. J. Dear. 1997. The changing dynamics of community opposition to human service facilities. *Journal of the American Planning Association* 63: 79–93.

Taylor, S., G. Hall, and R. Hughes. 1984. Predicting community reaction to mental health facilities. *Journal of the American Planning Association* 50: 36–47.

Trute, B., and S. Segal. 1976. Census tract predictors and the social integration of sheltered care residents. *Social Psychiatry* 11: 153–61.

Turner, M. A. 1998. Moving out of poverty: expanding mobility and choice through tenant-based housing assistance. *Housing Policy Debate* 9: 373–94.

Turner, M. A., S. Popkin, and M. Cunningham. 2000. *Section 8 mobility and neighborhood health: emerging issues and policy challenges.* Washington, DC: Urban Institute Press.

Turner, M. A., and K. Williams. 1998. *Housing mobility: realizing the promise.* Report from the Second National Conference on Assisted Housing Mobility. Washington, DC: Urban Institute Press.

Varady, D. P., and W. F. E. Preiser. 1998. Scattered-site public housing and satisfaction: implications for the new public housing program. *Journal of the American Planning Association* 64: 189–207.

Varady, D. P., and C. C. Walker. 1998. *Case studies of vouchering-out assisted properties.* Washington, DC: U.S. Department of Housing and Urban Development.

———. 2000. Vouchering out distressed subsidized developments: Does moving lead to improvements in housing and neighborhood conditions? *Housing Policy Debate* 11: 115–62.

Wagner, C., and C. Mitchell. 1980. *Group homes and property values: a second look.* Columbus, OH: Metropolitan Services Commission.

Wahl, O. F. 1993. Community impact of group homes for mentally ill adults. *Community Mental Health Journal* 29: 247–59.

Waldron, T. W. 1994. Parading politicians hear critics of housing program. *Baltimore Sun*, September 12, p. 1B.

Warren, E., R. M. Aduddell, and R. Tatalovich. 1983. *The impact of subsidized housing on property values: a two-pronged analysis of Chicago and Cook County suburbs.* Chicago: Center for Urban Policy, Loyola University of Chicago.

Weisberg, B. 1993. One city's approach to NIMBY: how New York City developed a fair share siting process. *Journal of American Planning Association* 59: 93–97.

Wenocur, S., and J. R. Belcher. 1990. Strategies for overcoming barriers to community-based housing for the chronically mentally ill. *Community Mental Health Journal* 26: 319–33.

White, H. 1980. A heteroskedasticity-consistent covariance matrix estimator and a direct test for heteroskedasticity. *Econometrica* 48: 817–38.

William L. Berry & Company. 1988. *A comparison of the appreciation rates of homes in Montgomery County communities with and without moderately priced dwelling units (MPDUs).* Bethesda, MD.

Wilson, W. J. 1987. *The truly disadvantaged.* Chicago: University of Chicago Press.

———. 1996. *When work disappears: the world of the new urban poor.* New York: Alfred A. Knopf.

Wolpert, J. 1978. *Group homes for the mentally retarded: an investigation of neighborhood property impacts.* Albany: New York State Office of Mental Retardation and Development Disabilities.

Yinger, J. 1998. Housing discrimination is still worth worrying about. *Housing Policy Debate* 9: 893–927.

Index

A

ACLU. *See* American Civil Liberties Union
AIDS, 12, 46
alcohol addiction, 45, 153
American Civil Liberties Union (ACLU), 63–4, 71
Americans with Disabilities Act, 14, 190
arson, 14
assisted housing. *See also* assisted housing, deconcentrate
    crime impacts, 81–2
    negative neighborhood impacts, 2
    roots of opposition, 11
    spatial concentration, 2
assisted housing, deconcentrate
    benefits, 2, 3
    for
        low-income households, 1, 5–8
        special-needs households, 1, 8–10
    housing sites analysis
        in general, 125–6
        lessons learned, 185–6
        property-value-impact model, 126–7, *127*
        reported-crime-impact model, 127–9, *128*
        sites not conforming to Denver ordinances, 129
    impact on neighborhoods, 17–8, 177–84
        homeowner focus groups analysis, 90–105
        in general, 74
        quantitative studies, 78–86
        statistical modeling approach, 74–8, 86–90
    innovative efforts, 2, 15–6
        in Baltimore City and County, 55–64
        in Denver, 31
    lessons learned, 176–86
    national policy context, 3–10
    neighborhood-friendly strategy
        burnish image of assisted housing, 198–200
        develop steps toward homeownership, 197–8
        in general, 186–7
        institutional mechanisms for policy delivery, 200–1
        intensify oversight of housing, 195–7
        rehabilitation of structures, 194–5
        siting to ensure sufficient deconcentration, 187–8
    overconcentration, 12
Atlantis (health care/housing agency), 45

B

Baltimore County, Maryland
    ACLU suit special certificates, 63–4
    County Housing Office (BCHO), 64, 97
    focus group, 91, 166–72
        Dundalk, 99, *101–2*, 103–4, 166, 168–71
        Millbrook, 100, *101–2*, 103–4, 166, 168–71
        Rodgers Forge, 100, *101–2*, 103–4, 166, 167, 170, 173
        Twelve Trees, 100, *101–2*, 103–4, 167–9, 171
    Housing Authority of Baltimore, City (HABC), 59–71, 197
    housing sales, 109–10, *110*, *111*
    Moving to Opportunity
        in general, 16–7, 60–3
    profile
        demographic context of controversy, 55
        education and employment characteristics, *51*, *52*
        housing characteristics, *51*, 54–5, *56–8*, 65
        in general, 50
        income and poverty status, *51*, 54
        population characteristics, *51*, *52*, *53*, 65
    protest, 2
    Section 8 program
        basic program, 59–60, 64, 192
        geopolitical context of controversy, 64–71, 176–7
        homeowner focus group, 99–100, 166–72
        impacts, 159, 160, *161*, *162*, 163–5, 166–72, 172–3, 177–8, *178*

Note: Italicized page numbers refer to tables and maps.

in general, 16–7, 55, 59
  occupancy sites and statistics, *116–21*
  program participants, 112, 115, 117
Baltimore Neighborhoods, Inc., 61
BANANA. *See* build absolutely nothing anywhere
  near anyone
Below-Market Interest Rate (BMIR) program, 79
Bentley, Helen, 70
BMIR. *See* Below-Market Interest Rate program
Boston, Massachusetts, 60
BRIDGE, 79
Buffalo, New York, 2
build absolutely nothing anywhere near anyone
  (BANANA), 11

C

California, 14, 188
CAN. *See* Community Assistance Network
Catholic Charities (Denver), 46
Center for Human Investment Policy, 46
Charlotte Housing Authority, 198
CHAS. *See Comprehensive Housing Affordability
  Strategy*
Chicago, Illinois
  community opposition, 2
  Gautreaux program, 7
  Housing Authority, 7
  Moving to Opportunity program, 60
  positive externalities with privately owned
    complexes, 78
  property values, 79, 81
Cincinnati, Ohio, 191, 192, 197
Cisneros, Henry, 71
City of Desmonds v. Oxford House, Inc., 14
class
  distinctions, 55, 65
  expand protected —, 189–90
  prejudice against tenants, 67
Cleveland, Ohio, 82
Clinton, Bill, 7, 9, 14, 60
Colorado
  AIDS project, 46
  Coalition for the Homeless, 46
  Department of Institutions, 42
  Division of Mental Health, 42
  Supreme Court, 42
Colorado Act for the Care and Treatment of the
  Mentally Ill, 42
Community Assistance Network (CAN; Balti-
  more), 61–2, 69, 70
Community Development Block Grant Program,
  189

community opposition, 2. *See also* neighborhood,
  concerns; not in my backyard
  economic motivation, 12
  in
    Baltimore, 63, 65–6, 71
    Denver, 21, 35
community reconnaissance, 18
*Comprehensive Housing Affordability Strategy
  (CHAS)*, 55, 65
criminal activity
  analyses, 18
  dispersed public housing impact (Denver),
    140–1, *178*
  impact model, 75–8, 88–90
  impacts of assisted housing, 81–2
  in
    Baltimore, 66–7
    Denver, 111–12, *112, 113, 114*
  in general, 11, 12, 17
  in tenant selection, 38
  reported-crime-impact model, 127–9, *128*
  supportive housing impact (Denver)
    impacts for different neighborhood types,
      152
    impacts for neighborhoods, 152, *178*
    in general, 144, 151
    mechanisms of crime impacts, 153–4
    trends, 151–2

D

Dallas, Texas, 2, 191
data quality, 205
Davis, Michael, 70
DeCarlo, Helen, 70
deconcentrate assisted housing. *See* assisted
  housing, deconcentrate
deconcentrate bonuses, 189
Del Norte Development, 46
Denver, Colorado
  Archdiocese of, 46
  Citizens Task Force, 35
  City Council, 15–6, 31–8, 43–4, 136, 191
  Community Development Agency, 16, 39, 42
  Consolidate Plan, 43
  crime trends, 88, 111–12, *112, 113, 114*
  Department of Health and Hospitals, 42
  dispersal program, 15–6
    adaptations in, 36–9, 141
    geopolitical context, 32–6, 176–7
    history of, 31–2
    impacts, 131–41, 177–8, *178*

occupancy sites and statistics, 117, 119–20,
        122, *123*
General Hospital, 42
Health and Hospitals Corporation, 31, 45–6
homeowner focus groups, 91–9, 136–9, 149–56
    Berkeley #1, *92–3*, 94, *96*, *98*, 103, 136
    Berkeley #2, *92–3*, 94
    Clayton, 95, *96*, *98*, 103
    Congress Park, 95, *96*, *98*
    East Colfax, *92–3*, 94, 103, 138
    Harvey Park, 95, *96*, *98*, 103, 150
    Hilltop, *96*, 97, *98*, 103, 150
    Montbello, *92–3*, 94, 97
    Montbello #1, *96*, *98*
    Montbello #2, 2, *96*, *98*, 103
    Platte Park, *92–3*, 94, 137
    South Park Hill, *96*, 97, *98*, 103, 150–1
    Speer #1, *96*, *98*, 99, 103, 150
    University Hills, *92–3*, 94–5, 163
Housing Authority (DHA), 15–6, 21, 31–9,
        42, 91, 133, 136, 143, 191
housing sales, 109–11, *110*, 111
profile, 21
    demographic context of controversy, 27
    education and employment characteristics,
        22, 26
    housing characteristics, *22*, 26–7, *28–30*
    income and poverty status, *22*, 26
    population characteristics, *22*, 23, *24*, 25
protest, 2, 45–7, 71
supportive housing initiatives, 16
    facilities, 124–5
    focus group study, 91
    history of, 39–43
    impacts, 143–56, 177–8, *178*
    legal restrictions on siting, 43–4
    neighborhood concerns, 45–7
DePazzo, Lou, 69, 70
desegregation suits, 6–7, 191
disabled. *See* special-needs households
"dispersal program," *See also* Denver, Colorado,
        dispersal program; "scattered-site"
        housing
    in general, 15–6
Dispersed Housing Program. *See* "dispersed
        program," in Denver; Denver, Colo-
        rado, dispersal program
drugs. *See* substance abuse
Dundalk, Maryland, 115
    focus group neighborhood, 99, 166, 168, 169,
        170
    neighborhood protest, 17, 61, 65–6, 68, 69

E

econometric issues, 205
education
    characteristics
        Baltimore County, *51*, 52
        Denver, *22*, 26
    enhance, 199–200
    higher, 7
811 Program, 9
elderly. *See* special-needs households
employment
    characteristics in
        Baltimore County, *51*, 52
        Denver, *22*, 26
    in general, 8
enrollment bonuses, 189
Essex, Maryland, 65–6, 68, 69
ethnic, 11, 12, 189–90
Experian, 109

F

Fairfax County, Virginia, 79
Fair Housing Amendments Act, 14, 190
Federal Housing Authority (FHA), 31–2, 80, 198
focus group analysis. *See* homeowner focus groups,
        analysis
focus groups. *See* homeowner focus groups
Foundations for Home Ownership (Denver,
        Colorado), 198
Freestanding Voucher Demonstration, 12
funding incentives, 189

G

gang activity
    in tenant selection, 38
    recruitment, 7
    violence, 141, 153, 156
Gateway program (Charlotte, North Carolina), 198
Gautreaux, Dorothy, 7
Gautreaux program, 7, 8, 191, 195
gay residents, 46
Goebel case, 16, 21, 42, 43, 45
government assistance. *See* Section 8
group homes, 45–6, 47, 80–1

H

harassment, 14
HIV/AIDS, 12

homeless population, 9, 12
homeless shelters, 13, 40, 44, 46
homeowner focus groups
  analysis, 18
  Baltimore Section 8, 99–100
    awareness of housing sites, 166–7
    impacts in less vulnerable neighborhoods, 170
    impacts in vulnerable neighborhoods, 168–9
    reactions in stagnant market, 170–2
  composition of, 103–4
  data analysis strategies, 105
  Denver dispersed housing, 91–5
    awareness of housing sites, 136–8
    reactions in booming market, 138–9
  Denver supportive housing, 95–9
    awareness of housing sites, 149
    comments about sites, 149–51
    insights regarding crime impacts, 154–6
  facilitation, 104–5
  in general, 90–1
  recruitment of participants, 100–3
  topic areas, 104
homeownership, steps toward, 197–8
HOPE IV
  ACLU's case against, 63–4, 71
  concerns over, 12, 191
  public housing reform, 6, 7
  replacement units, 63, 69
host community, 13, 16
housing
  analysis of sites. *See also* site selection, sufficient deconcentration and
  in general, 125–6
  property-value impact model, 126–7, *127*
  reported-crime impact model, 127–9, *128*
  sites not conforming to Denver Ordinances, 129
  characteristics
    Baltimore, *51*, 54, *56–8*
    Denver, *22*, 26–7, *28–30*
"housing as housing" approach, 9
Housing Opportunity Vouchers, 200
Housing Quality Standards, 172, 195
Housing Resource Directory (Denver Community Development Agency), 39
housing sales. *See also* property values
  in general, 17, 18
  price trends
    Baltimore's Section 8, 160, *161*, 162
    Denver's dispersed sites, 133
    Denver's supportive housing, 143
  single-family sales in

  Baltimore County, 109–10, *110–11*
  Denver, 109–11, *110*, *111*
housing values. *See* property values

I

income characteristics, *22*, 26, *51*, 54
"independent housing" approach, 9
infill construction program, 32
Internal Revenue Service, 189

J

Jung, Jean, 69

L

landlords, 156, 189, 196–7
land use regulations, 14
Large Residential Care Use Ordinance (Denver)
  criminal activity and, 157
  distinctions among facilities, 39–40
  limits on, 152
  neighborhood notification requirement, 45, 149
  passage, 16, 43
"level of care" approach, 9
LIHTC. *See* Low Income Housing Tax Credit Program
Los Angeles, California, 60
low-income households. *See also* Section 8
  deconcentrate assisted housing, 1
  opposition to, 10–11
  property value impacts of housing, 78–80
  push to deconcentrate assisted housing, 5–8
Low Income Housing Tax Credit Program (LIHTC), 191
Lowry Air Force Base, 46

M

Management Assessment Program, 189
Maryland, 188, 190
Maryland State Partnership Rental Program, 64
Massachusetts, 188, 190
McKinney Act, Stewart B., 9, 46
media events, 14
Medicaid, Targeted Case Management and Rehabilitative Services, 9
Memphis, Tennessee, 191
Mental Health Law Project, 80
mentally ill. *See* special-needs households
Mikulski, Barbara, 17, 69, 70

military bases, acquisition of, 46
Minneapolis, Minnesota, 2, 79
mobility
    counseling, 7
    -enhancing strategy, 6
mortgage interest payments, 189
Moving to Opportunity (MTO)
    authorization of, 6
    Baltimore County programs, 16–7, 60–4
        geopolitical context of controversy, 64–71
    concerns, 12
    impaction standards, 190–4
    positive impacts, 8
MTO. *See* Moving to Opportunity
multiple regression analysis, 75, 80

N

National Law Center on Homelessness and
        Poverty, 11, 12
national policy context
    in general, 3
    perils of poverty concentrations, 4–5
    push to deconcentrate housing
        for low-income households, 5–8
        for special-needs household, 8–10
neighborhood
    collaborative efforts with, 198–9
    concerns, 45–7. *See also* community opposition
    -friendly strategy
        burnish deconcentrated assisted housing
            image, 198–200
        in general, 187
        institutional mechanisms for policy, 200–1
        intensify oversight, 195–7
        rehabilitation of structured, 194–5
        siting, 187–94
        steps to homeownership, 197–8
    harm to, 17–8, 136
    impacts
        in general, 74
        lessons learned, 177–84
        quantitative studies, 78–81
        statistical modeling approach, 74–8
        use of focus groups, 90–105
    life chances and, 4
    nonpoverty, 2
    opinions on supportive housing, 47
    outreach, 38
    poverty, 4
    quality of life, 1
    reconnaissance, 46–7

    safety, 140
    security, 1
    upkeep, 136–7
"neighborhood impaction" standards, 6, 17, 139–
        40, 190–3
New Jersey restrictive zoning, 14, 188
New York City, New York, 60
NIABY. *See* not in anybody's backyard
NIMBY. *See* not in my backyard
noise, 11
nonpoverty neighborhood. *See* neighborhood,
        nonpoverty
NOPE. *See* not on planet Earth
not in anybody's backyard (NIABY), 11
not in my backyard (NIMBY)
    nature of, 10–1
    opposition, 2
        forms of, 13–4
        roots of, 11–3
        variations in, 13
not on planet Earth (NOPE), 11

O

Oakland, California, 2, 80
opportunity housing bonuses, 189

P

Paul, Ron, 33
pedophiles, 46
Peña, Frederico, 34, 36
PHA. *See* public housing authority
Philadelphia, Pennsylvania, 2, 80
Pittsburgh, Pennsylvania, 2
policy
    mechanisms for — delivery, 200–1
    reconnaissance, 18
population characteristics
    in
        Baltimore County, *51*, *52*, *53*, 65
        Denver, *22*, 23, *24*, *25*
property management
    mismanagement by local housing authority, 67–8
    monitor dwellings, 196–7, 172
    property-value impacts and, 147, 172
    rehabilitation of structures, 179, *180–3*, 184,
        194–5
    successful maintenance, 149
property taxes, 189
poverty
    characteristics in

Baltimore County, *51*, 54
Denver, 26
concentrated
abhorrence of, 4
in general, 1, 2
perils of, 4–5
subsidized tenants and, 67
correlation between property values and —,
139
rates, 192
property values
analyses, 18
correlation between — and poverty rate, 139
dispersed public housing (Denver)
evaluation of impaction standards, 139–40
focus group insights, 136–9
impacts for different neighborhood types,
134–5
impacts for neighborhoods, 133–4, 177–8,
178
in general, 132–3
mechanisms of impacts, 139
sale price trends, 133
group homes and, 47
impact of housing for
low-income, 78–80
special needs, 80–1
impact model specification, 75–7, 86–8, 126–7,
129
in
Baltimore County, 54–5, *56–8*, 65
Denver, 27, *29*, *30*, 31, 34
key variables, 208–9
level and trend, 76
lower, 11, 12
Section 8 (Baltimore)
impacts for different neighborhoods, 164–5,
177–8, *178*
impacts for neighborhoods, 163–4
in general, 160
sale price trends, 160, *161*, *162*
supportive housing (Denver)
focus groups insights, 149–51
impacts for different neighborhood types,
148–9
impacts for neighborhoods, 146–7, 177–8,
178
in general, 144
mechanisms of, 172–3
sale patterns, 144–6
undermined, 1
public housing authority (PHA), 187, 191–201
public safety, 140, 156

Q

Quality Housing and Work Responsibility Act,
197
quality of life, 1, 11, 149
quantitative studies
impacts with homeowner focus groups
Baltimore Section 8, 99–100
composition of, 103–4
data analysis strategies, 105
Denver dispersed housing, 91–5
Denver supportive housing, 95–9
facilitation, 104–5
in general, 90–1
recruitment of participants, 100–3
topic areas, 104
property value impacts of housing for
criminal impacts, 75–8, 81–2
low-income households, 75, 78–80
special needs households, 75, 80–1

R

racial groups, 11, 12
distinctions, 55, 65
prejudice against tenants, 67
Reagan, Ronald, 69
Regional Opportunity Counseling program, 6, 201
rehabilitation grants, 189
Replacement Housing Program (Denver), 32, 36
research approaches, 83
residential care facilities, 40, 44
"residential continuum" approach, 9

S

San Francisco Bay area (California), 79
Sauerbrey, Ellen, 70
"scattered-site" housing, 6, 7, 8, 31. *See also*
"dispersal program"
Schmoke, Kurt, 71
Section 8. *See also*, Baltimore County, Maryland
community concerns, 11–2
desegregation suits, 7
geopolitical context of controversy, 64–74
homeownership, 197–8
impaction standards, 190–4
landlord participation, 84
mobility of households, 189
property values and, 79–80
protest against, 2
tenant-based subsidy, 5

segregation, public housing and, 63, 188
sex offenders, 45–6
site selection, sufficient deconcentration and
    assist mobility of Section 8 households, 189
    fair housing and protected classes, 189–90
    impaction standards, 190–3
    incentives to spatially diversify, 188–9
    in general, 187–8
    monitor concentration of sites and households,
        194
social benefits, assisted housing deconcentration,
    2, 3
Social Services Block Grant, 9
spatial autocorrelation, 85
spatial dependence, 85
spatial economic issues, 206–8
spatial heterogeneity, 85
spatial patterns, 85–6, 151
    incentives to diversify, 188–9
special-needs households
    deconcentrate assisted housing, 1
    property value impacts of housing, 80–1
    push to deconcentrate assisted housing, 8–10
SSI. See Supplemental Security Income
statistical modeling
    alternative stratifications of regressions, 90
    crime-impact model, 88–90
    nontechnical overview, 74–8
    property-value-impact model specification, 86–8
St. Louis, Missouri, 78
St. Paul, Minnesota, 79, 81
subsidy programs. See government assistance
substance abuse
    in general, 12, 13, 67
    in tenant selection, 38, 45
    issue of concern, 141, 156
    mechanism of crime impact, 153
Supplemental Security Income (SSI), 9
"supportive housing." See also Denver, Colorado,
        supporting housing initiatives
    facility distinctions, 40
    initiatives, 9
    key characteristics of, 40–1
    opposition to, 11
    property values and, 80–1
    research, 10
Supportive Housing Program Competition, 9

T

Targeted Case Management and Rehabilitative
        Services, 9

tenant
    behavior, 66–7
    poverty concentration and, 67
    racial and class prejudice against, 67
    screen and monitor, 195–6
    selection in
        Baltimore, 60
        Denver, 38–9, 141
Tenant Readiness Training and Mobility Coun-
        seling (Baltimore), 60
threats, 14
traffic congestion, 11

U

undeserving poor, 68
Urban Revitalization Demonstration. See HOPE
        IV
U.S. Department of Housing and Urban Devel-
        opment (HUD)
    Baltimore County programs, 16–7, 63, 69, 70,
        71
    Denver Housing Authority and, 15
    811 program, 9
    focus group participants, 100
    foreclosure properties, 31
    housing for elderly, 9
    Housing Quality Standards, 172
    "neighborhood impaction" standards, 6, 36
    pilot programs, 188
    program participant guidelines, 38
    Regional Opportunity Counseling Program, 6,
        201
    Supportive Housing Competition, 9
    supportive housing programs, 13
U.S. Department of Veterans Affairs (VA), 31–2
U.S. Justice Department, 14
U.S. Supreme Court, 14

V

Veterans Affairs housing program, 31–2

Y

youth crime, 141, 156

Z

zoning
    expedited, 189
    inclusionary ordinances, 14, 188